THE

FIRST OF THE BOURBONS

VOL. I.

CONTENTS OF VOL. I.

———◆———

The First of the Bourbons. *BY*
CATHERINE CHARLOTTE,
LADY JACKSON

IN TWO VOLUMES
VOLUME I.

WILDSIDE PRESS

LIST OF ILLUSTRATIONS

Volume I.

THE
FIRST OF THE BOURBONS

———◆———

CHAPTER I.

INTRODUCTORY.

Vows of Vengeance Give Place to Dejection. — The King
Seeks Aid from the Huguenots. — The Baron de Rosny
Charged with the Message to Henri of Navarre. — The
Proposal Acceded to. — A Truce Signed. — Suspicions of
Treachery. — Meeting of the Kings. — A Wail of Despair. —
Advance on the Capital. — Henri III. Stabbed by a Domini-
can Monk. — Rejoicings in Paris, Consternation in the Royal
Camp.

FRENZIED excitement prevailed in Paris
during the early months of 1589, after
the assassination of the Duc de Guise
— the "grand Guise" of the populace — and his
brother, the Cardinal de Lorraine; the clergy
being further exasperated by the arrest of the old
Cardinal de Bourbon, the Archbishop of Lyons,
and the young Prince de Joinville, a youth of
eighteen, the late duke's eldest son, and now Duc
de Guise.

Suddenly, however, passionate vows of vengeance and reiterated imprecations on the tyrant Henri of Valois, "the last of his twice-cursed race" — excommunicated by the Pope, anathematised by the Sorbonne, and declared by the League, the priests, and the people to be no longer King of France — gave place to consternation, deep dejection, and mournful silence.* The vio-

---

* It was the popular belief that a malediction rested on the kings of the line of Valois, from their accession to the throne early in the fourteenth century to the extinction of the dynasty towards the close of the sixteenth, in the person of Henri III. In 1307 that cruel despot, Philippe IV., surnamed "Le Bel," whose cupidity was excited by the report of the vast wealth said to have been amassed by those warrior monks, the Templars, determined on abolishing the order and confiscating their property. To justify this act Philippe brought infamous charges against them, and fifty-five of the knights were sentenced in one day to be slowly burnt, after being duly tortured. A few years later the stronghold of the order in France, that fortified convent, the Temple, was taken by stratagem, and Jacques de Molay, the grand master, together with a high dignitary of the order, was hastily sentenced by Philippe to death, and burnt on the Place de Grève, March 17th, 1313. While the flames were rising high around him and his companion, Molay, in the agony of death, with uplifted arms, and eyes raised towards heaven, called down the vengeance of God on Philippe and his race, and summoned him and his partner in iniquity — Pope Clement V. — to meet him at the bar of God before the expiration of the year. Philippe, aged only 46, died in the following November, Clement a month or two earlier. Philippe's three sons, like those of Henri II., reigned each a short time, but left no male issue — the crown then devolving on Philippe's nephew, the Comte de Valois, who succeeded his cousin, Charles de Valois, as Philippe VI., inheriting with the crown the Templars' malediction.

lent harangues which fanatical priests continually addressed from their pulpits to the people, and which until then had sustained their wild desire for vengeance, now fell almost unheeded on their ears. For Henri of Valois had crowned his career of vice and crime by the greatest of all crimes, in the estimation of the fanatics of the League and the Parisian populace, — an alliance with the Huguenot chief, Henri of Navarre, and his heretic followers.

Many times in the course of his reign, notwithstanding his frequent public appearance as a penitent brother of the Flagellants, they had accused him of worshipping the devil, and his favourite, D'Épernon, of being " Satan *in propriâ personâ.*" Now they professed to stand appalled before the startling fact that a " son of the true Church, however vicious his life had been, should enter into a compact with devils," meaning that the king had been guilty of the heinous crime of appealing to his Huguenot kinsman to join the Royalist army with his troops, in order to aid him in suppressing the " Holy League," and wresting Paris from the grasp of their Spanish ally.

This bold step did not, however, originate with the weak and vacillating Henri of Valois, whose horror of an alliance with heresy was not surpassed by that of his superstitious and infuriated people. He was even at that moment secretly endeavouring to conciliate the chief of the League, the Duc de Mayenne, who repulsed his advances, declaring that no confidence could be placed in his word or promises. Yet often during the past few years it had occurred to him, when his sense of shame was roused by the indignities which the Guises and the League compelled him to submit to, that Henri of Navarre and his Huguenots might do him good service, could he win their aid by concessions. He would then, firm of purpose for the moment, rapidly pace his apartment, muttering, "*De inimicis meis vindicabo inimicos meos.*" But he was never able to make up his mind to put this threat into execution, but let "I dare not" wait upon "I would."

The king's army was far too small successfully to oppose that of the League. This was urgently pressed on him by many of the Royalist nobility and military chiefs of the "politique" party, who, from a reaction of sentiment, had resumed their allegiance to him. They suggested that he should communicate with the King of Navarre through the agency of the young Baron de Rosny (afterwards Duc de Sully), whom the Marquis de Rambouillet had seen and recognised in Blois, although he had sacrificed his Huguenot beard, and had otherwise assumed a disguise. He had, in fact, been secretly sent there by his chief to watch the movements of the armies, as Henri of Navarre was then warring against the League on his own account.

The king, as usual, hesitated to adopt the advice of his officers, but finally consented to see Rosny, whose brothers, having embraced Catholicism, were frequenters of the court. He was also personally known to him, from having been chosen in 1583 by the King of Navarre to inform the King of France and the queen-mother of the offers made to him by Philip II. of Spain, who proposed to supply him with money and troops and to restore that part of Navarre which his parents had been deprived of by Charles V., if he would declare war against France.

After some consultation with the Marquis de Rambouillet, the king thought it necessary, in order to prevent any misunderstanding, that the precise message to be conveyed from Henri of Valois to Henri of Navarre should be twice repeated by both the king and Rosny. For no letters or written assurances of any kind were given, the king fearing that, the bearer of them being, perchance, taken prisoner *en route*, they might fall into the hands of Morosini or the Duc de Nevers.

Having duly repeated the important message with which he was charged, the baron set off with all speed for Châtellerault, which had been besieged and taken that morning by the Huguenots. Henri listened very attentively to the king's proposals, then "several times asked me," says Rosny, "scratching his head as if much perplexed, if I thought his cousin of France was acting towards him in sincerity and good faith. I replied," he continues, "that I believed he was, the Marquis de Rambouillet's assurances to that effect having convinced me."

"You shall return, then, forthwith," said Henri; "and while you are taking your breakfast here in my tent, I will write my assent, under certain conditions, to his proposal; for, if he is afraid of the Duc de Nevers and the nuncio Morosini, I fear them not."

While Rosny was again on his way to Blois, the message he had brought was discussed in the Huguenot camp, where it naturally excited much surprise, and scarcely less suspicion. The Saint-Bartholomew Massacre, and the perfidy preceding it, then rose to Henri's mind, and to the minds of many of his followers. Yet, after the question had been fully debated, it was resolved, though still with many misgivings, to place patriotism and the salvation of the country far before any consideration of personal wrongs. In this decision both the Comte de Châtillon (Admiral de Coligny's son) and the brave La Noue fully concurred.

Henri III., though compelled to take the step he in his heart shrank from, was now so anxious that the alliance with heresy should be completed that, anticipating a favourable response to his overtures from Henri of Navarre, he set out from Blois with his whole retinue to meet Rosny on his way back, stopping, for that purpose, at the Château de Montrichard. Thither Rosny was conducted on his arrival at midnight. The king, for greater secrecy, was waiting in the uppermost room of the château to receive the Béarnais's reply. Rosny handed the king Henri's written response to his own verbal message.

The desired aid was promised, but a city of surety was demanded as a guarantee of good faith, while any interference with each other's religious worship was to be strictly forbidden to both Catholics and Protestants. The king was glad to accede to these moderate demands — promising the considerable city of Saumur as the city of surety, and urging Rosny to hasten back to Châtellerault, that the terms of his arrangement with his cousin of Navarre might be speedily concluded.

Before again setting out, being very weary, the baron desired to repose for an hour or two, but was informed that all available quarters were occupied, owing to the unexpected arrival of the king and his retinue. But just as he was putting his foot in the stirrup, a messenger from the Marquis de Rambouillet informed him that the quarters assigned to his brother, who had not yet left Blois, were at his disposal for the night. But the night was too far spent to take more than an hour's rest, for at break of day Rosny must be again in the saddle, and *en route* for Châtellerault.

On arriving he found that Henri had left that place and was at Argenton, whence he had dislodged the troops of the League before they could receive assistance to maintain possession of the town. It was from the pillage of these small towns, Henri being wholly without other resources, that the Huguenot army was supported and supplies of ammunition were obtained.

At Argenton the baron delivered the letters of Henri III. assenting to the conditions of the King of Navarre; the negotiators on either side were therefore to meet and conclude the treaty. But the fatigue of this journeying to and fro by night and day, together with the anxiety attending his mission, and the perils that beset him from surrounding parties of Leaguers, resulted in an attack of fever that confined the baron to his bed for twelve days.

The able Calvinist negotiator, Du Plessis-Mornay, was, in consequence, despatched by the King of Navarre to Tours to act on his behalf; and on the 3d of April a treaty was signed by him under the unusual form of a truce for a year. During that time the King of Navarre undertook to employ his forces and those of his party only as assented to, or commanded, by his majesty Henri III.; also to march direct on the Duc de Mayenne, respecting both the persons and the religion of the Catholics of those towns through which the march of his army lay. The places taken by the Huguenots, or which surrendered to them, were to be delivered to the king, certain privileges being conceded to the captors.

Very strangely, however, when after much consultation the terms of the truce were determined on and apparently approved by both parties, Henri III. became anxious to defer giving it immediate force by withholding his signature for a fortnight. Irresolution had resumed its sway, and now, at the eleventh hour, he repented of his daring deed, and would willingly have withdrawn from a transaction really contrary to his prejudices and sympathies.

He had been lately influenced by the Duc de Nevers, who denounced the "heretic alliance," and had recommenced secret communication with his half-sister, the Duchesse de Montmorency, natural daughter of Henri II., through whose intervention, together with the magnificent promises he authorised her to make in his name, reconciliation with the Duc de Mayenne he yet vainly believed was possible. But neither the Protestant nor Catholic negotiators were willing to consent to such trifling. They were resolute in declaring that the arrangement agreed to must be at once concluded or abandoned. Under the pressure, then, of stronger wills than his own, the king signed the truce, relieved, probably, by the fact that his mind had been made up for him.

It now remained only to appoint an interview, that the two sovereigns might confer together and arrange their plan of campaign.   Plessis-lez-Tours was named by the king for that purpose, and, accordingly, Henri of Navarre soon after set out to join him at that château.   A strong escort accompanied him, but less at his own desire than at the earnest request of several of the Huguenot chiefs, who could not wholly dismiss from their minds — and, perhaps, neither could Henri — a suspicion of evil intentions towards them and their leader.

At some two leagues' distance from the château the party came to a halt under a group of trees, and the question whether they had not embarked — and Henri especially — on a dangerous expedition was again discussed.   Henri was reminded of his own words after his escape from the court in 1575 — that "he would never again enter the private apartment of Henri III. unless guarded by a double line of his own soldiers."

"Why are you silent?" said the king, addressing Rosny.   "Have you no opinion to offer?"

"My opinion is," he replied, "that it is one of those occasions on which something must be left to chance, while contenting ourselves with taking such necessary precautions as prudence may suggest."

Henri reflected for a moment or two; then, turning towards his companions, "*Allons!*" he

said, "my resolve is taken ; we must hesitate no
longer." *

Very shortly after, Henri III. and his suite were
descried, the king having had the complaisance
to ride out with his gentlemen two or three miles
on the road to greet the King of Navarre. An
immense concourse of people had assembled on
the road to Tours, and the trees by the wayside
were full of eager spectators, all anxious to obtain
a glimpse of the meeting of the two kings after a
separation of fourteen eventful years. Their cor-
dial embrace seemed to give general satisfaction,
for the·unwonted cry of "*Vive le roi!*" saluted
Henri III., followed by "*Vive le Roi de Navarre!*"
and many hearty cheers.

* Rosny's silence on this occasion arose from dissatisfied
feeling towards his hero. Henri had given the government of
Saumur, his city of surety, to Du Plessis-Mornay. The baron
considered that he had a prior claim to it, his own part in
the negotiation having been more important, — fatiguing, too,
and even hazardous to liberty and life, had he fallen into the
hands of the Leaguers. At first he thought of retiring to his
estates, so much did the fancied injustice of the master he
was devoted to prey on his mind. He, however, soon after
changed his view of the matter, finding that the confidential
relations existing between him and his prince, which frequently
enabled him to do him great service, must have almost ceased
with his residence at Saumur, and his duties as governor. De
Mornay, whom the Catholics called "the pope of the Huguenots," resided there until 1621. He made many improvements
in the town, which became the headquarters of the French
Protestants. He also repaired the château, and founded a
Protestant college which obtained European renown.—*Mémoires
de Sully;* Dupuy.

Henri III., when it was his good pleasure to be gracious, had a very courteous and noble bearing, while the gaiety and gallantry of Henri of Navarre always won golden opinions. The animated air of the two sovereigns, as they rode towards the château conversing together, had apparently a beneficial effect on their attendants, good humour seemingly prevailing amongst them. But on entering the castle gates, only a part of the King of Navarre's retinue passed through them with him ; the rest remained outside, to be in readiness to rush to his aid should it prove needful. As Henri alone was in military dress, his suite wearing only the white scarf, the distinctive mark of their religious and political profession, their manœuvre excited no suspicion.

Henri's costume is thus described : * " His gray doublet was as usual worn at the elbows and sides, from the rubbing of the cuirass he was compelled so constantly to wear. His trunk-hose were of brown velvet ; his mantle was of scarlet cloth ; his broad hat of gray felt, with a tall waving white peacock plume, fastened by a fine medallion." Henri of Navarre had passed the greater part of his life in the camp, and had acquired there rather the habits and manners of *un bon camarade* than those usually associated with the dignity of a king and the authority of a commander-in-chief of an army. However, he could, on occasion, assume

* Palma-Cayet.

both ; and the energy and activity he at all times displayed, and the cheerfulness with which he bore the frowns and buffetings of fickle Fortune, were to those around less happily endowed in those respects both an example and a lesson.

Henri III. had known him as a participator in the too often dissolute amusements of their early youth, when detained by Catherine de' Medici as prisoners at her court. But the "Béarnais," as they still called him, had never sunk to the same low level of depravity as Henri of Valois and his favourite companions, who now appeared to be impressed by the manliness of character the King of Navarre had since developed ; and even fear of the military prowess of Duc Charles de Mayenne was also greatly subdued, since his cousin of Navarre had jestingly told him that "two Henris were worth more than one Carolus."

After an interview one may presume to have been satisfactory to both, the King of Navarre returned to his quarters at Maille, and on the following morning went on foot and unattended to the château of Plessis-lez-Tours. This appears to have satisfied his friends that, for the present at least, no attempt on his life need be feared.

The King of Navarre now laid before Henri III. his plan of assembling all the Royalist and Huguenot forces before Paris, and, by a general attack on the city, ending the war at one blow. The latter would doubtless have suggested a more dilatory method of warfare, but, roused from his inertia under the quickening influence of his more active heretic cousin — who temporarily, at least, appears to have imparted to him a little of his own energy and vivacity — he at once consented to carry out his views. The two kings passed several days together at Plessis, arranging with their respective commanders the details of the siege. A detachment of Huguenot troops, under Châtillon and Rosny, were ordered to besiege Chartres, which they took after a desperate engagement.

The great Huguenot captain, La Noue, with only 4,000 men, besieged and took the strongly fortified town of Senlis, and compelled the garrison, 10,000 strong, to surrender. Much more fighting took place, and with singular success, though unfortunately with immense loss of life — the combatants on both sides fighting with extraordinary fury. News of the capture of Senlis by the heretics reached Paris, together with the information that the Royalist and Huguenot armies were marching on the capital. A wail of despair ran through Paris. "O merciful God!" the people exclaimed in imploring accents, "let not the faithful city be defiled by the entrance of the accursed heretic and his Huguenot band!"

The Spaniard Mendoza — lately ambassador at the French court, but since the "great homicide of Blois" merely styled agent of Philip II. — in order to raise the spirits of the distracted people and induce popular reliance on Spain, assured them that the Prince of Parma, whose military reputation stood so high, was on his way to France to aid and save them. His harangue failed to fulfil its intention. Neither Mendoza nor Mayenne possessed the magic power of the "grand Guise," who on such an occasion would have kindled enthusiasm to its highest pitch, and subdued it at his pleasure. Of far greater effect on the public mind was the confident assertion of some two or three hundred "politiques," who had been arrested in Paris by the League and thrown into prison — that "the city could not hold out three days against the united armies, and that there would then be so many people to hang that in Paris and its faubourgs scarcely wood enough would be found for the gibbets." *

Meanwhile, the Royalist and Huguenot armies were advancing towards the capital, besieging on their way the towns held by the Leaguers — Henri III. often avenging the revolt of his rebel subjects by cruel deaths or punishments. These Henri of Navarre strove to avert or mitigate by appeals to his royal brother to spare life, or to obtain less onerous terms of capitulation, his clemency being much extolled by the Leaguers, in spite of his heresy, and occasioning, it was said, some slight feeling of jealousy in Henri of Valois.†

On the 25th of July Pontoise surrendered, and

<hr>

* L'Estoile, Cayet.   † L'Estoile.

on the following evening the united royal armies
were reinforced by 10,000 Swiss troops, 2,000
lansquenets, the Royalists of Normandy, and
1,500 cavalry, — their march being unopposed
by Mayenne, who dared not leave the capital.
On the 30th they secured the bridge of Saint-
Cloud, and distributed their quarters thence to
Argenteuil and to Vaugirard, — the King of
France establishing himself at Saint - Cloud, the
King of Navarre at Meudon. From 35,000 to
40,000 men were now encamped before Paris.*
The attack was to begin on the 2d of August,
and the chances seemed to be all in favour of the
assailants; for Mayenne had but 8,000 or 9,000
regular troops to oppose to them, and they clamorous for their arrears of pay, constantly desert-
ing, and generally so little to be relied on that it
was expected they would join the enemy in the
midst of the assault for the sake of pillaging
the city.†

Little was done, it appears, by the lieutenant-
general and others in military command, towards
putting Paris into a state of defence to offer the
invaders effective resistance. The chief hope of
those in power, as it eventually proved, apart from
the aid expected from Spain, was centred in assassination — in the successful crime, in fact, of a
fanatical young monk, Jacques Clément, hitherto
of most dissolute life, but who had become fired

* D'Aubigné.   † L'Estoile.

with the thought of atoning for his vicious courses
by murdering "the tyrant, Henri of Valois."
"Thus, while ridding the earth of a monster
whom France had hurled from the throne, he
believed he would secure the favour of Heaven
for himself."

The superior of his order (Dominicans), to
whom he applied to dissipate his only scruple —
"whether it was a mortal sin for a priest to kill
a tyrant " — informed him that "it was only an
irregular act." They cited instances from Scripture, and encouraged the demented youth to carry
out the sinister design which, as he said, he had
been charged with, in a vision, by an angel. He
was assured that "should his own life be forfeited
in accomplishing his purpose, the martyr's crown
awaited him on earth, but the fit reward of his
glorious deed would be conferred on him in
heaven."

The ladies of the Guise family, and especially
the Duchesse de Montpensier, the late duke's
sister — between whom and Henri the bitterest
hate existed — further incited the miserable fanatic to persist to the end in the fulfilment of his
"sacred mission." She promised him a cardinal's
hat and the highest ecclesiastical dignities on his
return to Paris. But he rather disdained worldly
preëminence, lest it should endanger his soul's
salvation, and occasion the loss of that higher distinction his superiors had told him to look for in

heaven, — placing himself as the so-called "saviour
of France" almost on a level with the "Saviour
of mankind."

On the 31st of July, being provided with a
forged passport and credentials purporting to be
signed by De Harlay, President of the Parliament,
Jacques, highly elated, set out on his holy errand.
On approaching the camp he was questioned by
the procurator-general as to the nature of his business there.   He replied that he was "the bearer
of letters and messages to the king from friends
in Paris."   That evening no access to the king
was permitted, but Jacques was invited to supper,
regaled himself freely, entered into the joviality
of the camp, and passed the night in sound
sleep.

In the morning he was summoned to the royal
presence.   Bowing profoundly, he mentioned in
a low, grave tone, as he handed the king the letters he had brought, that he had a private communication to make to him.   The guards and others
withdrew a few paces at a sign from the king,
who, leaning forward to hear the monk's message,
was stabbed by him in the abdomen with a knife
he had concealed in his sleeve.   Drawing the
knife from the wound, Henri struck the monk in
the face with it, exclaiming as he did so: "Ah,
the miserable monk!   He has killed me!"

The nobles and officers in attendance rushed to
the king's assistance.   The guards seized the

monk, threw him on the floor, stabbed him furiously with their daggers, and in their rage tore him almost limb from limb.   He was then thrown from the window, a bleeding, mangled corpse, which was speedily reduced to ashes and thrown into the river.   The king's death did not immediately ensue, and for some hours it was believed that the wound would not prove fatal.   A messenger was despatched to Meudon, and Henri of Navarre was quickly at the king's bedside, seeking to console and comfort him.

Towards evening an unfavourable change took place, fever supervening.   The king then, in the presence of all the Catholic nobility and officers in his camp, declared his "brother of Bourbon his legitimate successor," and required them then and there solemnly to swear allegiance to him, which, with apparent willingness, all present did. He afterwards exhorted Henri, in his own and the nation's interest, to embrace Catholicism.

Absolution and the Eucharist, at first refused by his confessor, were afterwards given on his promise to satisfy the demands of the Pope, should he yet survive.   He died on the 2d of August between two and three in the morning, in the thirty-eighth year of his age and fifteenth of his reign.*

While Paris, in the agony of suspense, was tremblingly awaiting news of the monk's success

* L'Estoile, D'Aubigné, Mathieu.

or failure, Clément's death was reported, but "the actual result of his deed concealed." The fact of the blow having been well aimed and its effects fatal was first made known in the city some hours later by the result of an encounter between a Royalist officer, Jean de Maurivert, and Claude de Marolles, of the army of the League, who had agreed on the previous day to break a lance "*en l'honneur des dames*" in the field behind Les Chartreux. Maurivert, who in the night had witnessed the king's death, hastened to the appointed spot at daybreak, full of resentment, and determined to avenge the assassination of his sovereign on one of his enemies.

The combatants were on horseback, each attended by his second. The combat was begun by Maurivert, who furiously attacked his adversary, while he, with more coolness, skilfully defended himself. Maurivert having in his fury broken his lance, Marolles took advantage of it to give him a mortal blow, and unhorsed him. " I am truly unfortunate," exclaimed Maurivert, " in being vanquished, yet most fortunate in not surviving the king, my master." Thus, it is said, was the fact of the king's death first announced.*

Marolles and his second, La Chartre, afterwards entered Paris triumphantly to the sound of trumpets, proclaiming the " good news " as they passed through the streets and squares. The League,

* *Histoire de Henri le Grand ;* Genlis.

the priests, and the populace were jubilant, the latter rushing from place to place shouting that "God had heard the voice of His people, and extinguished the accursed race of Valois." Madame de Montpensier, in her enthusiasm, fervently embraced the bearers of these good tidings.

"Welcome, most welcome, my friends!" she cried; "the perfidious tyrant, then, is really dead. One only regret I feel,— that it was not whispered to him when dying that it was I who nerved and steadied the hand that gave him his death-blow."

But while Paris was celebrating the extinction of the line of Valois, consternation filled the royal camp. Though personally unworthy of regret, the assassination of Henri III. occurred at a most unpropitious moment both for the nation and his successor. The Venetian ambassador, Moncenigo, in reporting the king's death to the Senate, states that "the influential men of the various cities and towns of France aimed at replacing the monarchy by municipal republics, while the nobles sought to elevate their governments into independent principalities." To this may be added that Spain looked to repairing the ruinous loss of her shattered Armada with the débris of France, and to swallow up the whole under the pretext of protection.

Such was the state of chaos into which the vices and misgovernment of Henri III. had plunged the nation. "Yet his death — occurring at a moment when his alliance with the French and foreign reformers seemed to afford him an opportunity of serving the state by wresting Paris from the grasp of the allies of Philip II. — was, in fact, a real misfortune for France, and foreign nations saw in it a threatened dissolution of the national unity."

CHAPTER II.

NO sooner was life pronounced extinct in
Henri III. than a great change was
observable in the tone and bearing of
a large part of the Catholic nobility and military
chiefs towards his successor. When danger
threatened, they eagerly sought the aid of the gallant Huguenot king and his troops. But when he
claimed to be their sovereign, although they had
sworn allegiance to him, they declared that it was
but conditionally on his immediate renunciation of
heresy and return to the true faith. "Otherwise,"
they exclaimed, adopting almost the exact words of
the Parisian populace, "rather a thousand deaths
than acknowledge a Huguenot as King of France."

"Some among them," says D'Aubigné, "in the
intensity of their rage, behaved like madmen;
stamping, dashing their hats on the ground, or

thrusting them on with great violence, clenching
their fists with a menacing air, and making many
significant signs among themselves, as though
some scheme had been secretly concocted, now
to be put into action. They then withdrew from
his presence, after a cold and constrained salute,
to confer together around the couch where,
stretched in death, lay the last of the Valois."

These were the rigidly zealous, or extreme,
Catholics, who absolutely rejected the King of
Navarre — placing, as they declared, the maintenance of the religion of the state before all
things. They declined to put any faith in his
promise to permit the exercise of no religion but
the Catholic, except in those towns where the
reformed worship was already established. No
more favourable reception was given to his declaration that "in matters of religion he was open to
conviction, and would be willing to receive instruction from a competent national council, when
the affairs of the realm allowed him leisure. The
test of sincerity proposed to him by those zealots,
of 'embracing the religion of the kingdom with
the kingdom, and — as enjoined on the sovereigns
of France by their coronation oath — suppressing
the religion pretended reformed,' he absolutely
declined to assent to." He even expressed much
indignation at being thus "taken by the throat, as
it were, on the very day of his accession."

Henri's great want at this crisis was want of

money.* He might have bought his kingdom at once had cash been forthcoming. Now he had both to conquer and to buy. He, however, gave those stern Catholics and patriots his word that no change should be made in the offices, pensions, and dignities then held by the princes, great officers of the Crown, or other faithful subjects of the late king. This appears to have had its due effect on those with whose interests it coincided ; for having aided by their shameless peculations in bringing the kingdom to the very verge of ruin, they were unwilling, while aught remained to appropriate, to be displaced.

It was resolved, therefore, by the majority, after due deliberation, to request the Duc de Longueville to inform the king that they were willing to swear fealty and obedience to him as their sovereign if he would place in their hands a promise to abjure heresy in the course of ten days. The "politique" duke refused to be the bearer of such an announcement. François d'O then offered his services. He was Governor of Paris and superintendent of the finances, — a man of the most depraved life. It was notorious that a larger part of the revenue of the kingdom went into the pockets of D'O, and one or two others of similar character, than into

---

* In writing to a friend (M. de Lannoy d'Entragues) at this time to borrow a few thousand crowns, Henri declared that he had "never before been in such straits. He knew not when he could pay, or if he ever could pay at all."—*Lettres de Henri IV.*

the coffers of the state. Of such were the late king's favourites, faithful subjects and ardent Catholics.

Again Henri declined to have a step demanding much serious reflection thus thrust upon him. " None," he said, " but a man wholly destitute of religion could accede to such a proposal." Nevertheless he renewed his promise to seek religious instruction at some future and more convenient season — naming six months as the earliest probable period, yet adding that in so serious a matter he could not submit to constraint.

The Protestant leaders were much displeased by this promise of Henri IV. to seek instruction in religion from an assembly of Catholic priests. The Duc de la Tremouille at once withdrew and marched south with his nine Protestant battalions. He " would never serve," he declared, " under the banner of a sovereign who bound himself to protect idolatry." He, however, allowed it to be understood that he " would not desert the cause of his chief if he continued loyal to his religion and his party." * Other defections followed, seriously diminishing the effectiveness of Henri's small army.

Yet, both among moderate Catholics and Protestants, he had many true friends, who, influenced only by a desire to serve him at this critical position of affairs, declared themselves perfectly willing

* L'Estoile, *Journal de Henri IV.* ; D'Aubigné.

to trust to his loyalty and good faith in the matter of religion, regarding it as ruin to the State should the ancient laws of succession be violated to the prejudice of the legitimate heir to the throne.

It was of the utmost consequence to Henri to retain the Swiss troops in his service. Already they were demanding payment of their arrears, and were preparing for departure. But the Marquis de Guitry, of the Huguenot army, and Harlay de Sancy, an able negotiator who had considerable influence with the Swiss commanders (from having been ambassador from Henri III. to the cantons), sought to impress on them that the salvation of France depended on their stay.* Further, too, that the treaty of their cantons being with the Crown of France, not with the late king personally, it would be a failure of duty on their part to abandon his successor. "With what perils," they were reminded, "would their return to their country be fraught, having no cavalry to escort them, — perils, too, from which neither profit nor glory could be reaped."

Henri IV. had not a crown to spare wherewith to enforce these arguments; but the Swiss commanders readily consented to serve the new sovereign for two months on credit, while the question of further service was referred to their cantons for decision. Sancy and Guitry returned to the king,

---

* Sancy was the possessor of the famous diamond known as "the Sancy."

accompanied by the colonel-commander-in-chief of the Swiss battalions, to confirm this good news. Henri, with that mingled courtesy and gaiety that made its way to so many hearts, cordially thanked and embraced them, declaring, with a little exaggeration perhaps, that to them he owed his crown.

Not they alone, however, were endeavouring to place it firmly on his head. Anne d'Anglure, Baron de Givry, a young officer who had greatly distinguished himself at the taking of Senlis, and who was much attached to Henri, was actively engaged in urging the young Royalist nobility of the Île de France, Picardy, and La Brie to acknowledge Henri IV. Some success he doubtless achieved ; for on returning from the Royalist camp, he said in a loud voice, after embracing the king's knee (the custom of the time on approaching royalty), " Sire, I have just seen the flower of your brave nobility. They impatiently await your orders. You are, as they justly say, the king of brave men, and only cowards will abandon you."

But while Givry, together with the Duc de Montpensier, the Duc de Longueville, and D'Aumont, Marshal of France, were striving to promote Henri's interests, others were considering how best they could turn this confused and unsettled state of affairs to account for their own advantage. Of this number was Maréchal de Biron (Armand de Gontaut), considered the most able general of the Royalist army, also a clever negotiator, but

Duc de Longueville.

Photo-Etching. — From an old Portrait.

one of the most avaricious of men. He proposed
to recognise Henri as captain-general of the kingdom until he should find it convenient to make his
abjuration, — a proposal which seems to have met
with some approval; but Henri at once rejected it.

Biron then made secret overtures to him, promising to devote himself wholly to his interests as
King of France, on condition of being rewarded,
when affairs should take a more favourable turn —
of which he appeared to have no doubt — with the
government of Perigord, and a considerable sum
of money, as soon as the revenues of the state fell
into his hands. This bargain Henri readily closed
with; promises alone were his to give, and very
largely he gave them, with little, if any, considera-
ation for the suffering and impoverished people on
whom would fall the heavy imposts to be levied
for their fulfilment. Biron, being for the moment
satisfied, undertook to make others equally so.

The result was that on the 4th of August a
declaration was made and signed by " Henri, by
the grace of God King of France and Navarre,"
setting forth his determination to maintain the
Catholic religion, and to convoke a national council
to enlighten him on religious subjects within six
months; to secure to all the retention of their
several offices and dignities, and to appoint only
good Catholics to them should vacancies occur
within the above-named period. Diligence also
was promised in seeking out and punishing the

real authors of the murder of the late king; and two gentlemen were to proceed immediately to Rome to inform the Pope of the object of this declaration.

To it was appended another document, "signed by the princes of the blood, dukes, peers, gentlemen and others, agreeing on their part to acknowledge Henri of Navarre King of France, according to the fundamental laws of the kingdom, and promising to do him service, to render him obedience and every assistance in dispersing and exterminating the rebels and enemies who sought to usurp the state." This also was signed and sealed at Saint-Cloud on the 4th of August, 1589, ratified and enregistered by the Royal Parliament, in session at Tours, on the 14th of August.

Many signatures were, however, wanting to this document, the question of precedence proving a stumbling-block to not a few of the grand seigneurs, while others availed themselves of it as a pretext for withholding the signature they had had no intention of giving. The arrogant Duc d'Épernon, for instance, in recent years only promoted by Henri III. to the rank of duke and peer of France, could not condescend to place his name after a marshal of France, as in the case of the Maréchal Duc d'Aumont, of an old ducal family. After so grave an affront to his dignity, D'Épernon left Saint-Cloud, taking with him 7,000 men who were under his command.

Others followed his example, the real motive for these desertions being anxiety to proceed to their respective provinces, there, as governors, to play the part of petty kings, and, with religion as a pretext, to appear in arms against their legitimate sovereign. Several also there were who, without any attachment to Henri or interest in his cause, chose to remain neutral, taking no immediate part in the compact between him and the nobility, but prudently waiting until events should declare on which side Fortune seemed likely to bestow her favour.

While these arrangements were in progress in the royal camp, the chiefs of the League had assembled for the purpose of electing a king. The " Council of Union "— as the representatives of the cities that adhered to the League termed themselves — were completely in harmony on the score of religion : "no Huguenot should sit on the throne of France." But as to which of the several claimants who aspired to occupy it was the most eligible, there was great diversity of opinion, the decision being rendered more difficult by the conflicting interests of those who were called upon to decide. The loss of the " grand Guise " of the Parisian populace was once more bitterly felt. He would have speedily solved the difficulty and cut the Gordian knot by ascending the throne himself.

Such a course was recommended to the Duc

de Mayenne. " So favourable an opportunity," his
sister urged on him, " might never again occur."
But he had not the promptitude, the audacity,
the indefatigable activity of the brilliant Henri
of Guise. Mayenne by no means would have
scrupled to seize the prize for which so many
were hankering, but drew back before the obstacles he, on reflection, saw rising up against him.
He was reputed an able general, though dilatori-
ness in his movements had occasioned him several
defeats. Latterly he had become exceedingly
obese, and too fond of the pleasures of the table,
betraying, as the people said, his German origin by
indulging, to an unlimited extent, his love for the
wines of the Rhine, which not unfrequently reduced
him to helplessness.

As chief of the League and a descendant of
Charlemagne, the Council of Union had expected
him boldly to assert his claim to the throne. As
he did not, they hesitated to name "the next
heir " — his nephew, the young Duc de Guise.
True, this youth was a prisoner in the Château de
Tours, where Mayenne, who regarded him as a
rival, was not unwilling that he should, for a time
at least, remain. The Duc de Lorraine, however,
as the husband of the late Madame Claude of
France, second daughter of Henri II., put forth a
claim to the crown. Catherine de' Medici had
greatly desired that this daughter, or one of her
children, should reign over France. With this

view she had strenuously, though vainly, endeavoured to secure the abrogation of the Salic law.
On those slight grounds the duke founded his
own claim, and afterwards that of his son, the
Duc de Bar, but the council would entertain
neither.

The pretensions of the Duc de Savoie, as a
grandson of François I. on the maternal side, were
also excluded from recognition by the provisions
of the Salic law. Equally untenable was the
claim of Philip II. His aim was to add another
province to Spain by enforcing the claim of his
daughter, the infanta Clara Eugenia, whose mother,
Elisabeth of France, Philip's third wife, was the
eldest daughter of Henri II. Philip believed that
by his own power and influence he could set aside
the Salic law and place his daughter on the throne
of France, under his suzerainty or protection, after
uniting her to his nephew, the Austrian Archduke
Albert. The archduke was then a cardinal, but it
was proposed to release him from his vow of celi-
bacy to marry the infanta.

Even to the zealots of the League, the idea of
France becoming a province of Spain was far from
agreeable. They were willing that Philip should
furnish the sinews of war and enable them to
exterminate the heretics and their leader. But
with all their devotion to Mother Church, they
were not prepared to welcome the gloomy bigot of
Spain as their ruler, or to establish in France a

tribunal the people had often been threatened
with, but always unflinchingly opposed — that of
the Holy Inquisition.   The Spanish priest Mendoza, who on Philip's behalf narrowly watched
the course of events, seeing at once the difficulty
of immediately and directly following up his
master's interests, arranged with Mayenne to
adjourn the discussion and, yielding to the evident
impulse of the majority, to nominate the old Cardinal de Bourbon King of France, under the title
of Charles X.

The cardinal was in very indifferent health; he,
too, was a prisoner at Chinon, whither Henri III.
had transferred him from Amboise, and was not
expected to survive the honor conferred on him
for any inconvenient length of time.   This arrangement seemed to suit all parties, and Charles X.
was declared King of France, — by the grace of
Mayenne and the League, of course ; while, until
his majesty could be delivered from captivity,
Mayenne, as lieutenant-general of the kingdom,
was appointed to govern in his name.   In this
arrangement, as has been observed, the right of
the Bourbons to the throne was unintentionally
acknowledged.

The lieutenant-general's proclamation was signed
and published on the 5th of August.   At the same
time, "all the princes, nobles, gentlemen, and
others, who had followed the fortunes of Henri
III., were invited, while awaiting the release and

presence of their sovereign lord, to rally to the
Union, and either to bear arms against the heretics
or to retire to their estates, making oath before
leaving the capital never again to assist those
heretics or their abettors." They claimed, they
announced, "from all Catholics the obedience due
to their natural, legitimate and Catholic sovereign,"
thus affecting to assert that the crown had been
lawfully transmitted from Henri III. to Charles X.

Defections in the king's army were now of daily
occurrence, while that of the League was receiving
reinforcements from the distant provinces. Many
officers, both Huguenot and Catholic, unwilling
entirely or openly to abandon their leader, made
private business or family affairs a pretext for requesting a *congé*, which he was not in a position
to refuse. In more than one instance, however,
the *congé* was but the preliminary step to passing
over to the League. The Comte de Montholon,
appointed by Henri III. keeper of the seals, on
being confirmed in his post by Henri IV., immediately resigned it. On handing to him the insignia
of that office, he declared that "his conscience
would not allow him to hold the keys of chancel
lor to a Huguenot king." *

Generally the Huguenots were discontented.
The officers for the most part had exhausted their

* Until Montholon's death, which occurred in the following
year, the post of chancellor remained vacant. From Henri's
letters it appears that he kept the seals himself, all documents
being signed in his presence.

resources in the service of their chief, whose sudden
elevation to the throne had been, so far as they
were concerned, a misfortune rather than an
advantage. An attempt was made by Henri IV.
to open a negotiation with Mayenne, through the
intervention of the late king's minister of state,
Nicolas de Villeroi, whom he invited to a consultation in the Bois de Boulogne. Villeroi had for the
second time joined the League, and Mayenne would
not allow him to attend. The lieutenant-general,
however, expressed himself in less discourteous
terms than was customary with the Leaguers,
with reference to Henri IV., whom he, nevertheless, called "the pretender," and said that he
"could consent to no discussion in disparagement
of the rights of King Charles X."

The position of the Royalist army under the
walls of Paris was becoming perilous, and the
Council of Union endeavoured still further to
embarrass the king in his relations with his new
allies. A pretended "letter of the Béarnais to his
coreligionists at Berne" was circulated amongst
them, setting forth that "his then critical situation compelled him for awhile to dissemble his real
sentiments and conceal his intention to maintain
and encourage throughout the kingdom the profession of the Protestant faith, in which he was
resolved to live and die."

This fraud had its effect by raising suspicion in
the minds of those who had believed they could

trust to his loyalty and good faith to carry out the promises of his declaration. His enemies also availed themselves of that document still more to disquiet the Huguenots, who, in a letter published at La Rochelle, menaced him with choosing a more steadfast protector, should he abandon his religion.

Convinced that he could not maintain himself before Paris with an army numbering less than half that of the allied forces with which the siege of the city began, Henri determined to withdraw. A report that he was about to retreat towards the Loire was purposely spread among the troops to deceive his adversaries. Such a retreat had indeed been suggested, but he did not propose to give so much satisfaction to the League as to adopt it. " It would be ruinous to your cause," exclaimed the Huguenot captain, Guitry, —D'Aubigné adding, in his usual plain, frank way, " Who would believe you to be King of France when they saw that you dated your letter from Limoges ? "

Henri, being of the same opinion, resolved to follow up the advantages the royal cause had obtained in the North during the last two months. He proposed, by occupying as many strong places as possible in that direction, to make it the principal seat of the war, returning South in the autumn to hold at Tours, as his declaration bound him, the " grand assembly of princes, nobles, and gentlemen,

further to deliberate on the affairs of the kingdom
before convoking the States General."

On the 8th he decamped, taking with him the
body of his predecessor, that it might not be
exposed to the indignities it was likely to meet
with from the populace of Paris and the Leaguers.*
He therefore proposed to deposit it in the Abbey
of Saint-Corneille de Compiègne until opportunity
offered to transfer it to Saint-Denis, as he had
promised the widowed Queen Louise, whose grief
for her worthless husband was so singularly intense
and prolonged.

Henri divided his army, which consisted of
about 15,000 infantry and 2,000 to 3,000 cavalry,
into three corps,† the first under the Duc de
Longueville, to hold Picardy, which the Spaniards
were then threatening to invade ; the second under
Maréchal d'Aumont, to protect Champagne, the
Swiss regiments and a few hundred cavalry sup-

---

* Another motive is said to have influenced him,— a predic-
tion of an astrologer of the time, that when the remains of
Henri III. should be placed in the Abbey of Saint-Denis, those
of Henri IV. would follow a few days after. Few were then free
from the weakness of giving heed to such prophecies, perhaps
because assassination so often fulfilled them when the death of
any great personage was predicted. Plots were then on foot to
take the life of Henri IV., not only in Paris amongst the Leaguers, but even in his own camp. It was an act of prudence,
then, as well as of respect to his predecessor, to remove the body
for temporary burial elsewhere.

† The number has been variously estimated from 10,000 to
20,000, besides cavalry.

porting them. The Princes de Conti and Montpensier, with Maréchal de Biron and 5,000 or
6,000 infantry and cavalry, accompanied the king.
The Seine was crossed at Meulan, whose importance for that purpose had been remarked by
Rosny. His plan for seizing it by surprise was
approved by the king, and carried out by the baron
and Maréchal d'Aumont.

Henri now marched rapidly towards Normandy,
taking Clermont and several small towns on his
way, and on the 24th, the anniversary of the Saint-
Bartholomew, reached Darnetal, whose governor,
appointed by Henri III., loyally delivered the fortress to his successor before departing to join the
army of the League. The troops, after their long
marches and occasional fighting, short rations and
no pay, were in much need of repose and refresh-
ment. Henri hoped to secure them both in the
fertile district of Caen, and possibly even a fraction
of pay, by depriving the League of the taxes
levied on Normandy, and on receiving the aid
from the German princes and Elizabeth of England, in money and troops, promised to him and
the late king.

An unexpected piece of good fortune put him in
possession of the seaport town of Dieppe, which
the governor, Aimar de Chartes, voluntarily surrendered to him without reservation or conditions. To this act Henri, then and oftentimes
after, declared that he owed his own and the

state's safety. The Governor of Caen followed the example of the Governor of Dieppe, and rallied to the royal cause. The commandants of Boulogne and Pont de l'Arche also sent in their submission.

News soon reached the king that Mayenne was setting out on his march against him, greatly reinforced by Spaniards, Swiss, and Walloons, and detachments of troops from the distant provinces. Crowds, it was further reported, were daily enrolling themselves under his banner. These, doubtless, were inspired by Spanish dollars to pursue with unwonted valour the "heretic pretender," who was flying, they were told, before the army of the League, and whom, unless warned beforehand to cross the sea and seek a refuge in England, it was proposed to lead back in triumph and imprison in the Bastille, there to await his final doom.*   So little did Mayenne dream of defeat that before setting out he wrote to Philip and the pope that he was "sure of victory."

As Henri had with him but about 9,000 troops and from 800 to 1,000 lansquenets, couriers were despatched to Maréchal d'Aumont and the Duc de Longueville to urge them to march with all speed to join the king. The Baron de Rosny, with a small detachment of cavalry, rode out to reconnoitre and ascertain the probable strength of Mayenne's army, a portion of which was passing

* L'Estoile, *Memoires de la Ligue.*

through the woods and plains of the baron's estates at Rosny. From the reports of scouts it was supposed to be not less than from 25,000 to 30,000 strong.

A source of yet greater disquietude to Henri at the moment of entering on a war with the League was the constant vigilance necessary to ensure the safe keeping of Cardinal Charles X. Intrigue succeeded intrigue with the view of effecting his release or escape, and the setting him up to play the part of king in Paris. But Mayenne much preferred to play the part himself. Courage, indeed, failed him to usurp it, yet eventually the League, he trusted, would thrust it upon him, so that he at least was not very energetic in his endeavours to set his king at liberty.

Du Plessis - Mornay suspected the Comte de Soissons of caballing with the Duc d'Épernon and his brother, the young Cardinal de Vendôme, to effect the old cardinal's escape in disguise. Soissons himself had recently escaped from the château-fort of Nantes, and because of the opposition he met with from Henri to his marriage with his sister, Madame Catherine, was rather disposed to thwart than to aid the king's cause. Mornay, however, so indefatigable where the interests of Henri IV. were concerned, succeeded in baffling all schemers and transferring the prisoner of Chinon from the hands of the suspected governor to safer custody at Fontenoy-le-Comte, in

Poitou.* His mind at ease on this matter, Henri then turned his thoughts to defending his crown and his life against Mayenne, which — unflinchingly and heroically — he resolved to do, supported by the justice of his cause, his courage, and the fidelity of a few attached friends.

* The old cardinal is said to have written to his nephew, acknowledging him as king, and, after referring to his state of health and infirmities, to have requested his liberation. (*Journal de Henri IV.*) Other authorities think it doubtful.

CHAPTER III.

N retiring on Normandy, Henri proposed
to attempt the siege of Rouen. But this
idea he was compelled to abandon on
learning that Mayenne was advancing, though in
his usual leisurely fashion, to give him battle at
the head of 30,000 men. The lieutenant-general
of the Leaguers expected to be further reinforced
en route by 5,000 or 6,000 cavalry, whom he was
anxious should join him and complete his force
before coming to an encounter with his enemy.
Henri's position seemed extremely perilous. Eight
thousand or nine thousand troops were the utmost
he could assemble to oppose the comparatively
overwhelming host commanded by Mayenne.*

* Some writers have stated the number of troops under
Henri's command as not exceeding 3,000 or 4,000; while Mayenne's army they increase to 38,000. It is probably more cor-

A council was held, and some of his generals
were of opinion that it would be a prudent step
on the king's part to cross the Channel, and seek
refuge for awhile in England, returning to France
with the troops and money promised him by
Elizabeth.   This was advice which by no means
found favour with Henri.   He is reported to have
indignantly exclaimed: "Have not I yet a few
brave Frenchmen under my command?   To counsel flight, then, is to give me counsel impossible
to follow!"   To which Biron added: "To leave
France but for twenty-four hours would be his
banishment forever."

It was, however, as clear to the king as to
others that it would be great temerity to attempt
with his small force to resist the large army about
to confront him.   Yet it would be no less dangerous, he considered, to shut himself up in Dieppe
than to march out with forces so unequal and offer
the enemy battle in the open country.   He decided
therefore, without abandoning Dieppe, to remove
his quarters a league and a half from that city,
and to take up an advantageous position he had
remarked on the side of the small towns of Arques
and Martin-Église.   He took possession of Eu and
Tréport, and established himself strongly around
Dieppe, having his camp at the foot of the château

rectly given by other historians at 30,000, and Henri's as between
8,000 and 9,000, the number with which, but a month earlier, he
and Biron left Saint-Cloud.

on the heights of Arques, and placing a sufficient garrison in Pollet, the principal maritime faubourg of Arques and Dieppe.

He was ill provided with artillery, but partly supplied the want of it by mounting his *cou-levrines*, or smallest cannon, on gun-carriages with wheels, and putting horses to them, being thus the first to make use of light artillery. The position taken up by the king appears to have been very wisely chosen, and every advantage it afforded most skilfully turned to account, art adding to its natural difficulty of access on every point. Henri and Biron were themselves the engineers, and by trenches and earthworks rendered impregnable every avenue leading to the town or château. Soldiers, citizens, and sailors worked with amazing diligence in digging moats and throwing up fortifications.

Mayenne's determination not to attack until every petty contingent he was expecting joined him had allowed his adversary time thus thoroughly to prepare for resistance. Not until the 13th of September did the army of the League make its appearance in sight of Arques. The two following days were spent by Mayenne in reconnoitring the position, and deliberating with his officers in council. An attempt was made to draw Henri into quitting his post; but as he remained immovable Mayenne divided his army into two corps, and attacked simultaneously the faubourg

of Pollet — the defence of which was confided to
Châtillon and Guitry — and the advanced posts of
the camp of Arques, and in both places was driven
back with extraordinary vigour. For three weeks
the assaults on the city and every point of the
entrenchments were continued unceasingly, and on
every occasion were effectually repulsed.

On the 20th Mayenne, having determined to
make a vigorous onslaught on the camp, silently
crossed the river Aulne in the night. A thick
mist in the morning favoured the aggressors by
preventing the Royalists seeing their approach
and pointing their cannon. The assaulting party
was headed by a regiment of lansquenets, who
feigned refusal to fight their countrymen — the
lansquenets of the royal army — at the same time
lowering their pikes, and crying " *Vive le roi!* "
as a sign of surrender. These traitors, on loudly
exclaiming that they were Protestants, were assisted by the Germans and Swiss to enter the
entrenchments. But no sooner were they there
than they fell savagely on those whose hands they
had grasped to enable them to enter, and took
possession of a " *maladrerie* " (a disused lazaretto)
which formed the defence of the camp on that
side.

Biron was soon surrounded, and two of their
officers penetrated even to the king's quarters, and
called on him " to surrender to M. de Mayenne."
For some minutes confusion was at its height, and

Henri, much excited, seized a lance to repulse the traitors, and demanded in a loud tone " if fifty gentlemen could not be found in his army to die with their king." A short but sanguinary conflict then took place, when Châtillon and Guitry, who had hastened from Pollet, arrived with their Huguenots, retook the lazaretto, dislodged the intruders, and not only were fifty gentlemen found ready to fight and die with their king, but every Huguenot in his army would have been proud to do so.

Rosny, who commanded a small detachment of cavalry on the opposite side of the camp, whose chief defence there was a deep morass, was attacked by a larger force, and in the *mêlée* that ensued was wounded, and his horse killed under him. "This," Rosny observes,* "was the beginning of a rout, which must have ensued had not the Swiss regiments so firmly and defiantly stood their ground, thus giving us time to rally and to make an effort to repulse the invaders. But another troop was riding up to support them, who in their eagerness to attack were unmindful, or perhaps were ignorant, of the nature of the ground they had to traverse. Dashing madly forward to charge us, the horses with their heavy-armed riders plunged into the soft, spongy earth overlying the morass, sinking to such a depth that but few of the animals could be extricated. The riders with

* *Mémoires de Sully.*

considerable difficulty released themselves, and were obliged to leave their lances and other parts of their accoutrements in the bog."

These skirmishes and hand-to-hand encounters took place during a thick mist early on a September morning — the besieged consequently being unaware of the full extent of the danger which threatened them. They were, in fact, on the very verge of destruction, though the besiegers would have had to pay a heavy price for their victory. Suddenly, however, the mists of morning rolled off, and the sun shone forth with great brilliancy, revealing the whole of the army of the League in motion. So near, too, had they silently approached, that none could hope to reach the earthworks which formed the Royalists' last entrenchments, though all resolved to resist unto death, and to sell their lives most dearly.*

Salvation came from what had been regarded as a great misfortune, inability to point the cannon of the château throughout the morning. Now, however, the royal batteries opened upon the enemy with deadly results, Mayenne having brought his army into a position (possibly misled by the mist) where their full effects were felt. Volley after volley was poured into their ranks, thinning them wonderfully. Unable to support this unexpected, and under Biron's direction well-sustained, fire from the guns of the château, the

* *Mémoires de Sully* ; Mathieu.

army of the League retired in disorder on the flank of the valley of Bethune, amazed, it would seem, at the greatness of their loss in killed and wounded, the *coulevrines*, drawn by horses, having followed the movements of the Royalist cavalry and completed the victory.*

Mayenne and his officers were greatly disconcerted by the determined and effective resistance they had met with from the royal army, resistance that had resulted in their defeat instead of the victory so confidently announced before leaving Paris. "The heretic Béarnais," too, who as a captive at his chariot-wheel was to have given added *éclat* to the lieutenant-general's triumphal return to the capital, was perforce left behind, master of the field.

It was a mortifying position, and Mayenne, having given two days to rest and reflection, determined on a pretended hasty flight in the night in order to deceive the king and his generals, while by a circuitous route of seven leagues he and the débris of his army reached the opposite side of the camp of Arques. On the 26th he appeared before Dieppe with the intention of

---

* This first employment of light artillery was due to the suggestion of Charles Brise, a gunner of Normandy. But its value and importance do not appear to have been perceived or followed up until many years later by Gustavus Adolphus in the Thirty Years' War and — again after a considerable lapse of time — by Frederick the Great of Prussia. — *Guerres des Français.*

again attempting to invest it. But Henri had
anticipated this manœuvre, and, after leaving a
sufficient garrison in Arques, had withdrawn with
the greater part of his troops to the faubourgs of
Dieppe. Perceiving his mistake, the lieutenant-
general would have fallen back on Arques, which
he supposed abandoned. But a vigorous sortie
from the château convinced him that the vigilant
and active adversary he had expected to deceive
had been more on the alert than he.*

For ten days the armies remained face to face,
cannonading and harassing each other, but coming
to no general engagement. On the 29th a detachment of 1,200 men landed at Dieppe, sent by
Queen Elizabeth, also money and ammunition,
and a promise to the king of a further reinforcement of 4,000 troops speedily to follow. On the
2d of October they arrived, while the Duc de
Longueville, Maréchal d' Aumont, La Noue, and
the Comte de Soissons and 500 gentlemen, having
effected a junction of their forces, were marching
to the king's assistance. An army of from 20,000
to 25,000 men being thus on the point of assembling, Mayenne, fearing to be hemmed in and his
army utterly lost should he wait their arrival,
began his final retreat on the 6th. He made no
attempt to oppose the advance of the king's

---

* Henri is said to have remarked on this occasion : "My
cousin of Mayenne is a great captain, but I am an earlier riser
than he."

troops, but marched steadily towards the banks of the Somme to meet the reinforcements of Spaniards of the Netherlands promised him by the Prince of Parma.*

Desertion among the troops, and dissension among the nobility, who brought each his contingent of followers to swell the army of the League, were frequent in Mayenne's camp. The principal command of the army, or at least the post of second in command to Mayenne, was expected by them. As it was impossible to gratify the ambition of all these gentlemen, several followed the example of the Marquis de Pont, son of the Duc de Lorraine, who, being a candidate for the throne, thought the supreme command of the Union belonged to him; but when he found that the lieutenant-general was not disposed either to cede the chief command or to guarantee his succession to the throne on the demise of the cardinal-king, he indignantly withdrew from the army, and with his 4,000 Lorrainers marched back to his country.†

Thus the army of the League became considerably diminished, and those who remained in it disheartened, while the success of the Royalists after the perils that had threatened them inspired both the troops and their leaders with renewed courage, confidence, and hope.

Mayenne sank greatly in public opinion as a general when the details of the engagement at

* J. Servan, *Guerres des Français.*   † *Mémoires de Sully.*

Arques, and its humiliating results to the army of the League, became generally known. A report was spread, by Madame de Montpensier it was supposed, that the "Béarnais" was killed. Whether this report of his death was believed by the priests or not, they availed themselves of it for the subject of some stirring harangues. Doubtless they gave credit to the information received from the army that "the pretender" was so far beaten that he was in no condition to resume hostilities. But the delusion could not last long, and while Mayenne, unwilling to return to the capital until the first clamorous outcry at his defeat had in some measure subsided, was lingering on the banks of the Somme for his long-delayed reinforcements, the "Béarnais" in person, at the head of an army 22,000 strong, and well provided with artillery, appeared at the gates of Paris.*

A little before daybreak on the 1st of November three columns of infantry attacked the faubourgs on the left bank of the Seine, — Henri's design being to spread alarm throughout Paris, to assault it, and, should he see opportunity for vigorous effort, to make himself master of it. With this object in view he had taken the precaution of ordering Montmorency-Thoré to destroy the

---

* Sully's Memoirs state that Henri, before leaving Dieppe, was twice fired upon — happily without effect — by a party of fusiliers lying in ambush near to a field where he and some of his officers were engaged in a military game. This may have given rise to the report of his death.

bridge of Sainte-Maixance, to prevent Mayenne from crossing the Oise and hastening to the relief of the city. "The sixteen," * no less terrified than the people, despatched couriers to their lieutenant-general with urgent requests for his immediate return. The faubourgs, attacked simultaneously, were all carried within an hour, and success would probably have been the result of this *coup-de-main* but that Montmorency — taken suddenly ill, it was said — failed to destroy the bridge.

News was soon brought to the king that Mayenne had crossed it without obstacle, and was approaching Paris, but from the opposite bank, that he might not encounter "the pretender." The assault on the city was therefore given up, and while the pillage of the faubourgs was going on — for Henri was compelled to allow his troops to take whatever they could lay their hands on in lieu of the pay he had not the means of giving them — he sought repose for an hour or two on some straw heaped up at the foot of a table in the hall of the Petit Bourbon.

On entering the Faubourg Saint-Germain, Châtillon's Huguenots raised the cry "Saint-Bartholomew!" which seems to have excited both themselves and the people, and to have led to much shedding of blood. Several hundred pris-

* Representatives of the League in the sixteen districts into which Paris was divided by the Leaguers.

oners were taken, and many more slain."* The booty appears to have been immense. Rosny, whose regiment took part with Châtillon's in the attack on Saint-Germain, states that his share "was 3,000 crowns, and that others fared equally well." He, however, seems to have been better pleased with the sum he obtained than with the mode of obtaining it. "For it was with feelings of extreme reluctance," he says, that he "struck down opponents who were already more dead than alive with terror; but it was necessary to overcome all who resisted."

He and Châtillon and several of their party entered the city, but drew back on perceiving that they were not followed. An order had been brought from the king to desist from the attack, the whole of Mayenne's army being in sight and the advanced guard about to enter. Though Henri and Biron believed that the city might have been taken, they "thought it the more prudent plan to be satisfied for a time with what had been done, and in spreading terror amongst those who had presumed to contemn the legitimate sovereign, but who now knew that he was not dead, and what in future might be expected from him."†

---

* Amongst the prisoners was the Prior of the Jacobins of Paris, le père Bourgoing, who was accused of having encouraged Jacques Clément to assassinate Henri III. He was taken with arms in his hands at the assault on the faubourgs.

† *Mémoires de Sully;* L'Estoile, *Journal de Henri IV.*

On the 3d of November Henri left the faubourgs of Paris, and on the 4th drew up his army
in order of battle on the plain of Montrouge. As
Mayenne did not think fit to accept this challenge,
the royal army on the following day withdrew,
marching in the direction of Tours. On their
march they invested and took Étampes, Janville,
Château-Dun, and Vendôme, the last named a city
of Henri's own private domain, which had declared
against him. He had with him the priest Bourgoing under arrest, intending, on his arrival at
Tours, to send him for trial and judgment before
the royal Parliament, in session at that city. While
at Étampes, he was reminded of his vow to avenge
the murder of the late king by the urgent request
of Queen Louise that the priest who had encouraged the assassin to take the life of his sovereign
might not go unpunished.

From the pulpit he had been loud in his praise
of the "glorious martyr's heroic deed," and had
held him up as an example to others,— the new
victim of fanaticism he indirectly pointed to being
unmistakably the "heretic Béarnais." The Parliament condemned Bourgoing to suffer death. His
punishment, the horrible one of quartering, he is
said to have undergone with great courage. To
the last he denied any participation in the murder
of Henri III., and before dying prayed aloud for
the conversion of Henri of Navarre. Several persons were hanged about the same time, some by

way of reprisal for executions that had taken place in Paris of partisans of Henri IV.*

Henri's entrance into his provisionary capital of Tours was by torchlight on the 22d of November, and, in a modified way, triumphal. His military reputation already stood very high, but the affair of Arques had raised it immensely. The magistrates of the Royalist party were in waiting to receive him, with Achille de Harlay, president of the Parliament of Paris, at their head. He had recently been liberated from the Bastille, where he and several of his colleagues were imprisoned for opposition to the views of the "sixteen," who now graciously permitted him to purchase his liberty for a considerable ransom. Two cardinals were also there, Lenoncourt and Vendôme, to offer their felicitations to the king on his accession to the throne; yet the latter — Henri's young cousin — had not wholly abandoned the hope of sitting on the throne himself.

Far more gratifying to the king was the presence of the Venetian ambassador, Giovanni Moncenigo, who awaited him at Tours to compliment him, and to present the congratulatory letters of the signiory with his own of reappointment as ambassador to Henri IV. It was a great satisfaction to the king to be acknowledged by so ably governed and influential a Catholic state as the Republic of Venice. This decisive step, so

* Palma-Cayet.

opposed to the views of Spain, and so calculated
to draw down on the signiory the anger of
Philip and the Pope, was taken by Venice partly
for the purpose of avenging herself for the
violent pressure put upon her in the preceding
year to compel her against her will to join in
the disastrous expedition on England of Philip's
"invincible armada."

Venice lost several of her finest vessels in the
storms and tempests encountered by the unfortunate Spanish fleet. The loss was severely felt,
for " *Venezi la superba*," though regarded then
and for some time after as a powerful and flourishing state, was gradually declining, and her East-
ern commerce, the source of her great wealth,
fast flowing into other channels. Yet she alone
of the Italian states dared openly to brave the
Escurial and the Vatican by acknowledging and
congratulating the Huguenot King of France.
Tuscany and Mantua, however, secretly sent him
assurances of their friendship.

The Sultan Mourad wrote him a very long
letter, in admiration of his bravery, his clemency,
his detestation of idolatry, and his soldierly qualities generally. He placed at his service his land
and maritime forces ; offered his " protection and
aid in subduing his enemies and establishing him
on his throne as the most powerful prince in the
world." He was himself very desirous of attacking Philip II., and was fitting out a fleet for that

purpose, but a revolt of his Arabian subjects put an end for a time to his projects.

The king's stay at Tours was but a short one. A few days only could he give to rest and receiving congratulations. The "assembly of princes, nobles, and gentlemen which was to have been held at Tours in October to consider the state of affairs" was, on account of the war, postponed until March; for Henri could not lie by for the winter. He must set out to rejoin his army, which he had left at Château-Dun, where envoys from the Swiss Protestant cantons had arrived with orders for the Swiss regiments to continue in the service of Henri IV., also to renew with him the treaties which united the cantons to the Crown.

War was raging throughout the kingdom; but many towns that Henri proposed to attack surrendered on his approach and declared their adherence to him, the garrisons frequently joining his army, of which Le Mans, Alençon, Angers, Laval, and one or two other small towns were instances. Pillage was not then permitted, and the terms of capitulation were always easy. A little money for his troops, with a supply of provisions, were usually all he asked, and were readily granted,— his clemency and soldierly bonhomie opening hearts and purses which excess and cruelties closed to the Leaguers. That "nothing succeeds like success" was soon very evident to the soldier-king. Within the space of a few weeks the whole of Normandy from the Seine to La Vire had either submitted to him or had been taken by force. Some among the people declared that " God must be on his side, Huguenot though he was, and would by and by work his conversion, for doubtless he was a valorous, humane and clement prince."

As the news of his prosperous campaign continued to spread, the number of his partisans increased, and several of the nobility of the "politique" party who had cautiously stood aloof as neutrals after the assassination of Henri III. now declared for him. Such powerful nobles as Montmorency (Damville) — almost king in his province of Languedoc — the Duc de Lesdiguières — a Protestant — with Alphonso d'Ornano, in Dauphiny, and La Vallette, in Provence, now rallied to his standard.

The Parliament of Rennes, with a part of Brittany, also made its submission. Even Sixtus V. is said to have shown symptoms of wavering in his determination never to acknowledge the Béarnais as King of France. From "good Catholics" he had heard most favourable reports of him, which, with a sort of admiration the pontiff was known to entertain for the Huguenot's energy of character and bold defence of his rights, might induce him, it was suspected, should heresy be renounced — as was hoped and prayed for by so many — not to refuse absolution.

At all events, he evinced but scant approval of

Philip's schemes, and showed little favour to the Leaguers, responding by no means liberally to their applications for money. He well knew that the greater part of the chief men among them were mere ambitious intriguers, actuated only by motives of self-interest, while others were in reality but imbecile fanatics. Mayenne had been at great pains to convince him that the old cardinal was really the chosen King of all France, — meaning himself and a few of his partisans. Sixtus did not oppose Mayenne's king, but had not formally recognised him. As he had a voice in the election of a sovereign to succeed the cardinal, Charles X., he despatched Cardinal Caëtano to Paris, towards the end of October, with the title of legate, and charged with the mission of " endeavouring to unite France under a truly Christian king," naming neither the cardinal nor any of the ambitious rivals who claimed the succession, but who, failing to secure the whole, would have been willing, Philip excepted, to divide the prey amongst them.

Sixtus inclined to the Catholic Bourbons, but by no means to the exclusion of the claims and the possible conversion of Henri of Navarre, who, as he stated, " appeared to be very active and difficult to subdue." On a previous occasion, on being told that Mayenne passed more of his time at table than Henri in taking rest, he declared that "the Huguenot, in his opinion, would eventually prevail over both Mayenne and the League."

Mayenne was unwilling to submit either to Spain or the Bourbons. He wished to reign in the name of the captive king, and had no objection to Spanish aid — but in dollars rather than troops. Philip, however, was not satisfied merely to play the part of banker to the League. He had made great sacrifices, both in men and money, with the view of annexing France to Spain. It was now time, he thought, to reap a little where he had sown so freely, and, as a beginning, he proposed that he should be proclaimed " Protector of France during the captivity of King Charles X." This was intended to prepare the way for the abolition of the Salic law and the elevation of Clara Eugenia as queen. The only part of his programme that Philip had changed was the substitution of a French for an Austrian prince to share the infanta's throne with the title of king, to whom on his marriage and coronation he proposed to transfer the county of Flanders, to be united to France.

The nobility, the magistrates, and principal persons among Mayenne's adherents urged him to refuse all countenance to proposals so insulting to the French nation. But he, replying adroitly to Philip's agents, Mendoza and Morio, declared that " the holy father would be deeply offended if any other than he, the Vicar of Jesus Christ, should assume the title of protector of the Catholic religion in France." It was therefore deemed prudent

by Mendoza and his colleague to refrain for the
moment from pressing on the lieutenant-general a
clearer understanding of Philip's views; the more
so as the project of marrying the infanta to a
French prince had in it no attraction for him.   He
knew, being already married, that he could not be
the prince selected for that honour.

Philip had in his pay both the democratic faction
of the "sixteen," and many of the members of the
Council of Union; all the monks, the preachers,
and most of the inferior clergy.   The "sixteen"
appear to have believed it possible to establish in
France, under the protectorate of the old demoniacal Spanish tyrant, a sort of theocratic republic,
governed from the pulpit.   But a heavy blow
awaited the "sixteen," threatening their overthrow, and upsetting all their schemes.

As lieutenant-general of the kingdom, acting in
the name of the captive cardinal-king, Mayenne
possessed a degree of power which under a protectorate would be considerably diminished.   He
determined therefore, by the exercise of that supposed delegated royal authority, to dissolve the
Council of Union, from whom the Spaniards were
intriguing to obtain a declaration in favour of
Philip's protectorate.   The council had not shown
themselves so docile in the furtherance of his
views as Mayenne expected, nor did they always
submit the result of their deliberations to him;
but, with his usual prudence, he chose as a favour-

able moment for his purpose the eve of his departure on a fresh expedition against Henri IV. Paris
was full of troops, and the lieutenant-general's
military staff assembled around him when the
Council of Union was summoned to his presence.

He explained to that body, consisting of forty
members, that, feeling himself overburdened with
affairs of state when on the point of taking the
command of the army, he found it necessary that
his council should accompany him. For that
object, and in virtue of the royal authority confided to him, he proposed to dissolve the present
Council of Union, and to form a more numerous
but private council. This announcement fell like
a thunderbolt on the "sixteen," who saw in it
their own inevitable doom. But Mayenne had so
well taken his measures and so forcibly asserted,
as it were, his royal prerogative, that they felt
compelled to submit.

The lieutenant-general, having deprived the
Bishop of Meaux (whom he suspected of being
inimical to him) of his post of chancellor and
keeper of the keys, transferred them to the
Archbishop of Lyons. He then appointed four
secretaries of state, charged henceforth with the
management of all public affairs; while, to prevent any outbreak of public opinion against this
secretly executed *coup d' état*, he convoked the
States General for the 3d of February, at Melun.

Continuing his preparations for resuming the

war, and being reinforced by 2,000 or 3,000 Walloons and Spaniards, Mayenne left Paris early in January to besiege Meulan, and, by more successful operations against the Béarnais, to retrieve his military reputation. For until he could reënter Paris wearing the laurel crown of victory, his views on that other crown he coveted had no prospect of realisation.

CHAPTER IV.

SCARCELY had the lieutenant-general, accompanied by a brilliant staff, set out to take the command of the armies, when the legate, Cardinal Caëtano, entered the capital, attended by a numerous escort of distinguished prelates, controversialists, and preachers. Amongst them was the Jesuit Bellarmino, a celebrated theologian ; also Panigarola, Bishop of Asti, whom Gregory XIII. sent to Paris after the massacre of the Saint-Bartholomew, as the fittest person, being the most eloquent preacher of his day, to offer the felicitations of his holiness to Charles IX. and the queen-mother, and to deliver an harangue on that "glorious event" and the victory achieved over heresy.

The legate was received in Paris with much

state and ceremony, after his leisurely journey.
He had made a rather long stay in Lyons and
Dijon, sowing discord, it appears, wherever he
halted, and wholly disregarding the instructions
he had received from Sixtus V.   These were to
the effect that he should not declare himself an
enemy of Henri of Navarre, so long as there was
hope of that heretic's conversion ; that he should
remain neutral regarding the pretensions of the
various princes to the throne, occupying himself
with the interests of religion only, and accepting,
without respect of persons, whoever should be
elected king, on condition of his being a French-
man, "professing obedience to the Church, and
approved by the nation."

But Sixtus had erred greatly in his choice of an
agent to carry out his views.   The mission was a
mission of peace ; the man it was entrusted to was
a violent fanatic, whose sole aim was the destruction of the Béarnais.   Caëtano seemed sent as a
firebrand to rekindle the flames of fanaticism,
which had recently shown some signs of abate-
ment towards Henri of Navarre — at least, among
the Parisian populace.   There was a longing for
peace, and the people would have been glad to
find it under the rule of a prince so gallant and
brave, and so merciful in the midst of victory, as
they had been led to believe, since truer reports
of his achievements and character had been circulated amongst them.

But this sort of feeling did not fall in with the views of the Leaguers, the priests, and the Spanish party, and Caëtano, far from holding aloof from them, threw himself headlong into the intrigues of the " sixteen," and openly and persistently promoted the designs of Philip II., and his agents. He expected all opposition to give way before him, and so great was his arrogance that, on the first occasion of his taking his seat in the Palace of Justice, he placed himself on the king's throne. The first president, Brisson — appointed to fill that office by the Leaguers since Harlay's imprisonment — immediately rose, and, taking the legate by the hand, conducted him to a seat below his own.

Except in this instance of rebuff for a great breach of etiquette and disregard of the dignity of the sovereign court of magistrates, the Parliament submissively adopted the legate's opinions, and acted on his suggestions. But Sixtus, who had himself indulged in indecently extravagant commendation of the assassin of Henri III., was now compelled to send instructions to his fiery legate to "moderate his zeal and restrain the violence of his language, which tended to encourage agitators whose harangues inflame the public mind."

Henri IV., on hearing of Caëtano's arrival, issued a decree from his camp ordering " all customary honours to be paid to the legate if he came to felicitate the king and to recognise him as the legitimate sovereign of France." But if with contrary intent, then he (Henri IV.) "solemnly protested against the proceedings of the Pope and his legate in favour of the League and the King of Spain." As a reply to the above, the Parliament of Paris annulled a decree of the "Pseudo-Parliament" of Tours, who had just declared "guilty of high treason whoever held any communication with the legate until he had sought his majesty's permission to reside in France." *

This greatly enraged Caëtano, who made strenuous efforts to revive the waning ardour of the "sixteen." They, however, with the prospect before their eyes of their office being summarily abolished by "the royal authority of the lieutenant-general"— who was expected, this time without fail, to return from the wars a conquering hero — were less extreme in their acts and denunciations than the legate, the priests, and the agents of Philip II. desired. But Caëtano could count on the Sorbonne. The anathemas of that enlightened body were at his disposal for all who were not in as full agreement as themselves with the pious aims of that worthy prelate.

* The sovereign Parliament of Paris was then divided between Tours and the capital. The magistrates who were members of the latter division were ardent Leaguers—those of the Parliament of Tours, partisans of Henri IV. Both issued decrees, and each in its turn declared those of the other " void and of no effect."

On the 10th of February, then, acting on his
suggestion, the learned doctors publicly denounced
the opinion held, as they understood, by some
persons, that the sovereign pontiff had no right
to excommunicate kings, and further, that " Henri
of Bourbon, a relapsed heretic, ought, or could
not be recognised as king, even should he again
become a Catholic." This was followed up on
the 1st of March by a mandate issued by the
legate to all archbishops and bishops, prohibit-
ing them from repairing to Tours should they
be invited there to instruct Henri of Bourbon
in the Catholic religion, seeing that neither
Bourbon nor those who were with him had
any authority to convoke the bishops, and that,
in fact, no council was necessary for such purpose.

A few days later a stringent decree of the
Paris Parliament commanded all persons to use
every means, not excepting force if needed, to
rescue King Charles X. from captivity, while all
communication with Henri of Bourbon or his
agents was "interdicted on pain of death." To
invest these various commands and prohibitions
with greater solemnity, and to further assure their
due enforcement, all the municipal authorities
assembled in the Church of the Augustins, and
there, in the hands of the legate, solemnly renewed
the oath of the union.*   On the 11th the Parlia-

* Palma-Cayet.

ment and all who held any office in the Government followed their example.

The part so directly taken by Rome, represented by the legate, in the affairs of the holy union imparted a certain increase of power to the "sixteen," which for awhile seemed likely to compensate that body for the abolition of the council.

Paris for upwards of two months had been almost entirely in the hands of the legate, the League, and the Jesuit preachers ; but meanwhile the Royalist army and that of the League had not been idle. The latter had set out to lay siege to Meulan, the defence of which was entrusted to Rosny, who greatly distinguished himself by his vigorous repulse of a no less vigorous attack, and the wise precautions which enabled the garrison to hold out until assistance came from the royal army.

The king had retaken several small towns, and was then engaged in assaulting the strongly fortified town of Falaise. He had called on the governor, the Comte de Brissac, to surrender; but he, trusting in the strength of his fortifications, replied : " I have made a vow not to listen to the word 'surrender' for at least six months to come." Henri, with his usual fondness for repartee, rejoined : " The count has made a rash vow, but I will undertake to absolve him from it, and to convert the six months into six days." Within that time Falaise was taken by storm and sacked, and Brissac surrendered himself prisoner.*

Henri then hastened to the relief of Meulan, and by a diversion on Poissy — taken by assault under Mayenne's eyes — compelled him to raise the siege.

While the two armies were in presence on the two banks of the Seine, both commanders received intelligence of the Marquis d'Alegre having taken the old château of Rouen by surprise. Immediately the king and the lieutenant-general began to march with all speed in that direction; but on reaching Gaillon, Henri was informed that a capitulation had been signed after a few hours' resistance. He resolved, therefore, on besieging Dreux; while Mayenne, leaving his army on the banks of the Seine, on the 26th of July went to Brussels to confer with the Prince of Parma. Ostensibly he sought reinforcements, but his real object was to request a further supply of Spanish doubloons to pay the Swiss, who had menaced desertion.†

Philip, though much displeased at Mayenne's opposition to the protectorate, yet would not, he said, allow the Béarnais to overwhelm the League. He therefore gave him 2,000 cavalry, Spaniards

* D'Aubigné.

† This was customary with these hardly used mercenaries, who, with no interest in the quarrel, risked their lives in fighting the battles of others for pay, which was rarely paid, and the chance of plunder.

and Belgians, commanded by the young Count Egmont. A small detachment of infantry was also allowed to join him, but to his appeals for pecuniary aid Philip turned a deaf ear. He was, indeed, so ill supplied with doubloons himself that since the loss of his Armada the King of Spain had repudiated his debts and become bankrupt.

On the 10th of March Mayenne returned, crossed the Seine at Mantes, and on the 11th marched to the relief of Dreux, which had held out for twelve days against the repeated attacks of the Royalists. The king on the 12th determined to decamp, but by no means to be put to flight. " Comrades," he said, addressing his principal officers, " we must efface the reproach of raising a siege by the gain of a battle ; and with men of proved courage like you, doubtless the result will be a signal victory. I need say nothing more to you."* That night he slept at Nonancourt, where, with Biron and other officers, he arranged his plan of battle. On the morrow he deployed his army on the plain of Ivry, near Nonancourt and Dreux.

Henri intended to combat the enemy at the passage of the Eure, but Mayenne crossed the river at Ivry, and the day had passed, as the king wrote to Rosny, " in mere skirmishing, taking up quarters, and securing all possible advantages, the general action being deferred till the morrow."

* Péréfixe; Mathieu; D'Aubigné.

Rosny and the three companies of mounted arque-busiers under his command at Passy hastened to join the army, yet fearing, as he states, that they would arrive too late to assist the king — whose troops were greatly inferior in number to Ma-yenne's — by taking any part in the battle. He was, however, rewarded for his diligence by reach-ing Ivry before the fighting began.

Mayenne, it appears, would have been content to relieve Dreux and avoid a battle — indeed, that for the time was his only aim; but his officers imagined that an opportunity of overwhelming the Béarnais at one blow then presented itself, and must not be lost. A council was held. The lieutenant-general was constrained to fight, his desire for delay being overruled, chiefly by the vehement reproaches of Count Egmont, who vauntingly declared that "with his squadron alone he would vanquish the pretender's whole army." This was decisive, and Egmont, elated by his victory in the council over Mayenne, and the prospect of that he had rashly promised over the Béarnais, rushed from the council exclaiming excitedly, "Battle! battle!" Mayenne, however, took every precaution to assure his retreat, issuing orders to prepare for the destruction of the bridges on the Seine. Henri also, in case of a reverse, was advised to ensure his retreat, but he replied that "there was no retreat for him but the field of battle."

On the morning of the 14th of March, while preparing for action, Henri IV. sent for the commandant of the Swiss troops, Colonel Schomberg. This officer, importuned by his soldiers, had asked the king on the previous evening to pay the arrears due to them. As usual, he was without funds, and the request, as he thought, was made at an inopportune moment. He therefore hastily replied, "Is it the act of a man of honour to ask for money on the eve of a battle?" Schomberg, much mortified, retired without answering. On the morrow Henri repented of his harshness and injustice. "Colonel," he said, addressing Schomberg, "I insulted you yesterday; to-day may be the last of my life, and as I would not like to take away what I could not restore — the honour of a gentleman, whose valour and merit I know so well as yours — I ask you to pardon and embrace me." "Your majesty yesterday wounded me, certainly," replied Schomberg, "but to-day you kill me, for the honour you do me obliges me to die in your service." He was killed in the battle.*

As soon as the king appeared at the head of his squadron, the charge was sounded. Rosny was riding by his side. The king desired that he should see the disposition of the two armies, and, as he said, learn something more of his trade. There was, however, yet a short prayer to be said, and a few last words to be addressed to his army;

* Mathieu.

and very devoutly the army listened while the
king, bareheaded, said the following prayer:

" O God, thou knowest my thoughts and seest
my heart. If it is to my people's advantage that I
should possess the crown, then favour my cause
and protect my arms. But should I be one of
those kings whom thou givest in thy wrath, take
from me both life and crown, and grant that my
death may deliver France from the calamities of
war, and that my blood be the last to be shed in
this quarrel." A prolonged shout of " *Vive le
roi !* " rose from the troops as an amen to the
prayer.

" Behold, they pray!" had been a cry often
heard on the battle-field during the long wars of
religion, and was regarded as a sign of the Huguenots' conscious weakness in the presence of their
Catholic foes. But on this occasion Catholics and
Protestants rivalled each other in invoking the aid
of the God of armies; and while the Calvinist
minister, Gabriel d'Amours, prayed as usual, standing before the king, ere the battle began, a Cor-
delier monk, bearing a large crucifix, marched
at the head of the Walloons, anathematising both
" *hérétiques* " and " *politiques.*"

The minister's appeal to heaven for a blessing
on the Huguenots' arms being ended, Henri,
turning towards his troops, said : " Friends and
comrades, you are Frenchmen, and so am I, your
king. Behold, our enemy is before us ; the greater

their number the greater the glory. If to-day
you risk life for me, I also risk it for you ; for I
will either vanquish or die with you. I pray you
keep well your ranks ; but should you be carried
away by the excitement of battle, think immediately of rallying ; it is the winning of the combat.
And should you lose your ensigns, do not lose
sight of my white plume; you will find it always
in the road to glory and honour." Another shout,
loud and long, of " *Vive le roi!*" rent the air.
Henri then put on his helmet, decorated with a
tall plume of the feathers of the white peacock, the
head of his charger being similarly ornamented.*

The action began by several effective volleys
from the artillery of the royal army, to which
that of the League, being less advantageously
placed and less well served, replied but feebly,
perhaps it should rather be tardily, as Palma-
Cayet asserts that "nine volleys were fired from
the Royalist guns, spreading confusion amongst
the Belgian *reîtres*, before any reply was given by
the Leaguers." But the principal shock, and,
indeed, nearly all the fighting, was between the
squadrons of cavalry commanded by the impetuous
Count Egmont, the Chevalier d'Aumale, and the
bulky lieutenant-general on the one side; by the
dauntless Henri IV., the Duc de Montpensier, and
the experienced and valorous Maréchals d'Aumont
and de Biron on the other. With the exception

* D'Aubigné ; Mathieu.

Maréchal d' Aumont.

Photo-Etching. — From Painting by Mauzaisse.

of the German and Belgian *reîtres*, all the cavalry on both sides was composed of gentlemen.*

Rosny, who was in the king's squadron, states that "Egmont charged them with extraordinary fury," and, he admits, with "great bravery, like a man determined to vanquish." But his *reîtres*, being Protestants, and unwilling to fire on their coreligionists, gave him no support. Notwithstanding, part of the left wing of the king's squadron was put to flight, the right was broken and gave way. Egmont a second time charged with 1,300 cavalry, to complete, as he imagined, the defeat of the Royalists. Maréchal d'Aumont, however, had succeeded in rallying the fugitives, while Henri in his turn had rushed headlong on the Spanish and Walloon lancers, and carried confusion and dismay into the ranks of the enemy. So far did he plunge with desperate valour into their midst, followed by the more ardent cavaliers of his troop, — whose courage, like his own, was animated by the perils surrounding them and the glory of issuing from the contest as conquerors, — that a terrible *mêlée* ensued.

The conflict was sharp and short, but sanguinary in the extreme, and soon the plain of Ivry was

* The Spaniards and Walloons were armed with long heavy lances, requiring much space to be effectively used. In Henri's army they had for some time been abandoned, and his cavalry armed with sword and pistol, which enabled them, as appears from some accounts of the battle, to pass under the upraised lances of their adversaries and attack them *corps-à-corps*.

covered with the dead and dying of both armies.
Great anxiety prevailed for a time respecting the
fate of the king.   For more than a quarter of an
hour it was not known what had become of him.
His white plume was not discernible, and many
feared that he was either amongst the slain or a
prisoner ; for once engaged in that desperate
struggle which he had vowed should end in death
or victory, " he fought like a paladin of the Middle
Ages," and as though he felt that he must conquer
his crown by the sheer force of his own right arm.

The Royalists, discouraged by thus temporarily
losing sight of their chief, began to waver.   But
at that moment reappearing, he calls to his troops
to face about, and if they will not fight, at least to
break not their ranks till they have seen him die !
The cheering sight of his draggled white plume
and the imposing sound of his voice suffice to rally
them, and into the thick of the fight they follow
him, his presence and example inciting them to
wondrous feats of valour.   The Leaguers fall back.
A pistol-shot lays low the valiant but rash Count
Egmont.*   The rout is complete, for Mayenne,

---

* This young man, so devoted an adherent of his countrymen's persecutors and his father's murderers, was the son of
L'Amoral d'Egmont, who, with Count Horn, was decapitated at
Brussels by order of the ferocious Duke of Alva in 1568.   His
father being mentioned in his presence with much respect, he
interrupted the speaker and impatiently desired him to "say no
more about L'Amoral d'Egmont, who was a traitor and deserved
the fate he met with."

Nemours, and the Chevalier d'Aumale take flight before the advancing *corps de réserve*, under the orders of Maréchal de Biron.

The king, having reformed his squadrons, followed up his victory by pursuing the fugitives. The number of men killed during the flight or drowned in attempting to ford the rivers was estimated as not less than that of the killed and wounded in the fearful *mêlée* which preceded it. Frequently during the pursuit Henri's voice was heard crying, " Quarter to the French, but spare not the foreigners ! " Notwithstanding, the excited savage soldiery committed terrible atrocities, regardless of the country or creed of their victims.

Mayenne's destruction of the bridge of Ivry partly interrupted the pursuit, by compelling the king to cross the Eure a league and a half up the river, at Anet. Thence he continued the chase of the enemy to within a short distance of Mantes, where the inhabitants, on being told that the Béarnais was killed and the loss to both armies about equal, consented, after some hesitation, to open the gates of their town to Mayenne. The escape of the lieutenant-general, with that of the two or three princes and noblemen who were with him, was thus secured. It has, however, been asserted that Mayenne, by breaking the bridge of Ivry after passing it, sacrificed the lives of many hundreds of his soldiers to ensure his own safety. A more active general, it is said, would have gathered the

fugitives in a body on the opposite side of the
Eure, and there making a stand, have offered an
effective check to the pursuers, and have saved a
part of his army.*

A corps of Swiss alone stood firm and refused
to surrender. Biron was about to bring cannon
to bear on them, when Henri preferred to offer
them quarter, which they accepted and passed over
to him. The completeness of this victory, so
essential to the king's cause, was really astonishing considering the inequality in the number of
troops composing the two armies. Besides innum-
erable prisoners, five cannon, all the baggage, forty
or fifty infantry banners, twenty or more *cornettes*
or cavalry standards, including the standard of
Count Egmont — red and gold — and the lieutenant-general's white one, embroidered in black with
fleurs-de-lys, were taken. The last-named standard
fell into the hands of Rosny, whose part in the
battle was a rather extraordinary one.

He was wounded and his horse killed under him
during the first headlong charge of Egmont's cavalry. His equerry, le sieur Maignan, risking his
own life, sought and secured him a charger which
had just become riderless, and with some difficulty
Rosny was once more mounted. Egmont now
charged a second time, and Rosny received a lance
wound ; his horse also was severely wounded in
the nostrils and the flank. Both sank together on

* Servan, *Guerres des Français.*

the field. Rosny fainted without having seen the issue of the battle. A considerable time elapsed ere he recovered consciousness. He then found that he was lying amongst the dead and dying, his helmet by his side, his armour battered and bruised, and his limbs so stiff that he could not rise.

Only with much difficulty did he succeed in sitting up to gaze around him. Of troops he saw none, friends or foes, and no one was near to help him. He imagined the battle lost, the king slain or a captive, and the débris of the royal army flying before the Leaguers. A domestic in the suite of the army at last passed that way, mounted — as described by Rosny — on a scrubby little pony. This man could give the baron no details of the combat; but he believed, though for a certainty he knew not, that the Royalists were the victors. This scanty news, however, raised the poor baron's spirits, and at once he made an offer to the man for his pony. The place he was going to was near at hand ; he was willing, therefore, to part with the animal for a startling sum, and Rosny was not unwilling to pay it ; for although it was his prudent habit not to give more for anything than it was worth, the occasion in question was not, he considered, one suited for bargaining.*

With some difficulty Rosny, assisted by the man,

---

* More than once, in his Memoirs, Sully speaks of his habit of providing himself with money when going into battle. He had found it useful, he says, to do so.

mounted his sorry nag, and slowly proceeded in the direction that would enable him, as he hoped, to join some portion of the royal army. Presently he is saluted with "*Qui vive?*" by seven cavaliers of Mayenne's army. He declares himself, and is ready to surrender, being too weak to offer resistance. But what is his surprise when four of the cavaliers humbly request him to take them prisoners! He imagines for a time that it is a mere illusion, arising from the pain of his wounds and his extreme weakness; for these cavaliers appear to be safe and sound, while he is covered with dust and dirt, his hands and face are stained with blood, and he is scarcely able to support himself.

But they persist, and in sign of surrender one of them, Charles de Sigogne, Mayenne's standard-bearer, places in his hand the white banner of the Guises, with his black *fleurs-de-lys,** and gives him the details of the battle. A battalion of the Royalists appearing in sight, the remaining three cavaliers — one of whom was the Chevalier d'Aumale — put spurs to their horses, and, bidding Rosny and his voluntary prisoners adieu, galloped off at full speed.

Friends are now within hail, and Rosny is relieved of the burdensome white banner by one of the king's pages. A surgeon attends to his wounds, and, after resting for a day at a

---

* Adopted by them in memory, and "in horror," of the Saint-Bartholomew massacre.

neighbouring château, a litter is prepared and placed in a boat which, under the charge of Maignan, whom again he here meets with, is to convey him down the river to the Château de Rosny. As he approaches he perceives that the plain is covered with cavaliers, horses and dogs. The king has been hunting.

When following Mayenne, as night was drawing on, the king gave up the pursuit of the fugitives when Mantes was approached, and took up his quarters at the adjacent Château de Rosny. There supper was prepared for him and his officers. As the latter with their several detachments successively arrived, Henri rose to greet them, to extol their valour, to thank them for the zeal displayed in his service, and to invite them to sit down with their soldier-king to the banquet. It was but just, he said, "that those who so loyally had borne their part in the burden and heat of the day should partake of the feast that followed it." "Sire," said Biron, in reply, " you have to-day, in incurring such risks, done Maréchal de Biron's duty, and the marshal has done the king's."

As at the affair of Arques, Henri received neither wound nor scratch in the desperate encounter of the 14th — though his helmet and armour were battered, broken, and useless, and the once white plume besmeared with dirt and blood. It would almost seem, as some of his Huguenots really believed, that he bore a charmed life. Many brave officers were, however, absent from the banquet — dead or wounded. Of the latter number was the Baron de Biron, the marshal's son. But Rosny, the devoted, was not accounted for amongst either the slain or wounded.

His arrival at the château, though borne on a litter, is both a surprise and a pleasure to the king, who had feared that his friend and confidant must be reckoned among the slain. He embraces him heartily, is amused by the stories of his adventures and his possession of so glorious a trophy. His voluntary prisoners are also welcomed; for, as may be supposed, they are not unknown to the king, and are not very rancorous enemies. Having ascertained from the surgeon that a little patience only is needed to restore Rosny to health, unmutilated and unmaimed, Henri turns to the officers who accompany him and says aloud, " I here give my friend Rosny the title of true and stanch chevalier, which I consider a far superior one to that of a chevalier-in-waiting on me." The chevalier cannot rise to thank his king; but he protests that he is willing to suffer a thousand times more than he already has done in his service.

After his two or three days' sojourn at the château and two or three hunting parties in the forest, Henri was leaving for Mantes, which, with Vernon, had surrendered to the Royalists.

" Adieu, my friend," he said, again embracing Rosny ; "take every care of yourself, and be assured that you have a good and grateful master."*

* *Mémoires de Sully;* Péréfixe; Mathieu ; Palma-Cayet.

CHAPTER V.

GREAT was the consternation of the Parisians when, on the 15th of March, an officer of Mayenne's staff arrived in the capital with the disastrous news of the Béarnais' victory over the lieutenant-general, and the destruction of the army of the League. Immediately the Archbishop of Lyons, chancellor of the League, and other members of the privy council, the chiefs of the municipality, and the principal preachers, assembled at the legate's residence. Such was the general state of alarm that all were expecting from one moment to another to see this redoubtable Béarnais with his conquering hosts encamp under the walls of Paris. So bewildered with fear were several of those who were present at the conference, that they advised "that proposals of peace at once be made, arranging any terms found possible with the victorious enemy."

"Paris," they urged, "was in no condition to stand a siege. Already a long course of civil war had impoverished it, and almost ruined its commerce. Ammunition and provisions were wanting; the artillery lost at Senlis and at the taking of the faubourgs had not been replaced. One cannon alone was in a serviceable condition, and the walls of the city were in a ruinous state. It might be very long," they said, "ere Monseigneur de Mayenne could again raise a force sufficient for the defence of the capital; perhaps, indeed, he never could." Prudence, therefore, dictated that no time be lost in despatching negotiators to treat with the King of Navarre.

These views were, however, far from acceptable to the fanatical priesthood and zealous theologians. Especially were they disapproved by the doctors of the Sorbonne, who very sternly rebuked those whose advice, they declared, proved them to be "culpably distrustful of Divine protection." The legate, who had listened with growing anger to the proposal to treat of a general peace with the "heretic Béarnais," now rejected entirely so preposterous an idea, and joined the Sorbonne in severely rebuking it. As regarded the city of Paris, he said, his proposal was "to defer coming to any decision until opportunity offered of conferring with M. de Mayenne;" but it was unanimously agreed that couriers should instantly be despatched to Rome, Spain and the Netherlands, with a special request for aid to the Duke of Parma,* then at Brussels; also that on the morrow the preachers should more fully inform the people of the real result of the battle.

The famous preacher, Père Christin of Nice, was one of the priests selected for that duty. Lincestre, Boucher and Roze, Bishop of Senlis, also addressed the people, and while seeking to inspire them with intense hatred of the excommunicated Béarnais, consoled them with the gratifying intelligence that the Divine anger was great against him, and that, in consequence, he had been most severely wounded and had lost the larger part of his heretic army. Christin preached on the text, "Whom the Lord loveth he chasteneth," and proved, of course, that Mayenne's overwhelming defeat and the destruction of his army were indications of the Divine favour being on their side; while to quell the fears of the more timid, and to brace up the nerves of the people generally, the legate published a promise that, happen what might, *he* would not quit Paris.

Mayenne meanwhile was at Saint-Denis; he dared not show himself in the capital after so

* Alexandro Farnese, Duke of Parma and Placentia, son of Octavio Farnese and Marguerite d'Autriche, natural daughter of Charles V.

signal a defeat. Yet he was not cast down by his misfortune, and was even more averse to the proposal his friends urged on him, to attempt negotiations with Henri of Navarre, than when, after the victory of Arques, Count Belin, sub-governor of Paris, who had been taken prisoner, was released by Henri and charged to offer terms of peace to Mayenne in his name. When the legate, the Duchesse de Montpensier, the Arch-bishop of Lyons, and others went to Saint-Denis to visit the lieutenant-general, he informed them that he was about to leave for Soissons, there to reorganise his army and await reinforcements from Spain. He appointed the young Duc de Nemours Governor of Paris in lieu of the Chevalier d'Au-male; wrote to Philip II. to ask aid on a larger scale than hitherto, and to Sixtus V. to reproach him for having entirely withheld assistance. He then exacted from those present a renewal of the oath of union, and immediately after took his departure from Saint-Denis.

On the 17th, Henri IV. left the Château de Rosny for Mantes. This city, with that of Ver-non, voluntarily surrendered to him, and was almost the only advantage he derived from the brilliant victory of Ivry. He had fought battles and gained victories enough for the conquest of two or three crowns, yet that for which he was contending he was apparently no nearer the chance of wearing than before. Another battle

was fought, another victory gained for him in
Auvergne, on the same day as that of Ivry, and
the commander of the Leaguers' troops, the
Comte de La Rochefoucauld, was slain on the
battle-field.　A body of Breton Leaguers was also
repulsed with great loss, while throughout France
the fame of the Royalist troops, their bravery, and
the brilliant achievements of their gallant leader,
were spreading far and wide.

Yet the month of March had passed away, and
Henri IV. was still at Mantes.　The Parisian
populace, so startled at first, took courage as day
after day went by and the conqueror came not to
lay siege to the city that would so readily have
opened its gates to him — demanding only that
the clemency he had shown elsewhere should be
extended to the capital.　That he was disabled by
wounds and his army destroyed, as the priests had
told them, though the people doubted it then, was
now believed ; but in case of a surprise, all began
to work diligently at repairing the fortifications,
casting cannon — the church-bells supplying the
metal — and generally putting the city into a
condition to resist the tardy invader.

Many excuses have been made for Henri's
inaction.　First, his want of money to enable him
to profit by his victory.　His troops are said to
have mutinied, the Swiss especially demanding the
arrears of pay due to them before they would
move forward another step in his service.　Appli-

cations to the superintendent of the finances,
François d'O, were of little avail. In the then
disorganised condition of the Government, the
royal revenues barely sufficed to satisfy the avid-
ity of the financiers, and Henri was not then in
possession of that absolute authority which alone
could effectively impose restraints on those harpies.

The king at that time had no knowledge whatever of financial affairs.* He was compelled,
however, in his great need to give some attention
to them. Nor was it difficult, as Rosny says, to
discover that the Seigneur d'O had lately received
some very large sums altogether unaccounted for.
On further and more pressing applications being
made to him, he handed over, not too willingly,
a portion of the sum he had appropriated. With
this the king appeased for awhile his loudly murmuring troops. Yet the active and energetic
Henri IV. still continued a laggard at Mantes.
There was a want of good feeling, it is asserted,
among his officers; they were jealous of each
other, and when a town surrendered or was taken,
each eagerly sought to be appointed its governor.
Even Rosny, as he regretfully confesses, considered that the king acted unjustly towards him by
giving the government of Mantes to a Catholic,
though that Catholic was his own brother. But
the difference in their religious profession had
made them brothers only in name. The Catholic

* *Mémoires de Sully.*

nobility in the Royalist camp are said to have
been averse to Henri's too speedy conquest of his
kingdom.   Biron certainly desired to prolong the
war, and twice gave advice that led to a check, if
not actual defeat.

That the troops needed rest, that the weather
was bad, and the roads in a state too terrible for
the march of a ragged, shoeless army, were also
among the reasons given for delay.   But with all
these disadvantages it was the opinion of contemporary writers * that had Henri but marched on
Paris without delay, while his troops were flushed
with victory, the city would have capitulated and
Henri IV. have been master of his capital without
abjuration, by the force alone of his own heroism,
and a right purely civil and laic.†

Often his troops, both officers and men, while
lingering at Mantes and Vernon, would exclaim :
" À Paris ! à Paris !" from which one would infer
that their murmuring and disaffection were caused
by their leader's unwonted inaction.   He, however, is supposed to have resisted these cries, and
sometimes earnest entreaties of both men and officers, because he discovered in them, and, of course,
more especially in the Huguenots, an intention to
seek an opportunity of avenging the victims of the
Saint-Bartholomew massacre by carrying fire and
sword into Paris.

It needed, however, but little discernment to

* Palma-Cayet. D'Aubigné, Mathieu, L'Estoile.   † Henri Martin.

discover that the king was under the spell of some
enchantress, who held him captive at Mantes, fast
bound by the silken chain of love. As at Coutras,
in 1587, he sacrificed all the advantages that might
have resulted from following up his victory for the
gratification of laying the colours taken in that
battle at the feet of "la belle Corisande," so now
the trophies of the victory of Ivry — a victory
whose fruits, like the former, must be lost if not
seized without delay — were at all hazards borne
by him to the lady to whom, for the time being,
he had given his heart.

Corisande was no longer in possession of that
priceless treasure. She had lost the symmetry of
youth, it appears, and the graces of form and
feature in a too ample development of her charms.
She had resented her gay cavalier's infidelity by
screening from his knowledge the stolen meetings
of the Comte de Soissons, recently escaped from
the château-fort of Nantes, and Madame Catherine, which took place at Madame de Grammont's château. In this way, and apparently to
her intense satisfaction, she annoyed her former
lover greatly. Her successor was "la belle
Antoinette de Pons," the beautiful widowed
châtelaine of La Roche-Guyon, who dwelt in
the vicinity of Mantes. But victory did not
attend Henri's ardent siege of the lovely young
widow. She was by no means disposed to surrender and become his mistress, though he wrote

with his blood a promise of marriage, and presented it on his knees. The promise, however,
could not be fulfilled until abjuration, absolution,
and divorce had taken place, none of which events
could then be deemed of probable early realisation; at most, they were but dimly perceptible to
some keen eyes in the misty future.

The fair widow had not the gift of second sight,
so Henri in despair rose from his knees to seek
conquest elsewhere. His thoughts then turned
to another *cruelle et belle maîtresse,* as he sometimes named the good city of Paris, and once
more he dons his battered and bruised armour,
obtains a new white plume for his casque, and
sets out with his army for the capital.

The League, on hearing that the king was
preparing to leave Mantes, sent negotiators to
him — Villeroi, and Gondy, Bishop of Paris — but
gave them no powers to treat, the real object of
their mission being merely to delay the advance
of his army, while Paris was enrolling her citizens,
laying in provisions and ammunition, and drilling
a regiment of monks, of which Caëtano was
expected to take the lead, and thus raise the
frenzy of the populace to the highest pitch.
Meanwhile the legate vehemently urged the
people to resist the heretic Béarnais to the utmost,
and induced the Sorbonne doctors, who were ready
enough to obey him, to issue a declaration to the
effect that "all who should render any assistance

to the said heretic, Henri of Bourbon, would be considered in a state of permanent mortal sin, while those who resisted him unto death might look forward with hope to the palm of martyrdom."

After leaving Mantes, Henri besieged and took the strong town of Dreux, and then marched towards Sens with the intention of assaulting it. But the determined and effective manner with which that city had prepared for its defence, and laid up stores of every kind for a protracted siege, induced him to forbear from attacking it, and to hasten on to Paris, hoping to bring the Parisians to terms before the expected arrival of the Duke of Parma. He therefore resolved on blockading the capital rather than assaulting it.

On his way thither he took Corbeil, Montereau, and Lagny, called the " keys of Paris." The posts on the lower Seine were already occupied, which, with those of the upper part of the river and its affluents, would enable him to intercept all supplies of provisions for the city. By this means he believed that the Parisians, so fond of good living, and accustomed to be supplied without stint, not only with necessaries, but every luxury of the table, would be eager to capitulate as soon as they were threatened with scarcity.

The royal army consisted of from 10,000 to 12,000 infantry, and between 3,000 and 4,000 cavalry. The first detachment passed close to

the city very early on the morning of the 1st
or 2d of May, sounding the reveille as it passed.
This was the cause of considerable dismay.   People
rushed from their beds greatly excited, imagining
that the heretics had taken Paris by surprise.
Henri was amused.   His mistress, he said, "evi-
dently loved not soft music."

On the evening of the 7th of May — a few hours
after the publication of the decree of the Sorbonne
consigning him and all who did not repudiate him
to everlasting perdition — the king deployed his
army in sight of the northern faubourgs.   He
had crossed the Marne at Lagny, and came to
place his troops in battle array between the faubourgs of Saint-Antoine and Saint-Martin.   The
Duc de Longueville and La Noue had joined him
with a corps of 2,000 German auxiliaries, with which
on the morrow he attacked Saint-Maur and Charenton, and carried them on the 9th.   Of this exploit
he informed the châtelaine of La Roche-Guyon,
adding, what was scarcely in the lady's eyes a
merit, one would suppose, that he had hanged the
captain of that post and all his soldiers.*

In the place of the unfortunate captain, the king
established Givry at Charenton with a strong detachment of infantry.   Maréchal d'Aumont took

---

* This barbarous act, which Henri, with his reputation for
clemency, would have done well to omit, took place in con-
formity with an ancient custom, which prescribed death as the
merited punishment of both captain and soldiers who ventured to
defend against a royal army any post — *non-tenable.*

charge of Saint-Cloud, and the greater part of the rest of the army was quartered between Paris and Saint-Denis. On the 12th, La Noue, commanding a numerous body of troops, attacked the faubourgs of Saint-Denis and Saint-Martin. But the French troops, together with the Germans and Swiss of the League, being supported by a company of citizen soldiers, defended themselves with so much vigour that La Noue, who was severely wounded, was compelled to beat a retreat. Henri had partly expected that a movement in his favour would be made by the "politique" party on his appearing before Paris. They were, however, restrained by the resolute opposition of the more zealous Catholics.

The attack on Saint-Martin was not renewed, and Mayenne being absent in quest of the Duke of Parma and an army, the king addressed a letter to the Governor of Paris, calling on him to "surrender, and recognise him as his sovereign and *bon ami.*" This having no effect, an order was given to burn all the mills in the environs of Paris, and Henri drew his troops in closer circle around the city. The small towns and châteaux in the vicinity were all garrisoned by Royalists, leaving less than the interval of a league between them, the blockade being completed by detachments of cavalry, who scoured the surrounding country incessantly.

CHAPTER VI.

WO days after the assault of the faubourgs, the priests and monks of the mendicant orders, together with several scholars of the University, formed themselves, to the number of 1,300, into a regiment, ostensibly to assist the citizens in repelling the heretic invaders. In reality, their purpose was to keep up by frenzied harangues, and their appearance in the streets in a sort of semi-military costume, the violent agitation they had already kindled among the people by their ravings in the pulpit.

At the head of these ecclesiastical masqueraders marched Roze, Bishop of Senlis, and with him the curé of Saint-Côme as his serjeant-major. The fanatical preachers, Boucher, Lincestre and le père Christin followed, and after them the priors of the Feuillants, the Chartreux, the Carmelites, and Minimes, the priests of each order bringing up the rear, four abreast.*

Their robes were tucked up, and capuchins thrown back; a gorget over the surplice, sword by the side, and halberd or arquebuse on the shoulder. Generally, their heads and beards were shaven; but several wore helmet and corselet. A large crucifix served for an ensign, and for their grand standard a banner bearing an embroidered image of the Virgin was carried in front of the bishop-commandant. This division of the church militant defiled before the legate on the quays and bridges, singing psalms and hymns, intermingled with salvoes of musketry, while Caëtano gave them his benediction, and saluted the pious warriors as they passed him with the title of " true Macca-bees." Several among them are said to have deserved this appellation from the bravery they displayed some weeks after while fighting in defence of the ramparts.†

Yet this grotesque association of the cassock and the cuirass gave occasion for much ridicule and raillery. The Benedictins, Celestins, Génové-fains and monks of Saint-Victor took no part in this warlike demonstration of the mendicant orders. The Jesuits are said to have advised it, and to have been spectators of the review, but did not commit themselves to joining it. So little accustomed

* Pierre de l'Estoile.   † Palma-Cayet; Mathieu.

were the soldier-monks to handling firearms, that they pointed their arquebuses without knowing whether they were loaded or not. When they saluted the legate, his almoner, who stood beside him, was shot dead by one or two of their bullets. The poor man was by no means pitied. His fate was rather regarded with envy.

To be laid low by the random shooting of an awkward squad under ordinary circumstances would have been thought a deplorable end; but that awkward squad being engaged in the holy act of saluting his holiness's legate, changed the face of the thing altogether, and the bullet became a passport ensuring immediate admission to heaven. It was indeed whispered about that the shot was really well aimed, though its destination was not the almoner's breast, but that, in the confusion which occurred by the crowding of the people to see the novel spectacle of a review of warrior-monks, a swaying movement took place, occasioning the failure to hit the right mark.

And it may well have been so, for not every priest was an enemy of the Béarnais, while many were decidedly hostile to the arrogant, fanatical Caëtano, "the centre of resistance in Paris, and, in spite of the Pope, the representative in France of the extremest views of the ultramontane party." Sixtus V. certainly held a favourable opinion of Henri of Navarre. He expressed regret at having too hastily excommunicated him, and promised the

Duc de Luxembourg-Pinei (deputed by the Catholic Royalists and "politiques" to explain their
motives for adhering to his cause) that he "would
embrace him, should he ask to be again admitted
within the pale of the Church." Though Caëtano's
ill-judged violence was so greatly censured at the
Vatican that the Pope almost disavowed his legate
and gave him no support, yet he dared not, it was
said, recall him,— such was the state of excitement into which he had plunged Paris by his
vehement denunciation of the "heretic band,"
together with those whom he called "traitors
towards God" (the "politiques"), who followed
the Béarnais while still professing to be Catholics.
His mission, he declared, was "to uphold the true
faith;" and again he vowed that, happen what
might, he would not leave Paris.

But while monks were shouldering the arquebuse, marching and countermarching, and preachers
were raving from the pulpits, some successful sal-
lies were made on the advanced posts of the Royalists by the Chevalier d'Aumale and the Parisian
militia. They drove them from the Abbey of
Saint-Antoine, and thoroughly pillaged the church,
which the heretics had respected and left un-
touched. Some small villages were also surprised
by the Leaguers, and evacuated by the Royalists.

These small advantages were, however, of little
profit to them; the blockade was not less strict;
the villages were retaken, and the city more closely

invested, while day by day provisions grew scarcer
and apprehensions of approaching famine spread
dismay among the people.   Even the chiefs of the
Union begran to take alarm, and were generally
reproached with having neglected to provision the
city to the extent they might have done.

News was received at this time of the death of
the king of the League, Charles X., on the 8th of
May, at the Château of Fontenay-le-Comte. He
was sixty-six years of age, and succumbed to a
painful malady from which he had long suffered.
A mere shadow of a king, his death was an event
to which the Parisian people were utterly indifferent
— the more so that their thoughts were then fully
occupied by the terrible doom which seemed to be
hanging over them.   Mayenne was the person
most interested in the cardinal's death.   To him
it was a grave event, rendering his position with
reference to Spain more difficult than before.   In
his absence, the choice of a successor was entrusted to the States General — not then sitting,
and, in the actual state of things prevailing in
Paris, not likely to be very speedily convoked.

Henri reckoned on the threatened famine for
bringing the Parisians to negotiate, greater vigilance in every direction being used to cut off any
attempt to obtain or send in supplies.   By this
means he thought to dispirit and dishearten them.
But D'Aubigné asserts that he did but inspire
them with hatred more intense, a greater desire

for vengeance, and, for a time, the power of en-
during the pangs of hunger, and uncomplainingly
supporting the fatigue of the harrowing kind of
warfare then being carried on. He speaks of this
attitude of the Parisians as having in it a something
that appeared to him both "just and glorious."

On Ascension Day the Duc de Nemours, the
Chevalier d'Aumale, the military officers and magistracy, after walking in procession through Paris
— priests bearing before them the reliques most
venerated by the people, together with the silver
shrine of Sainte - Geneviève — swore on the high
altar of Notre-Dame to die rather than surrender
the city to the heretic King of Navarre. All present
at this ceremony repeated the oath. A letter purporting to be from the Duc de Mayenne was afterwards read; it promised his speedy arrival and
prompt relief to the famishing Parisians. Letters
from the lieutenant-general more and more cheering were constantly read to the people. But, alas!
he and his longingly looked-for army came not;
for the letters were written by the "queen of the
League," Madame de Montpensier, or by some of
the "sixteen."

Gaunt famine in all its horror began to be
severely felt. Hundreds of wan, emaciated crea-
tures might daily be seen wearily dragging their
spectre-like forms along the walls of the city for
the chance of finding some plant or herb — often
fatally venomous — or of plucking here and there

from between the stones a blade or two of grass.
Such food could scarcely appease the pangs of
hunger; but among these miserable people there
were some who, to the last, could not overcome
the natural feeling of horror and disgust at par-
taking of a meal of human flesh, or even that of
rats and cats, whilst there were others — women
— who, in the fancied sublimity of patriotism with
which Panigarola and such-like preachers had im-
bued them, declared that they preferred to slay
and eat their own children rather than it should
be said that famine had induced the Parisians to
surrender to the heretics.

In more than one or two instances, mothers did
indeed overcome for a moment natural affection
and sacrifice their children to the maddening crav-
ing for food, — dying, ere the revolting repast
was finished, horror-stricken on awakening to a
sense of their terrible crime.

The preachers themselves had become sharers
in the passions with which they had so zealously
sought to inspire others. The provincial of the
Jesuits died in a state of delirium ; but it was not
from want of food. The ecclesiastics had taken
better care of themselves than the government
had of the people. The monasteries were all well
stocked, that of the Brotherhood of Jesus particularly so. Salted provisions were stored there in
abundance, corn and flour, and the fruits and
vegetables of their gardens. Very comfortably

were the Jesuits prepared to pass through the rigours of a long siege, while they charitably bought up daily all the dogs, cats, rats, and mice that were brought to them. These they skinned, gave the carcasses to the poor, and sold the skins at a great profit.*

When, however, the noble and the wealthy began to find the necessaries of life difficult to procure, and agonising cries for bread were heard in every street, then the monasteries, hitherto exempt from the general search, were visited by the governor's order. So well were they still supplied, though the siege had endured about two months, that they were required to relieve the famishing people with food for at least a fortnight. During that time supplies were duly forthcoming, but gradually diminished in quantity, finally ceasing altogether.

The king and his officers, who had expected the Parisians to be willing to surrender when the first pangs of hunger assailed them, were now amazed at their endurance. Hundreds were dying daily. Of the soldiers of the garrison, many had succeeded in escaping and joining the Royalists, many more were dead, and others dying of hunger and exhaustion. Henri is reported to have

---

* The leather-dressers and furriers who bought the skins, hoping for better times, were often waylaid by famished wretches, who took the skins from them and made of them some sort of horrible food.

said that he would rather give up Paris entirely than possess it ruined by the death of so large a portion of its inhabitants.*

Several attempts were made to negotiate, publicly and privately, both on the part of the king and the Leaguers, but no satisfactory issue was arrived at, because of the interference and intrigues of the legate and the Spanish ambassador Mendoza, both anxious, since the death of the cardinal-king, to enforce the claim of the infanta to the throne of France. In some respects, also, failure was due to Henri's absolute refusal to consent to the question of his change of religion entering into the discussion and being made the subject of barter. He offered the famine-stricken city very easy terms of capitulation; renewed his promise to seek religious instruction when the cessation of war enabled him to do so, and his assurance meanwhile that Catholics and their form of worship should neither be molested nor interfered with. Thus Henri strove to conciliate both Catholics and Protestants, — a difficult task, for neither had confidence in the other, — while in the camp their mutual jealousy engendered strife and increased their leader's difficulties.

* Thirty thousand persons are said to have perished during this siege — perhaps an exaggeration. The number of inhabitants was merely guessed at, and was given as ranging, from the time of François I. and Henri II., from 250,000 to 500,000, — the number generally accepted being 300,000, and the number of deaths from famine as low as 13,000.

Distress in Paris had now attained its height. Horses, asses, and mules, after the cattle failed, had all been consumed, then the lower animals, and as the needs of the people increased, some had recourse to reptiles and vermin. Vegetables, fruits, herbs, and every kind of cereal had long since disappeared from the markets, and existed only in the gardens of the monasteries. Even the dead, at the suggestion of Mendoza, were torn from their graves, and an attempt made to use their crushed bones for bread — or, rather, a revolting kind of paste, said to have caused the death of those whom raving hunger induced to partake of it. They were, however, consoled in the agony of death by the assurance of the priests that " no martyrdom was so pleasing to God as the martyrdom of hunger." Fevered in mind and body, over-excited by fanaticism, they invoked with delirious ecstasy the death that was to open to them the portals of life eternal.*

But what pen can adequately describe, or imagi-

---

* In an Italian account of the siege of Paris by P. Corneïo, one of the ecclesiastics in the suite of the legate, a contest is described between a man and a dog, both famishing and furious, and ravenous for each other's flesh. The struggle between them was short and desperate, and ended by the dog overcoming the starving man. But when about to devour his prey both he and it were seized by several men who, standing apart, had watched the contest with anxious, eager eyes that seemed almost starting from their sockets, as impatiently they waited its termination, and finally bore both man and dog away, to banquet upon themselves.

nation even picture to itself, the intensity of the
sufferings endured by those two or three hundred thousand human beings pent up in that
beleaguered city struggling for months together
against the horrors of famine, disease and lingering death ?   So many unburied corpses lay in the
streets, and upon them fattened toads, asps, and
other noisome reptiles, that the air had become
pestiferous, and plague was said to be spreading.
Yet, under the idea of stimulating the ignorant
populace to further endurance, these fearful reali-
ties were mixed up with such childish folly and
miserable superstition as that of the curés of
Paris pretending to write letters to Sainte-
Geneviève (how they reached her we are not
informed), cajoling her, as it were, as patron
saint of Paris, into relieving the misery of the
capital by flatteringly representing to her that she
was "too patriotic a Frenchwoman to allow a
heretic to reign in her own good city."   Whether
she ever sent any answer to the curés' letters is
not recorded ; but it does not appear that she in
any way troubled herself to move in the matter.

The Corporation of Paris also — instigated by
the fanatical preacher Boucher — "walked in procession to the cathedral to implore the intercession
of Notre-Dame de Lorette on behalf of the inhabitants of the besieged city," and "solemnly to
vow that, when through her prayers they were
released from their sufferings, by the dispersion of

the heretics, they would present her with a new silver boat of the weight of 300 marks."

The sainted lady of Lorette evinced no less indifference to the prayer of the city magistrates and their promised bribe of a silver boat than had the sainted Geneviève to the flattery of the curés. The heretic Béarnais was possibly not so much out of favour with those ladies as their petitioners supposed. They may have been as tolerant as the Abbesses of Montmartre and Poissy, who fearlessly accepted the homage of the gallant Huguenot king, who had taken up his quarters with them, and by their amiability and graciousness enabled him to while away pleasantly in their society many hours of that tedious siege.

The poor people, however, who had faith in the power of images to release them from their misery, continued to linger on in the hope that, moved by pity at the sight of their sufferings, they would put an end to the blockade. The disappointment of that hope was fatal to many; others, in their despair, strove to drag their weary limbs to the churches, and if life became not extinct by the way, sat quietly down in the house of God to await the welcome visit of death.

Some writers state that Henri IV., with his accustomed gallantry and humanity, sent frequent presents of provisions to the ladies of the Guise family ("the princesses of the League"). Yet he well knew that they were in less pressing need of

them than others, and were also his most active
and persistent enemies, — exerting their utmost
influence in strenuous opposition to him and to
every attempt then made to arrive at terms of
capitulation, lest the relief of the city should tend
to overthrow their absent relative's views on the
throne.   Again, it is often asserted that his pity
for the sufferings of the Parisian people was so
extreme that he was moved to tears, and had the
weakness to permit the revictualling of Paris while
he was besieging it ; or that if he did not actually
authorise it, he at least shut his eyes to the traffic
in provisions carried on by his officers with the
inhabitants of the beleaguered city.

"Legend," remarks a French historian, " is
often found side by side with history." *   To the
Henri IV. of legend belong the acts above mentioned, with many others of equal veracity.   The
Henri IV. of history severely reprimanded Givry,
D'O, and other officers who attempted to pass provisions into the city to their friends.   It was, of
course, undoing with one hand what was done by
the other, and prolonging the blockade the king
was anxious to raise.   He was far too astute for
that ; *trop madré*, as was remarked by D'Aubigné,
who so well knew and so much esteemed him.
Henri IV. doubtless was very humane.   His
clemency was a strikingly conspicuous trait in his
character, the more so from its almost total absence

* Dupuy, *Histoire de France.*

in the men of that age, who had passed so much of their lives in camps, as indeed Henri himself had done, having been a soldier from his boyhood, when Jeanne d'Albret buckled on his sword, and presented him to the Huguenots as their future leader.

The so-called religious wars had brutalised the minds of most of those engaged in them, while the fearful massacres by which they were generally preceded or followed had rendered murder and assassination in their most horrid form too familiar. The quality of mercy was then rarely, if ever, exercised. But Henri was endowed with so genial a temperament that, although he yielded to none in bravery on the battle-field, he was naturally inclined to remember mercy in the midst of victory, and to be lenient where others were disposed to be rigorously severe.

An instance of this occurred during the blockade of Paris. The governor, with the view of affording some slight relief to the necessitous citizens, had ordered the expulsion of some thousands of beggars and others (*bouches inutiles*) who had been driven to seek shelter within the walls of the city when the Royalist army appeared. They were now more than willing to leave, it appears. The whole population would indeed have been glad to be thrust out with them. They had assembled at the gates, but when in the act of leaving, the advanced posts of the Royalists opposed them.

Resistance was impossible, "the king's order was imperative," and the gates of their prison must again close on them. A cry of intense anguish then rose in the air, the wail of a despairing, disappointed people, who had hoped to escape, when thrust out of that famine-stricken city, the death that threatened them within it. This mournful cry, this appeal of a starving multitude for pity, reached the king's ears.

For awhile policy struggled in his breast with pity, but pity triumphed, and he gave his consent for three thousand of the most miserable and distressed inhabitants to pass his lines on leaving the city, ordering also rations of bread to be given them. Nearly four thousand contrived to push their way through. As many more desperately strove to follow, but the Royalist troops were now ordered firmly to bar their passage.

Three months had passed away, and there was still no sign of surrender. It was high time, the king thought, to awaken the League from its fancied security by a very decisive blow. His army had increased in numbers, was well provided, and more efficiently organised. Reinforcements to the extent of 7,000 or 8,000 infantry and cavalry had recently been brought to him, levied by Turenne and Châtillon from among the Huguenots of Languedoc and Guyenne. The Royalist nobility of the provinces of the Loire had joined him, with the Prince de Conti as their leader. The Duc de

Nevers also, with five hundred gentlemen, renounced his neutrality, " recognising," he said,
" in the victory of Ivry, the decree of the God of
armies."

Twenty-five thousand excellent troops were now
under the king's command. These he divided
into ten corps, in accordance with the number of
faubourgs to be forced, and chose a starlight but
moonless night — the 24th of July — for the execution of his projects. The general attack was
overlooked by Henri from an upper window of
his quarters in the Abbey of Montmartre. The
Baron de Rosny and Du Plessis-Mornay were with
him. The former gives the following account of
the nocturnal assault of the faubourgs : *

" It began at midnight by a terrific volley of
artillery, which was vigorously responded to, and
so unintermittingly was the cannonade kept up on
both sides that utter destruction seemed to be the
inevitable doom of that immense city. A spectacle
more capable of inspiring horror has probably
never been witnessed. Thick whirling volumes
of smoke rose in the air, pierced at intervals by
long trails of flame, overspreading the whole sur-
face of the capital, now plunging it into deepest
darkness, now burying it in a sea of fire.

" The roar of artillery, the clash of arms, the
cries of the combatants, the shrieks of the people,
added terror unimaginable to the fearful scene,

* *Mémoires de Sully.*

which was further intensified by the natural horror and darkness of night. For two full hours this desperate attack on the faubourgs continued. All were then reduced and in possession of the Royalists, the long rambling suburb of Saint-Antoine not excepted. The gates of Paris were then strictly blockaded. Nothing could enter, none pass out." Monks and priests were the gunners, for they had suffered but little or nothing at all from the famine, and were therefore physically better able than others to take those duties upon themselves.

The presence of Rosny at the assault of the faubourgs seems at first unaccountable. He was very severely wounded at Ivry, and had retired to his château, firmly resolved that on his wounds being healed and strength regained he would renounce henceforth both camp and court, and — faithful adherent though he from boyhood had been of Henri of Navarre — wholly devote himself to his own private affairs, the cultivation of his lands and management of his estates. No sooner, however, was he informed that the royal army was before Paris, than his firm resolutions immediately vanished. He could not overcome, he says, his strong desire to witness that expedition and its results. Besides that, the invincible regard he had for the king, which ever drew him to his side, then asserted itself more forcibly than ever.

His wounds were not nearly healed; he had

one arm in a sling, and only supported by a crutch was he able to walk at all. Yet he determined to go to the army. Accordingly he was placed on a horse, and, assisted by his servants, was able, it appears, to retain his seat. His equerry and a few gentlemen accompanied him. Proceeding at a leisurely pace, the cavalcade reached, without accident, the king's quarters, where Rosny was received and welcomed by the king with his customary bonhomie and frank good-humour; apparently also with entire forgetfulness of the ruffled temper publicly displayed by the young baron when —having appointed his brother Governor of Mantes in preference to himself — he bade him adieu at Rosny.*

Henri already knew full well the worth of the future Duc de Sully, and policy led him to overlook Rosny's too plainly and too openly expressed dissatisfaction with his arrangement respecting Mantes. "He has a quick temper," replied the king when, on a future occasion, some surprise was expressed by courtiers then present at Rosny's plainness of speech and Henri's toleration of it — "he has a quick temper, but he is a man of scrupulous honesty and stainless honour." With the exception of a few of his old attached Huguenot friends, there were not many of his then professed adherents of whom so much could truly be said.†

After the taking of the faubourgs, the principal

* *Mémoires de Sully*.　　† Mathieu.

citizens entreated the Duc de Nemours to authorise them to capitulate. They were sure of easy
terms, and it was believed that he was beginning
to waver, and to feel that in vowing he would
never surrender he had made a rash vow. The
people, too, were bitterly reproaching Mayenne,
whom they stigmatised as "a coward, indifferent
to their suffering, who had withdrawn from the
city that he might not share their privations. He
had an army at Meaux; why had not he the courage to come and save Paris, or bury himself under
its ruins?" Patience had been carried to its
utmost limit. "Make peace," the people cried,
"or give us bread!" Even the legate thought
peace was desirable. Still, with the hope that aid
would arrive,— nay, must, he thought,— Nemours
urged that they who so heroically had hitherto
borne the delay should yet linger on a day or two
longer.

A promise of aid did, in fact, arrive on the 1st
of August. A disguised messenger from the
Duke of Parma contrived to elude the vigilance
of the guard, and to enter Paris to announce that
the duke, then about to begin his march, expected
to effect a junction with Mayenne's army in the
course of a fortnight. For Philip, on receiving
news of the cardinal-king's death, immediately
hastened to fulfil a promise already made to the
League of both money and troops, and gave further orders to the Governor of the Netherlands to

send a sufficient force of his best men to France, and to take the command himself. The duke obeyed these instructions very unwillingly, and took a considerable time to make his arrangements for the expedition. His repugnance to it arose from his conviction that it was risking the loss of Belgium, then persistently attacked by Maurice of Nassau, for the doubtful chance of gaining France.

When, however, the people were informed of the joyous news, as it was represented, of the advance of the Duke of Parma, but that fifteen days must elapse ere he arrived, "one heavy despairing sigh," we are told, "one long heart-rending wail of anguish, was raised throughout Paris. Impossible to survive so long! The cowardly and base Mayenne, the inhuman Spaniard, would then find Paris one immense tomb!"* The "politiques" — secretly protected by the chief magistrates of the Parliament — strove to turn the prevailing agitation to account, and to incite the people to seize the Spanish ambassador and drown him in the Seine. The will to do the deed was not wanting, but they who were willing had not the strength to accomplish it.

To lay violent hands on Mendoza was to attack an army of priests,— priests ever on the alert to detect and defeat mutinous projects. The one in question was speedily known to, and denounced by, them, and two or three of the would-be actors

* L'Estoile, *Journal de Henri IV.*

in it were hanged. The president of the Parliament, Augustin de Thou, and other magistrates, were permitted "to purchase their expulsion"— ransom their lives — for a considerable sum. Perhaps the state of excitement caused by this attempted revolt enabled many of the Parisians to drag out life through those weary fifteen days. But, alas! not even then did "the Liberator" appear. Yet another fifteen days must elapse ere he could reach the beleaguered city; but during that period the friendly hand of death became the liberator of many hundreds of the unhappy people from the misery of hopeless agony. That the flickering spark of life should have survived in any through that terrible month of August was regarded by all as a miracle.

On the 23d the Spaniards — 14,000 or 15,000 of the *élite* of Parma's Belgian army — joined Mayenne's forces at Meaux. The lieutenant-general had expected to take the chief command of this detachment; but on learning that the duke headed his own troops, and would suffer no interference with his command of them, Mayenne was not only disappointed, but resented the arrangement as an offence, and as placing him under the Spaniard's orders. The latter disliked his mission, and bore himself haughtily; no very friendly feeling, therefore, subsisted between the two generals.

The Archbishop of Lyons and the Bishop of

Paris were at Mayenne's quarters when the Spaniards arrived, soliciting his authorisation to treat,
if not for a peace, at least for a truce of some
months. But in his anger with Philip and his
general, Mayenne resolved to throw all the responsibility of such a permission on the latter. To
him he referred the two ecclesiastics for the
answer to their request, the result being an
authoritative command from Farnese that "all
pourparlers with the heretic should cease."

His arrival in France came as a thunderbolt on
Henri IV. The news was brought by his scouts,
and at first he disbelieved it. He had constantly
averred that the duke would never withdraw his
best troops and risk the loss of Belgium to bring
them into France. Still there was time — and
many of his officers urged him to avail himself of
it — to take the city by assault, as he might have
done at any time during the four months' siege,
had he cared to do so. However, he still persisted
in his refusal, fearing, he said, "the excesses of
his army, which he would be unable to prevent."
Yet his lengthened blockade of his "good city,"
attended, as it had been, with all the loathsome
horrors that famine and disease give rise to, and
causing suffering and lingering death to so many
thousands of its inhabitants, would seem to be
inflicting a greater measure of evil upon it than if
it had been taken at once by force of arms.

So deplorable was the state to which the city

and its wretched inhabitants were reduced at this time, that the priest Cornei͏̈o, in his "Narrative of the Siege of Paris," writes: "But two days longer and the Parisians would have been compelled, not only to have opened the gates of their depopulated city to Henri IV., but even to have implored him to enter." The Royalist army was then anxiously awaiting this speedy surrender, and officers as well as men, calculating on an immense booty, were eagerly looking forward to the pillage of Paris, to partly compensate them for the ruinous losses Henri's wars had brought on many of his followers, Huguenot and Catholic.

Great, then, was their disappointment, and equally great their leader's mortification, that, in order to avoid being hemmed in between Paris and the French and Spanish armies, he was compelled to raise the blockade, and march to meet the advancing foe. He would speedily terminate this quarrel, he declared, by a decisive battle, which should be for him a signal victory or death on the battle-field.

During the night of the 29th, the king and his army decamped without beat of drum; and in the morning the monkish sentinels (only priests and monks then went to the ramparts) raised a shout of joy so loud and long that it tempted such of the poor emaciated people who still were able to leave their homes to inquire its cause. "The Royalist *corps de garde* are empty!" is the news rapidly spreading through Paris. "The blockade is raised, and the enemy has wholly disappeared." The mere announcement gave renewed life, as it were, to many, while to others, who had lingered on hoping against hope for relief, the glad tidings came but as the messenger of death, exciting deep emotion, and murmuring "Thank God!" they died.

A procession was formed chiefly of priests and some members of the municipality of Paris, and thanks were offered to God at Notre-Dame for the release of the city from the horrors of the siege. But no *Te Deum* was sung. The joy of the people was saddened by the loss of so many friends and relatives, — victims of the severity of the famine.

CHAPTER VII.

" I write you a line, my mistress, on the eve of a battle, the issue of which is in the hands of God, who already has decided its results as He knows will be most expedient for His glory and the safety of my people. If I am vanquished, you will see me no more, for I am not a man to fly before the enemy, or to retreat. Yet truly can I assure you that if I am slain in this conflict, the last but one of my thoughts will be of you, and the last of God, to whose protection I recommend you and also myself.

"*30th of August, 1590.*"

THE above was addressed by Henri IV. to the châtelaine of La Roche-Guyon. Critical as was his situation at that moment, with an army for the greater part in a ragged, desperate condition, disappointed, dissatisfied, and inclined to be mutinous, he yet, with his accustomed chivalric feeling, could not refrain from sending a word of adieu — which might be an adieu forever — to the lady for whom he constantly professed the highest respect and regard, long after the ardour of his love had subsided, and he again and again had sighed, an adoring slave, at the feet of other and younger *belles*.

He was then expecting to draw Farnese into accepting battle, and had decided on taking up an advantageous position at Claye, between Meaux and Paris. His light cavalry had already advanced so far, and some slight skirmishing had taken place. But the chief man in his camp played a treacherous part towards him, and so strongly insisted that the plain of Chelles was the spot where the advance of the enemy to Paris might be most effectually checked, that Henri — with the deference customary with him, and which he required his officers also to pay to Maréchal de Biron's opinions — at once adopted his views.

It was not wholly without misgivings, it appears, nor was it long ere he became fully conscious of his error. His army, in numbers almost equalling that of the enemy, but greatly inferior in artillery and other munitions of war, occupied an eminence having a deep valley and morass on one side, effectually preventing the possibility of acting in that direction. The Duke of Parma was considered the greatest captain of the age. He was as remarkable for prudence as Henri for temerity and reckless bravery, and no sooner perceived his adversary's error than he hastened to turn it to advantage.

He encamped on an eminence also, immediately opposite the Royalists, but beyond the range of their cannon, and secure from sudden attack. He had no intention to hazard a battle, but merely to keep the king in check while he carried out his plans with the least possible risk. His camp was fortified with earthworks, thrown up by his soldiers in a single night; and as both French and Spaniards remained immovable in their lines, Henri, on the 1st of September, sent a herald to offer battle to Mayenne, who referred him to Parma.

With exceeding haughtiness the duke replied: "Tell your master that I have come to France, by command of the King of Spain, my sovereign, to defend and uphold the Catholic religion, and to compel the raising of the siege of Paris. Without much trouble I have already done one, and by the grace of God I hope to succeed in the other. If I find that the shortest way of attaining that end is by giving battle, I will give it, and compel your master to accept it. Otherwise, I shall do what may seem to me best."

For several days the armies remained face to face, the king vainly attempting to draw his adversary into the plain. On the 6th the decisive moment so anxiously desired he believed had arrived, — the cavalry of the united French and

Spanish armies being drawn up on the ground separating the hostile camps and apparently preparing to advance. But this manœuvre was really but a *ruse de guerre* to conceal the movements of a company of infantry then crossing the Marne on a bridge of boats, for the purpose of attacking Lagny. A thick fog and a contrary wind appear to have favoured this expedition, which fully succeeded.

When the king became aware of it, and would have sent troops to its aid, Lagny — badly fortified — had been carried by assault and the garrison with every barbarity put to the sword. Whatever were the military abilities of the Duke of Parma, he yielded to none in fanatical religious zeal and savage brutality, for which the Spaniards of that day were notorious. The taking of Lagny raised the blockade of the Marne, and a flotilla of boats, laden with provisions of every kind and protected by soldiers, soon covered that river and were conveyed to Paris. The people had already received several hundred chariot-loads of provisions, brought by the Spanish general, and had begun slowly to revive under the new régime.

Henri was both embarrassed and enraged at what had occurred, the more so as it would have been impossible had he remained in the position he first took up at Claye. His reputation also as a general was compromised by it, he feared, in the eyes of his soldiers. He, however, felt that with

an army such as his, clamouring for pay, bare-
footed, and their clothing for the greater part in
rags, he could not successfully maintain a struggle
with troops well supplied with everything wanting
to his own.   He proposed, however, to make yet
another effort to take Paris by surprise.

Accordingly, on the 9th of September, at midnight, an attempt was made to scale the walls of
the city.   Jesuit priests kept watch that night
in the garden of the Abbey of Saint-Geneviève.
The saint herself was also supposed to have kept
her eyes well open, and to have directed those of
the priests to the tops of the ladders just then
appearing above the walls.   The tocsin was
sounded, the valiant priests seized their halberds,
and vigorously drove back the assailants, who
were compelled to beat a speedy retreat, leaving
their ladders, which were seized by the triumphant
priests, and "long preserved as a trophy of the
victory which had rescued Paris from the grasp
of the heretic." *

Henri, having determined on retreating for
awhile, broke up his camp at Chelles.   All around
him were murmurings and complaints, and there
being no longer any hope of pillaging Paris, the
nobility of his army, with but few exceptions,
demanded their *congé*, and were dismissed to their
several governments.   Yet he placed sufficiently
strong garrisons in the places held by the Royalists

* L'Estoile, *Journal de Henri IV.*

in the Île de France — which seemed to announce
that his absence would be but temporary — and
retired, with only a sort of flying camp, towards
the river Oise, establishing himself at Creil.
Thence he watched the movements of Farnese,
who after a siege of three weeks took Corbeil,
which sanguinary exploit was his only attempted
conquest in France.

Mayenne entered Paris on the 14th of September, and was very coldly received. The Duke of
Parma accompanied him, but *incognito.* He was
anxious thus to see what ravages the four months'
siege had caused in that immense city, as it then
was called, and its effects on the unfortunate
people. Paris was half depopulated, and fearful
maladies prevailed. The results of such long
endured privation could not be readily effaced,
and the people were still suffering too deeply both
mentally and physically from the great affliction
they had passed through to be animated with any
sort of enthusiasm towards Mayenne or the tardy
"Liberator," so that neither profuse cursings nor
blessings — whichever his *incognito* was intended
to spare him — met his ears.

Unfavourable reports of revolt and disturbances
in Flanders induced the duke to hasten back to
his government. His retreat was accomplished
with infinite trouble, being hindered by perpetual
skirmishing with the Royalist troops, and otherwise harassed unceasingly by Henri, who, ac-

companied by 3,000 cavaliers of the northern
provinces, pursued him to the utmost limits of the
frontier.   It was in an engagement at the passage
of the river Aisne, during this retreat and pursuit, that the king saved the life of Baron de
Biron, the marshal's son.   "Imitating his sovereign's recklessness, he rushed so far into the midst
of the enemy's battalions that his death was inevitable, had not the king (as Mathieu relates) at the
risk of his own life instantly advanced with several
of his cavaliers, and by one supreme effort released
him, though already wounded, from his perilous
position."

Corbeil and Lagny were retaken by Givry,
Governor of Brie, a few days after Parma's departure.   Messengers from the legate and Mayenne
were therefore sent after him to strongly urge his
return.   The Spanish general was inflexible to
this request.   The desperate resistance he had met
with at Corbeil, and the great loss he had sustained
there both in infantry and cavalry during the three
weeks' siege, had disinclined him to risk dim-
ming the glory he had acquired by his masterly
relief of Paris by undertaking further expeditions.
The object for which he came to France was
accomplished, as he informed Mayenne.   He,
however, sent him 3,000 or 4,000 of his weary
troops to recover Corbeil and Lagny, if he were
able; then with the remainder of his army he
hastened his march to Brussels.

Having seen the Spaniards well out of the country, the king with his cavaliers retraced his steps, and on the 10th of December entered Saint-Quentin, where he was received with enthusiasm. The inhabitants being anti-Leaguers, at once acknowledged him as their sovereign, making none of the usual bargains with him for special privileges, exemption from taxes, or other concessions. There awaited him also at Saint-Quentin a deputation from the Parliament of Bordeaux, hitherto neutral, to inform him of their recognition of him as king, and the publication of their decrees in the name of Henri IV. To this was added an earnest prayer that he would not long delay embracing Catholicism, to which he gave his usual answer. He also received at this city the news of Corbie being taken by surprise, which assured him a good post in Central Picardy.*

These varied successes revived his hopes, for though rarely cast down, the ill success of his last campaign, and the general fruitlessness of his victories, appear to have temporarily weighed on his usual buoyant spirits.

During the last few months the general aspect of affairs had in a measure changed. Sixtus V. had unexpectedly died, and Philip II. — with whom

---

*The library of the Abbey of Corbie—celebrated for the number and importance of its ancient MSS. and rare works of the fourteenth and fifteenth centuries — was pillaged and dispersed.

he was on very bad terms, and by whom he was
mortally hated — was strongly suspected of having
brought about that event.   The League detested
this "crafty, wily Pope, who would give no ear to
their demands for money and troops."   The Jesuits
and the Inquisition held him and his religious views
in strong suspicion.   He was seventy years of age,
and felt assured that he would outlive Philip, who
was about six years his junior, but supposed to be
so worn and debilitated by a complication of maladies that his death, anxiously desired, was from
day to day looked forward to.

Sixtus was full of projects, for the realisation of
which he had heaped up treasure in the Castle of
Saint-Angelo.   The conquest of Naples and abate-
ment of the power of Spain he had especially at
heart, together with the destruction of the projects
of the League.   The fear of Spanish tyranny he
imagined to be the only obstacle to the reconciliation of England and the Protestant States of
Germany with the Holy See.   This reconciliation
he hoped to effect as the distinguishing event of
his pontificate.   His suspiciously sudden death put
an end to his schemes and immediately restored
Philip's ascendency at Rome.   Sixtus V. died on
the 27th of August.   This event was announced
to the Parisians from the pulpit by the curé of
Saint-André des Arts on the 13th of September.
"God," he told them, "had delivered Christendom
from that wicked Pope and politique, Sixtus V."

Pope Sixtus V.

Photo-Etching. — From Portrait in the Gallery of Versailles.

It was generally circulated, and believed by many amongst the people, that Sixtus had made a bargain with Satan, who had agreed to give him the triple crown for a certain number of years if he consented at the end of that time to give him his soul, for which he would come at the end of the period named (five years). The unwelcome visitor, according to some versions of this wonderful tale, came, as Sixtus thought, rather before his time, as he had not nearly completed the task he set himself to accomplish when, throwing off his languid air and kicking aside the needless crutches which had gained him his election as "a stop-gap Pope," he briskly mounted Saint-Peter's chair, and harangued his cardinals in stentorian tones.

Yet, hated as he was, no Pope, it is said, more strictly fulfilled his duties as a sovereign pontiff than Sixtus V., and his exaction of the same strictness in others resulted in a greater degree of general prosperity and safety in the Papal States during his five years' reign than had been known for a considerable time. Henri IV. sincerely regretted him. His death he regarded as most unfavourably affecting his cause. True, he had anathematised him at the beginning of his pontificate, but had since regretted that step, and taken another view of Henri's character, listening with much satisfaction to the accounts he received respecting him from his partisans amongst the Catholic nobility.

"What a trick Spanish policy has played me!" exclaimed the king on hearing that Sixtus was dead. "I have lost a Pope who was everything to me."* Doubtless he would have facilitated Henri's possession of his kingdom by his readiness to absolve him and welcome him back to the fold of the faithful. He had recalled the preacher Panigarola, and remonstrated with him for giving his support to the aims of the League, and he was about to summon Caëtano to Rome, where some striking mark of his holiness's displeasure awaited him.

The energy suddenly displayed by this refractory Pope in his opposition to the League and Spanish policy alarmed Philip II. He was determined to use every effort and brave all hazards to place the Infanta Clara Eugenia on the throne of France, and if he could not in this matter bend the Pope to his will, he could, as he had ofttimes done with others, if not with Popes, compel him to silence and inaction. The first step was to render him odious in the eyes of the fanatically zealous Catholics of Spain. A Jesuit preacher who had taken for his subject the "deplorable condition to which the Church was reduced by those sons of perdition, the heretics, and those false brethren who were their abettors and followers," though speaking in general terms, greatly excited his hearers. But what was their horror

* L'Estoile, *Journal de Henri IV.*

when, referring to Venice, he said : " Not only does that republic favour the heretics, but —" and he placed his finger on his lips and whispered, " Silence ! — silence ! " Then with a shudder, as though he scarcely dared give utterance to the words, murmured, "The Pope himself protects them."*

What more thrillingly terrible announcement could have been made to a congregation of blindly bigoted men and women! They dispersed in silence, dumb with terror. Sixtus V. had been so zealous a persecutor of heresy that it must have greatly perplexed them to learn that he had fallen so low as to become its protector. However, he did not long survive his fall. Satan soon after carried him off. Some boldly declared that they had seen him ; and not improbably they had seen somebody or something representing the prince of darkness and his victim.†

Urban VII. succeeded Sixtus V., and reigned only the suspiciously short period of thirteen days. The conclave, then under Spanish influence, elected the Bishop of Cremona, who took the name of Gregory XIV. He was a Spaniard, — a man of rigid piety and narrow views, but perfectly suited blindly to serve the political objects

---

* Ranke, History of the Papacy.

† Sixtus V. was the founder of the Vatican Library. He restored the Lateran Palace, and erected a magnificent fountain on the Quirinal Hill.

of Philip II.   While the Spanish king was securing this victory at Rome, his troops, under the
Duke of Parma, had accomplished the purpose of
their mission to France, and were on their way
back to Belgium.

Though so diligently harassing the march of
the Spaniards, Henri IV. yet found or made an
opportunity at Attichy of secretly stealing away
in disguise from his troops, and riding with incredible speed to the Château de Cœuvres, to
judge with his own eyes of the beauty of the fair
Gabrielle d'Estrées.   She had been described to
him as of surpassing loveliness.   But Henri found
that description very far from doing justice to the
vision of youth and beauty that met his gaze
when, as a wayfarer and a suppliant for a draught
of milk and some bread, he was admitted within
the castle gates, and his wants graciously supplied
by order of the Baron de Cœuvres's amiable and
lovely daughter.   " That he might not excite the
baron's suspicions " (says the contemporary historian, P. Mathieu), " he then contented himself
with thanking the fair Gabrielle for her hospi-
tality ; adding, as he again mounted his horse,
that he was going to join in the pursuit of the
enemy, and that she would soon hear what he
had done for love of her.   Ere his absence was
generally noticed, he rejoined the pursuing party."

The Baron Antoine d'Estrées — the head of a
family of ancient lineage, in Picardy — had held

the hereditary post of grand-master of the artillery, succeeding to it on his father's death. He was also one of the "politique" party who favoured the cause of Henri IV. The family resided at the fortified Château de Cœuvres, and, like many ladies of high rank in the sixteenth century, "la belle Gabrielle," as she was then called, and still lives in song, had been trained to defend her home, in case of need, against the attacks of straggling and lawless parties of marauders who, in those turbulent times, would often seek to surprise and plunder a château from which the owner and his retainers were known to be absent. During the religious wars in France, there were many instances of ladies successfully repelling such attacks with great spirit and bravery.*

Gabrielle had been taught by her father to apply the match to the *coulevrines*, to fire off an arquebuse, to defend herself with a dagger. A daring and graceful horsewoman, she was his constant

---

* Almost at the precise moment that Henri made his first visit to Cœuvres, Marguerite d'Ailly, the wife of François de Coligny — then with the Royalist army — was besieged in her Château of Châtillon-sur-l'Oise by the Marquis de Bouron, Governor of Montargis, for the League. Placing herself at the head of a small party of soldiers left at the château for her protection, she sallied forth suddenly on her assailants, killed a part of them, drove out the rest, and recovered the booty — the pillage of the château — which they had placed on carts for removal — took the marquis prisoner, and locked him in the tower of the château until he was ransomed for a considerable sum. Both Royalists and Leaguers had their heroines. — MEZERAY.

companion in the grand hunting and hawking parties which then formed the favourite recreation of the *vie de château,* as she afterwards was in the royal hunts with Henri. Her family appears to have been remarkable for personal beauty, in the paternal line. This she fully inherited, together with the grace, fascination, and amiability of temper of her mother, Françoise Babou de la Bourdonière.

Henri, being desirous of securing the support of the Royalist Catholic " politiques," soon devised a means of paying further visits to the Château de Cœuvres. He suddenly showed much anxiety to know the baron's opinions on various points connected with his army. The post of grand-master of the artillery at that moment was really nothing more than a sinecure. Nevertheless, the hope that at no distant period its duties might become more weighty gave Henri occasion for frequent discussion of his projects with the baron, and for lingering at the château for awhile when the discussion was ended.

He dared not then, at least openly, speak of love to the fair Gabrielle. As a Huguenot, his prospects of becoming ruler of France were still but dim and hazy. To use his own words, he was " a king without a kingdom, a husband without a wife, and a soldier with an empty purse," while his personal appearance could hardly be considered attractive in the eyes of a young lady of eighteen.

He was never considered handsome, but from his seventeenth to his twenty-first year he is described by some writers of his day as of an agreeable, animated countenance, with dark complexion, and black wavy hair.

At thirty-six, but for the buoyancy of his spirits, he might have been taken for an elderly man, so worn and aged in appearance had he become from the hard life he had led and the excessive fatigue and disquietude of years of civil warfare. His once clear olive skin was now swarthy, rough, and wrinkled from constant exposure to all the changes of weather. He had a long hooked nose (generally, in his portraits, art has converted it into an aquiline of moderate proportions), and wore the heavy Calvinist beard and moustache, already profusely streaked with gray. Yet a pair of sprightly keen black eyes still sparkled from under his bushy eyebrows, and his face wore a good-humoured, if a rather bantering, smile, while there was in his bearing less of the courtier than the soldier — frank, jovial, dauntless.

Indeed, his widespread reputation for gallantry and bravery, notwithstanding all personal disadvantages, — for he was sometimes called the "ugliest gentleman in France," — might well win for him the favourable notice even of the lady whose admirers claimed for her the title of "the loveliest in the land." There were moments, too, when his weather-worn face was lighted up with so much animation, and fun gleamed and sparkled so merrily in his eyes, as, in conversation, jest succeeded jest, that an impression was left on the minds of those who saw and heard him that he was handsome in spite of his ugliness.

Gabrielle probably felt this when, with an eager earnestness that gave force to his unstudied eloquence, he told her of his perilous campaigns in the Rouergue and Languedoc; of the heroism of the little army that fought so valiantly for the fugitive King of Navarre; of his own hairbreadth escapes both in assault and repulse, till, like Desdemona with Othello, "she loved him for the dangers he had passed, and he loved her that she did pity them." For by his own confession, her gentleness and sweetness of temper were even greater attractions to him than her dazzling beauty. Thus Henri strove to interest her in the success of his cause and the operations of the war. That he did succeed in interesting her both in himself and his cause is, of course, well known. To see her but for a few minutes, he would disguise himself as a peasant, steal away from his quarters, and pass through the enemy's lines when the two armies were encamped near each other, risking recognition at the outposts or by reconnoitring parties.*

The Baron d'Estrées could scarcely flatter himself that this assiduousness on the part of the

* *Mémoires de Sully.*

heretic king was due to his *beaux-yeux*, or because
of any great value set on his advice and opinions.
He is said to have been desirous of putting an
end to Henri's visits — which, by detaining him at
Saint-Quentin, exposed not only himself but his
troops also to great hazards, and was the cause of
much murmuring — by marrying his daughter to
the Sieur de Liancourt, Nicolas de Lamerval, a
gentleman of a wealthy and influential family, residing at his château at Creil.   The chroniclers of
that day, amongst whom is the Baron de Rosny,
assert that the marriage was a mere conventional
one, concerted by the king with his friend Liancourt, who consented to lend himself to the
furtherance of Henri's purpose of releasing Gabrielle from parental control.   Others declare that
D'Estrées connived at this arrangement.

Had Henri been free, he would have offered
her marriage, and the chance of some day being
Queen of France.

Marguerite's levities had long since annulled
her union with Henri, according to the laws of
the reformed faith, and very gladly would his
austere Calvinist ministers and friends have sanc-
tioned his marriage with a Protestant princess
whose connections would have given support to
their cause.   Henri, however, was not desirous of
a divorce in order to marry a German princess.
His right to wear the crown of France could not be
contested ; but his Protestantism lay in the way of

securing that right, and he would but have added another obstacle to it had he attempted to free himself from his marriage yoke without the aid of the Pope.

Pope Gregory XIV. had but just sent his nuncio Landriano to Paris ("the bulwark of the true faith," as he was pleased to call that city) with a full budget of furious bulls, anathemas, briefs and admonitory letters, all of which were eventually burnt in the public square by order of the Parliaments of Tours and Châlons-sur-Marne. Henri could therefore only present another promise of marriage, signed with the customary crimson fluid, to the lady of his affections. This he appears to have done without loss of time; for M. de Liancourt after his marriage kept so entirely in the background, or absented himself altogether from his youthful bride, that it was judged better, their mutual consent being obtained, that the marriage should be at once dissolved, and means seem to have been readily found for effecting the desired result. Gabrielle then became her royal lover's acknowledged mistress, changing the name of Liancourt for that of Marquise de Monceaux, which title, with the château and extensive estate of that name, near Meaux in Brie, he conferred on her.

True, Henri had not brought matters to quite so rapid a close, when the murmurs in his camp at his protracted inaction compelled him to tear himself from the enchanted spot where dwelt his newest idol. He had, however, prepared the way for their due accomplishment, for he never neglected his affairs of gallantry, though generally he had so much besides on his hands, with his diplomacy, his wars, and religion. None knew the king's weakness in this respect better than Maréchal de Biron, and none regarded it with less disfavour. It fell in with his views of prolonging the war, and by various devices rendering Henri's victories abortive, as they had hitherto been, while a total defeat was avoided.

As Paris was surrounded by Royalist garrisons, there had been almost incessant fighting during the winter, but the failure of a night attack on Saint-Denis, headed by the Chevalier d'Aumale, who was killed by a ball from an arquebuse, led the Parisian Royalists to urge the king to make another attempt to seize Paris by surprise. A council of war approved the suggestion. So Henri, after taking a tender leave of the "belle Gabrielle," confided the conduct of his love affair to his friend, M. de Liancourt, who, as he knew, would not fail speedily to bring it, as he faithfully did, to the desired termination.

CHAPTER VIII.

THE renewed attempt to take Paris by
surprise was made in the course of the
night of the 19th and 20th of January.
Henri gave the rendezvous between Senlis and
Saint-Denis to his captains of Picardy, Champagne,
and the Île de France. The royal troops entered
the Faubourg Saint Honoré in silence. A *corps
d'élite*, disguised as millers, leading horses, asses
and mules, and having with them a number of
carts apparently laden with sacks of flour, but each
containing a man, had preceded them by an hour
or two. Their design was to block up the gate,
make themselves masters of the *corps-de-garde*, and
give entrance to the arquebusiers and *gens-d'armes*
concealed in the faubourg.

At four in the morning the millers presented

themselves at the Porte Sainte-Honoré ; but their
number exciting suspicion, entrance was refused
them. The millers persisted. The priests in
response sounded the tocsin, and the Parisians
in great alarm flew to arms. Henri's dispositions
being made for a surprise, and by no means for an
attack by open force, he at once withdrew his
troops. Not a single shot was fired, yet the
priests chanted a *Te Deum*, as though a great
victory had been gained. An annual *fête* was
also instituted to commemorate the great event —
" the check given to the heretic Béarnais " being
regarded by the Leaguers in the light of a revenge
for their own discomfiture at Saint-Denis, and the
loss of the depraved and ferocious Chevalier
d'Aumale, the most audacious and intrepid of
their military men. They had named him their
" lion rampant," to express the *mélange* of courage, meanness, and ferocity which formed the
basis of his character.

The day, or "*fête* of the flour-sacks," gave
occasion for numberless *bons-mots* and *calembours*
ridiculing Henri and the Royalists. But a result
of far more importance, and more damaging to
Henri's prospects, was the opportunity it afforded
the Spanish ambassador of enforcing the necessity
of admitting a Spanish garrison for the safety and
defence of Paris, a proposal which hitherto had
been firmly rejected. With exceeding regret the
municipality now yielded to the ambassador's ar-

guments, then the Parliament gave way, and Ma-
yenne, though most unwillingly, also consented.
Four thousand Spaniards, under the Duc de
Feria, then entered Paris.

Henri consoled himself for this disgrace by the
taking of Chartres, called the Granary of France.
This city was defended with so much vigour that
the king was about to raise the siege when the
Comte de Châtillon arrived with a corps of cavalry,
and a second time an attack was made, but again
with little effect; for the place was strongly
fortified, and surrounded by a very deep moat,
which the besieged greatly relied on for their
security. Châtillon, however, imagined a way of
overcoming this difficulty by constructing a mov-
able and covered bridge, to be pushed over the
moat, thus enabling the attacking party to mount
to the assault. The Chartrains failing in their
attempt to set fire to this bridge, or to drive
their assailants from their walls, disappointed also
of expected support from Mayenne, capitulated,
after a two months' siege, on the 19th of April.

The city retained its municipal privileges; but
Henri exacted a considerable indemnity in money
and provisions. The capitulation also gave assurance to the inhabitants that no public exercise
of the Calvinist form of worship should take place
at Chartres. Notwithstanding, upwards of eight
hundred persons, including many of the *bourgeoisie* and nobility, influenced by the preachers,

left Chartres with the garrison, rather than remain in a city under the rule of a heretic king.

When Henri made his entry into Chartres he was met by the mayor and corporation, the former being prepared to deliver an harangue in the name of the inhabitants. " Sire," he said, " we recognise that we are compelled to obey you by laws both Divine and human." " And," rejoined the king, as he rode on, for he hated long harangues, "you may add by *cannon law* (*le droit canon*) also."*

When it was known in Paris that the capital of the fertile province of Béarn had fallen into the hands of the Royalists, the rage of the priests knew no bounds. Mayenne was censured, declaimed against, and almost as fervidly anathematised as the heretic Béarnais himself. Paris was still suffering from the effects of the famine, and, excepting the monasteries, was but ill supplied with provisions, owing to the Royalist garrisons in its neighbourhood, though Henri had left no cavalry to keep up any strict blockade. To cut off the supplies from Chartres was therefore the cause of much privation. " The common people," says L'Estoile,† " wished both Mayenne and the war at the devil, and began to care not which side gained if they were but assured of food and repose." The Spanish garrison and the faction of the " sixteen " alone restrained them from throw-

* Mathieu, *Histoire de France.*   † *Journal de Henri IV.*

ing open their gates and inviting the king to come
to their relief.

The city of Noyon was next invested by Biron,
and afterwards taken by the king.   The Duc de
Mayenne, who, with the Duc d'Aumale,* had
advanced to its relief, yet allowed it to be taken
under his eyes, fearing to be forced by Henri
into giving battle.   The troops of Mayenne and
D'Aumale were therefore attacked by the king,
and beaten in several skirmishes.   The Vicomte
de Tavannes, who commanded a corps of 500
arquebusiers for the League, was made a prisoner,
and the Duc d'Aumale, to save himself, was compelled to take to flight.   Mayenne then assembled
the débris of his wounded, vanquished troops, and
retired to Havre.

On the morrow, Henri, at the head of his
cavalry, with his infantry ready to follow, as he
was about to mount his charger, said, addressing
his captains in his usual lively manner : " M. de
Mayenne is now so near a neighbour that he would
say we were wanting in courtesy should we fail to
pay him a visit this morning to inquire after his
health."

Henri and his army then marched directly to
him.   Mayenne made no response to this courteous visit, but remained closely shut up in his
fortress ; and as the Royalists were not in suffi-

* The elder brother of the Chevalier d'Aumale, killed during
the attack on Saint-Denis.

cient force to lay siege to the famous château-fort, the king retired, satisfied with having proved that his enemy, though stronger in troops than he, yet dared not risk a battle.

Notwithstanding the many demands on his time, and the difficulty he experienced in maintaining peace and concord in his camp, Henri yet found leisure to keep up a correspondence with the fair Gabrielle, as well as other ladies, sometimes sprightly, sometimes serious, but always breathing tenderness and devotion. At about the time now in question, when Pope Gregory XIV. was launching his thunder against him, promising to send troops to the League, to supply money to promote the cause of Philip, and to uphold his designs on France and its throne, he wrote :

"I am so overwhelmed, *ma belle*, with troubles, and perplexed by affairs great and small, that I must necessarily soon become a madman or a very clever fellow."

He might well indeed be perplexed, for beside the insane violence of Gregory XIV., who continued to fulminate his censures and anathemas against him (of which he had lately complained with dignity and moderation), new pretenders to his throne had arisen. All were clamorous for the convocation of the States General — to whom the election of a successor to the late King Charles X. was to be entrusted. His cousin, the Cardinal de Vendôme—who since his uncle's death had assumed the title of Cardinal de Bourbon, and now aspired to the throne, to the prejudice of its legitimate claimant, Henri IV. — was a young man of very feeble capacity, if not exactly of weak intellect. Partly aided by his younger brother, Soissons, an intriguer of far greater ability, the cardinal endeavoured to form a third party between the League and the Royalists.

At first this apparently was in Henri's interests, though in fact entirely in his own. Soissons did not join it, his motive for suggesting ambitious schemes to his brother being to annoy Henri, who was averse to his marrying his sister, between whom and Soissons an engagement existed. The cardinal had two able but unprincipled counsellors, Touchard, Abbé de Bellosane, and Jacques du Perron. They appear to have been very active agents, endeavouring, though without success, to corrupt the governors of those towns who acknowledged Henri IV. The cardinal, however, had none of those qualities that ensure popularity.

A lady of Madame Catherine's little court of Nérac readily joined the third party, in revenge for the neglect of an unfaithful lover. This lady was Corisande d'Andouins, Comtesse de Grammont, who for the same spiteful purpose, as already observed, had favoured the loves of Catherine and Soissons, when Henri partly forsook her to kneel at the feet of the Châtelaine of La Roche-Guyon. She was entitled to his gratitude certainly, for she had more than once supplied him with money to enable him to continue the struggle for his crown: she had cut down the timber on her estates; sold her jewelry; parted with a portion of her domains; and had twice sent a troop of a hundred arquebusiers to join him, all well equipped and receiving their pay from her. But in spite of these sacrifices for the sake of an almost penniless soldier-king, though he still corresponded gaily with her, he could not resist doing homage to younger and "more symmetrical beauties" (Corisande was several years his senior, and had grown fat and florid), to whom he offered his heart and a doubtful promise of marriage, while professing to honour and regard the countess, as also the lady of La Roche-Guyon, above all other women.

His devotion to Gabrielle was doubtless the result of a deeper love, a sincerer attachment, than any he had previously felt; and it may be inferred that the fair Corisande regarded his new infidelity in this light, as her resentment was strong enough to induce her to employ her influence in furtherance of a political intrigue to the king's prejudice. But in all those intrigues of the time there was always some one concerned in them who for a consideration was willing to play the traitor — utterly indifferent whether he served Catholic or heretic.

Such an one Henri was able to buy in the person of Jacques du Perron — the most able and

confidential of the young cardinal's advisers. He
was the son of a Huguenot doctor who had sought
refuge from persecution in Switzerland, and is
described as "a man without principles rather than
a bad man." Agreeable in manners, he was also
subtile, penetrating and unscrupulous ; learned,
ingenious, and a great friend of the arts and letters. To all these qualifications for an able
intriguer, he possessed the further advantage of
a great flow of language, and was an interesting,
eloquent, and persuasive speaker.

Henri probably knew the kind of man he was,
from Du Perron having been reader to Henri III.
To obtain that post he had renounced Protestantism, and to put his sincerity beyond doubt he
became an *abbé*. He amused the frivolous Henri
III. by his lively conversation and ingenious para-
doxes. One day, having proved to the king the
existence of a God by clear and evident reasons,
Du Perron then offered to prove to him, by reasons no less evident, that there was no God.
Henri stood aghast with fear, then fled from the
room in dismay. He would see his reader no
more. He probably thought him Satan incarnate,
as many of the royal sinner's subjects believed
their king to be.

In the hands of such a man the poor, weak cardinal's schemes were soon frustrated. Du Perron
revealed all his patron's projects to Henri IV.,
and placed himself at his service to entirely thwart

them. His patron's correspondence with Gregory XIV. and his secret instructions to an agent in Rome were intercepted and laid before him. In them the cardinal entreated his holiness to aid him in obtaining recognition of his rights to the throne, of which the head of his house had rendered himself unworthy by his persistence in heresy. He declared his own profound submission to the Holy See, and protested that he had hitherto attached himself to the King of Navarre's party only from necessity, and in the hope that his promised conversion would be fulfilled. This hope being at an end, he feared that in allowing the evil to continue he should become its accomplice. If the holy father would interpose in his favour with the League, he promised to draw all the Royalist Catholics from their allegiance to his cousin.

But the Pope, notwithstanding his frenzied opposition to Henri IV., seems to have been aware of the cardinal's personal nullity. He therefore contented himself with praising his good intentions, refraining from making promises until he knew more of the extent of his credit with the Royalist nobility and his capacity as an opponent to the Béarnais. Henri, aware of this, no longer feared the intrigues of his treacherous cousins. He, however, thought that dissimulation would be more prudent in this matter than punishment. Consequently he summoned them to join him at Mantes, his temporary court, where he could keep a strict eye upon them. There, too, the cardinal — who, strangely enough, frequently unbosomed himself to the staid Calvinist Rosny, with reference especially to his amorous intrigues, which, as was the custom of the Bourbons, he carried on simultaneously with his political schemes — would have the advantage of the general good advice and supervision of his Huguenot friend.

As Gregory continued to send anathema after anathema, bulls of excommunication, briefs and monitory letters "to all and every," whether bishops or archbishops, who favoured the heretic party, the royal Parliaments of Tours and Châlons-sur-Marne returned him thunder for thunder. Decrees were issued by the latter, declaring his "bulls, his briefs, etc., utterly null, being abusive, scandalous, seditious, full of impostures, and contrary to the holy decrees, approved councils, rights, and liberties of the Gallican' Church." The decrees of the Parliament of Tours were even more violent. They declared "the *soi - disant* Pope Gregory an enemy of peace and of the unity of Church, king, and state; an adherent of the Spanish conspiracy; an abettor of rebellion, and guilty of parricide committed on the person of Henri III., he having as cardinal approved it."

The king returning at this time from Louviers, which he had taken by surprise, on the 4th of July convoked at Mantes an assembly of the princes,

the nobility, the Royalist bishops, and general
clergy. His purpose was to consult with them
respecting the reëstablishment of the edicts of
pacification granted to the Protestants in 1577
and 1580, and the revocation of those exacted by
the League in 1585 and 1588 from Henri III.
Induced by the denunciations of Gregory XIV.,
he had recently reiterated his promise of seeking
religious instruction from a general or national
council of bishops so soon as a cessation of war
gave him leisure, and in the interim to maintain
inviolate the religion of the state.

The Huguenots were dissatisfied with his leaning, as they considered it, towards the Catholics,
and the preference shown them over those by
whose constancy to him his cause had been mainly
supported. Henri himself felt that he owed to his
faithful followers, whom he still called his coreligionists, some compensation for the promises and
assurances of good faith circumstances had made
it incumbent on him solemnly to renew to the
Catholics. The above-named edicts, so favourable
to the Huguenots, had been granted to them
merely to serve the momentary designs of Catherine de' Medici and Henri III., and were scarcely
promulgated ere they were declared rescinded.
Henri now proposed to revive them, "until," he
said, "it shall please God to give us grace to
reunite our subjects by the establishment in our
kingdom of a good and solid peace."

The apprehension that the Protestants would exact concessions much more favourable on the arrival of the Vicomte de Turenne with the auxiliary English and German army, alone, it is said by the historian Floquet, prevented the clergy from opposing the king's intentions.   The Cardinal de Bourbon, however, being present at this council, thought the moment favourable for hoisting the flag of the third party.   Timidly he rose from his seat, and, murmuring some words of protest, was about to leave the council-chamber, expecting to be accompanied by some at least of the clerical members of the council.   But neither bishops nor archbishops seemed disposed to follow their would-be leader; while the king, in an imperious tone and manner, ordered his cousin to return to his seat.   Sullenly he obeyed.

The Royalist prelates then undertook to send a strong remonstrance to the Pope.   Also they invited all good Catholics to join their prayers to theirs for the king's speedy conversion, of which he then gave them hope.   A document to this effect was drawn up as the result of the council's discussion, and was signed by all present, including the Cardinal de Bourbon, who dared not refuse to place his signature after that of the Cardinal de Lenoncourt.   Although the Royalist cardinals spoke with extreme caution when referring to Rome, it was yet considered that the obtaining of any manifesto on the part of the Church of France, in favour of the heretic king, was a great point gained.

The ensuing campaign was looked forward to as one from which great results were expected. The siege of Rouen was to be attempted; but Henri, unwilling to weary either his cavaliers or his troops, determined on remaining quiet until the arrival of the English and German forces. Meanwhile he secretly betook himself to Compiègne, assigning as a reason for his journey a desire to receive an expected corps of *reîtres* in that neighbourhood.

CHAPTER IX.

The Baron de Rosny Again Fired upon in the Forest of Mantes, and Severely Wounded. — Rosny at the Court of Catherine de' Medici, in 1583. — His *Valet de Chambre* Prevents Him from Forming a *Mésalliance.* — He Marries Then Mdlle. de Courtenay. — Bontin. — The King in the Following Year Requires the Services of His Partisans. — Death of Mme. de Rosny. — Escape of the Duc de Guise. — The Magistrates Hanged by Order of the " Sixteen." — Mayenne Returns to Paris. — Henri Assembles His Troops.

THE real object of the king's journey to Compiègne, as stated by the Baron de Rosny, was to pass some time with Madame de Liancourt, whose divorce was on the point of being accomplished. He was not sorry, he says, that Henri had chosen to absent himself at that time, as it afforded him also an opportunity of enjoying the society of a lady whose acquaintance he had recently made at Mantes, and to whom he had become more sincerely attached on every occasion of visiting her, — so much so that he had begun seriously to think of contracting a second marriage. Though so severely wounded at Ivry by lance, sword, and arquebuse that his survival seems almost marvellous, he had for several months past thrown aside his crutches, slings and ban-

dages. But at about the time of the king's departure for Compiègne, the baron, while riding through
a part of the forest some two or three leagues from
Mantes, with eight gentlemen and four attendants,
was suddenly attacked by a party of twenty horsemen.

As they wore the white scarf of the Royalists,
they were supposed to be friends, and to their
challenge "*Qui vive?*" the response of "*Vive
le roi!*" being returned, these "brigands or
Leaguers," he knew not which, immediately un-
covered. This courtesy, however, was instantly
followed by a volley from their arquebuses,
especially, it appears, aimed at the baron, whose
attendants rode up, shouting "*Vive De Rosny!*"
The whole party then charged their assailants,
who after another volley rode off into the thickest
part of the forest, leaving one of the baron's party
unhorsed and wounded, though not very seriously.
On Rosny himself they fired three times, one
shot only taking effect; but this inflicted so
serious a wound, "piercing his lip and passing
out at the nape of his neck," that, after the many
similar injuries he had so lately recovered from,
it is surprising that it did not cause death. A
charge of small shot also temporarily disfigured
his face.

A proposal was made to pursue these men, but
Rosny objected to being drawn further into the
forest. He was also suffering much pain; and

losing blood, and feeling very faint in consequence, he was anxious to reach the château of
his friend, M. d'Auteuil, half a league distant.
There his wounds were attended to, and thence in
a litter he returned to Mantes, where he was six
weeks, he says, in the hands of a surgeon. His
wounds and honourable scars did him no dis-
service, one may reasonably suppose, in the eyes
of the lady to whose hand he aspired,— Madame
de Châteaupers, a young and wealthy widow of
twenty-three, seven years Rosny's junior, whose
husband had died in 1589. She was, of course,
of distinguished family, for M. de Rosny was very
far from being indifferent to the advantages of
birth and wealth.

Eight years earlier he was on the point of
marrying a lady whose only dower was youth and
beauty. Rosny was then playing the gay gallant
at the voluptuous court of Catherine de' Medici,
narrowly observing all that was passing there, and
taking note of the various intrigues by which,
under many disguises, Catherine sought to further
her own plans or thwart those of her enemies.
Rosny was playing the courtier in the interests of
Henri of Navarre, with the view of frustrating the
aims of the League. Naturally grave and sedate,
the depravity of the court repelled rather than
attracted him; but as he says, the nature of the
mission with which he was charged compelled him
to frequent it, also to mix in the most brilliant

society of the capital, and to take part in its
pleasures and idle amusements.*

Being then, he pleads, in the flower and force
of early manhood, it will scarcely be thought
surprising that he should have paid the ordinary
tribute of youth to love, and have become passionately enamoured of the daughter of Président
Saint-Mesmin, "one of the most beautiful of the
young ladies of France." It was an excellent
match for mademoiselle, who appears to have
been well pleased with her suitor, who was also
welcomed in the most friendly manner by "her
respectable father," "a very worthy man, but not
nobly descended."

M. le baron had a *valet de chambre* named La
Fond, an ancient retainer of the house of François
de Béthune, Duc de Rosny, who had observed
with dismay the progress of the young baron's
love affair, and its probable termination in a
mésalliance. There was also the stumbling-block
of difference of religion. Rosny, however, had
made no proposal to M. de Saint-Mesmin for the
hand of his daughter; but seeing that it was
expected of him, he duly endeavoured to check
the ardour of his feelings while he reflected on
the matter. Then suddenly it flashed on his
mind that Mdlle. de Saint-Mesmin, all lovely,
amiable and worthy though his heart told him she
was, nevertheless was no suitable bride for him.

* *Mémoires de Sully.*

Now was La Fond's opportunity to step in and
help the love-lorn baron to shake off the silken
fetters that still held him a captive to love.   This
staid young man, who, as some writers have
asserted, was from childhood to manhood a
stranger to youthful feelings, says he suffered
agony in the conflict between love and duty, —
victory ever inclining to the former.   It was a
desperate struggle, and never, he thought, should
he have succeeded in freeing himself from the
fetters of first love if La Fond had not powerfully
aided him.   This ancient servitor suggested a
diversion, namely, that he should pay his court to
another young lady, and named Mdlle. de Courtenay.   " You will find there, monsieur," he said,
"wealth, royal extraction, and no less beauty,
when in the course of a year or two the personal
charms of Mdlle. de Courtenay are fully developed
as are Mdlle. Saint-Mesmin's."   She was two
years her junior, it appears.

Rosny confesses that La Fond gave him excellent advice, which he at once acted upon by paying
a visit to the De Courtenay family, with whom he
was distantly connected, his great - grandfather,
Guy de Béthune, having married a Mdlle. Françoise de Courtenay-Bontin.   His admiration of the
beauty of the now deserted Mdlle. Saint-Mesmin
had blinded him, he found, to the charms of his
new mistress.   For on more attentively observing
her than he had hitherto done, the only difference

he perceived in the ladies' attractions was but as
that of two fresh and lovely rosebuds, one of which
was about to unfold its roseate leaves, the other
having already partly done so.

The gentleness of disposition, the qualities of
mind and character, the care that had been bestowed on the education of Mdlle. de Courtenay,
were closely observed by M. de Rosny, and met
with his general approbation; and as he succeeded
in making himself agreeable to the young lady,
they shortly after were married.*

Rosny, having been attached to Henri of
Navarre from his childhood, dedicated, or given
to him, in fact, by his father to be the friend and
confidant of the prince through life, with an in-
junction never to forsake him, may be regarded
as having been a man of war from his youth. He,
however, on the occasion of his marriage refrained
from returning to Navarre, and from taking part
in the harassing and unceasing warfare then going
on in every province of France, and, indeed, every
town and hamlet in it. His devotion to his amiable and charming young bride detained him a
whole year at his château and estates of Rosny,
occupied with the duties, the pleasures, the sports,
and exercises of a country life, — a life as new to
him, he says, as was his life at the French court,
though a far more agreeable one.

He had a taste for fine horses, and bred a large

* *Mémoires de Sully.*

number, which were eagerly sought after, and very
large prices paid for them. He was also felling
timber, and attending to his crops, raising money,
though not exclusively for his own use, but chiefly
to enable Henri to carry on the wars against the
persecutors of his religion. But towards the end
of 1584 the King of Navarre — who seems to have
acknowledged Rosny's right, on Scriptural authority, to spend his first year of marriage with his
wife — reminded him that he had then need of the
services of his partisans ; that religion and the
state were menaced with heavy misfortune if
measures were not promptly taken to avert it, and
that almost immediately he should be engaged in
a fierce and furious war.*

Rosny obeyed the summons of his prince, taking
with him for his use 48,000 *francs*, the product of
a sale of full-grown forest-trees, felled for that purpose. But his gentle, delicate wife was perforce
left behind, naturally full of anxiety for her husband's safety. Her life, from that cause, and the
disquietude, inconvenience, and even danger the
war personally occasioned her (being at times
obliged to leave her home and live concealed in
Paris under a feigned name, and to suffer many
privations), was an unhappy, anxious one. Rosny's
visits, though as frequent as possible, were of
necessity comparatively few and far between.

*It was in this year that the daring projects of the League
first became apparent.

But in 1589, soon after the King of Navarre had joined his forces to the army of Henri III., and their march to Paris was determined on, tidings of his wife's dangerous illness were brought to the baron. Immediately he gave up his command, and, with a strong escort — the route being infested by straggling parties of Leaguers — hastened to Rosny.

On his arrival he found his own château closed against him, the drawbridge raised, and by his elder Catholic brother's orders entrance refused him. This unnatural and cruel act, he says, both amazed and enraged him. He vowed that he would enter or perish in the attempt. His escort being sufficiently numerous, they were about to scale the walls when the hard-hearted brother, either from fear or repentance, let down the bridge and gave him admission. Madame de Rosny was still living, but without hope of recovery. She died on the fourth day after Rosny's arrival.

He appears to have deeply lamented her, the thought of her short married life having been so lonely, so full of anxiety and trouble, adding much poignancy to his grief. Time, however, had its usual soothing effect, and between two and three years having elapsed, the Baron de Rosny sought the hand of Madame de Châteaupers. The incident of the attack on him in the Forest of Mantes interrupted for a while the progress of his suit;

but on his recovery, finding the lady, he says, favourably disposed towards him, he made his proposal : it was accepted, and their marriage arranged.*

The satisfaction the king had felt on the success of his arms and his affairs of gallantry was suddenly dampened by the lamentable news of the death of François de La Noue on the 4th of August, from a wound received at the siege of Lamballe. Men of all parties and of different creeds regarded him as one of the noblest men of the sixteenth century — a man of stainless honour, *"sans peur et sans reproche."* Not many days after, another death was announced, that of François de Coligny, Comte de Châtillon. He died at his Château de Louve, to which he had retired to rest awhile,— the many hardships and the excessive fatigue he had undergone in the wars having ruined a constitution naturally far from strong.

His untimely death — he was but in his thirtieth year — was deeply lamented by the Huguenots ; and Henri, in the difficulty he found in replacing so able and zealous an officer, became aware of the irreparable loss he had sustained in the man he had but lightly regarded while living, and to whose usually excellent advice in the council, both as a

* It did not take place until the following year, May, 1592, when it was celebrated at Mantes, on the same day that the Duke of Parma passed with his army by Houdan, near Mantes, and effected his famous retreat.

François de la Noue.

Photo-Etching. — From Portrait in the Gallery of Versailles.

statesman and a soldier, he had rarely given any
heed. Like the admiral, his father, François de
Coligny was a sincere yet not bigoted Protestant ;
but his sedateness of manner was as little in
sympathy with Henri's more buoyant Calvinism
as his sincerity with Rosny's ingenious sophisms
for quieting the qualms of conscience with reference to the king's suggested abjuration.

Another event which at first Henri was disposed
to regard as likely to lead to further embarrass-
ments occurred in the same month — the escape of
the young Duc Charles de Guise from the Chateau
de Tours, where he had been a prisoner since the
assassination of his father in December, 1588.
Here was another candidate for the throne,— also
a formidable rival to M. de Mayenne ; but this
new element of discord the king on reflection perceived would eventually turn to his own advantage.
Though zealous Leaguers received the young
duke with almost furious joy,— recognising in him
the successor of their "grand Guise,"— yet when
the enthusiasm of his reception at Bourges,
Orléans, and Paris was described to Henri, he
exclaimed : "The escape of M. de Guise will
prove the death-blow of the League."

The Duc de Mayenne, of course, did not show
the frenzied delight of the Leaguers. His bulky,
unwieldy person formed an unfavourable contrast
to that of his nephew,— a youth of twenty, slight,
elegant in figure, active, courageous, spirited, re-

joicing in his freedom, and bent on avenging the
late duke's death.   Scarcely so well provided with
all the requisites for a popular hero as his father
had been, there was still a sufficient likeness to
him in feature and a certain confident bearing,
to which "time," it was said, "would add new
touches," to revive the memory of their former
leader, and to inspire a hope that the mantle of
the father had fallen on the son.   Already the
"sixteen," then tottering towards their extinction,
looked forward to a renewed term of power and
increased influence under the youthful head of the
house of Guise.

His escape was contrived by his servant, who
procured a rope and attached it to' the window
of his apartment, keeping the guards (who were
probably in connivance with him) in conversation
while the young duke glided down to the court-
yard.   With equal facility the servant followed his
master.   They passed through the gates, which
would seem to have been conveniently wide open,
while horses awaited them at a short distance
from the château.   The Jesuits, however, claimed
the credit of this successful flight.   They had
prayed for it unceasingly to Our Lady of Lorette
and celebrated mass daily, with the same object,
by their general's order; and lo! on the 15th of
August, Our Lady's *fête*, the prison doors flew
open and the captive was released.   From this
miraculous occurrence it was inferred that the

duke was favoured by Heaven and Our Lady, and sent to the support of the "sixteen," those zealous upholders of the true faith.

Since Mayenne's suppression of the Council of Union he had treated the "sixteen" and their projects with indifference amounting to contempt. They were excluded from all offices of importance, and were doomed by the lieutenant-general to be finally crushed as soon as a suitable pretext presented itself. They were desirous, in their zeal for religion, to establish a sort of Inquisition at Paris, which was intended to lead to a second Saint-Bartholomew, the victims in this instance to be the "politiques," or "encouragers of heresy." Gregory XIV. had been secretly communicated with, and had given the scheme his entire approval and pontifical blessing, promising also to support it with money and troops. But when it was revealed to Mayenne he positively refused to consent to the establishment of any such tribunal.*

Mayenne's own power was already with difficulty sustained, and his views on the throne, which he dared not openly avow, more than ever were jeopardised by the unlooked-for appearance of his nephew on the scene. Believing that he had put a curb on the "sixteen" and their schemes, Mayenne withdrew to Laon, resolving to keep a vigilant eye on them. They in return resolved to profit by his absence to put to death the presi-

* Palma-Cayet.

dent of the Parliament of Paris, Brisson, and two or three of his colleagues.   They had given judgment contrary to the expectation of the League in the case of a man denounced for having written a letter to his uncle, who was a Royalist.   As the letter was one of no sort of importance, the Parliament declared him innocent of crime.

The "sixteen" were furious : they accused the magistrates of being sold to the Royalists, and swore to avenge the "good cause," of which they were the only incorruptible defenders.   Brisson was arrested as he was crossing the bridge Saint-Michel, on his way to the Palais de Justice. He was taken to the Petit-Châtelet, where were assembled several of the factious "sixteen," wearing long black robes, with a red cross in front. Brisson, who was a learned and eloquent man, requested to be allowed to finish a work he was engaged on, being shut up in his cell meanwhile and allowed only bread and water.*   To this appeal they were, of course, inexorable, and Brisson was immediately hanged inside the prison.

A band of fanatical priests, headed by the curé of Saint-Côme, arrested two other magistrates, — Larcher, the oldest counsellor of the Grand Chamber, and Tardif, counsellor of the Grand-Châtelet.   They also were hanged, and in the morning the Parisians passing the Place de Grève

---

* He had already written a work, then much esteemed, on jurisprudence, and another on the ancient Persian monarchy.

beheld the three men who had been carried there in the night, hanging on gibbets in the centre of the Place. To each was attached a paper setting forth that "these men were traitors, and favourers of heretics." They had calculated that this spectacle would incite the people against the Royalists, and that, led by the "sixteen," they would at once proceed to slay all who were pointed out to them as tainted with the "damnable sin of heresy."

The effect of this exhibition on the minds of the people was directly opposite to that expected. They seemed struck dumb with terror and amazement at the audacity of the men who had so long filled Paris with grief and misery. Instead, therefore, of uttering the vociferous applause the murderous band expected, — and had they received it they would have made themselves masters of the capital, — the people gazed with horror, then turned silently and sadly away.

Bussy-Leclerc, whom the "sixteen" had made captain of the Bastille, then requested the chiefs of the foreign garrison to begin the execution of those " politiques " whose names were on the lists of proscription he handed to them, and which were named significantly the "red papers" (*papiers rouges*). Both the Spanish and Italian colonels declined to take upon themselves so frightful a responsibility ; though they also refused to assist Count Bélin, Governor of Paris, in repressing the violent conduct of the "sixteen," while the count himself would not accept the proffered aid of the "politique" part of the *bourgeois* militia.*

Letters to Philip II. from the "sixteen" and the leading men of the University, having been intercepted by one of Rosny's agents and sent to Henri IV., were afterwards forwarded by him to Mayenne. In them Philip was told of the great desire of the writers to place the sceptre of France in his hands. But as that could not be, and he had no second son to give them, they would joyfully receive the infanta, in whose veins flowed the blood of France and Spain, and who therefore was doubly agreeable to them. They prayed that a husband for her of Philip's choice might be selected. But they humbly put forward the claims of the "young and valiant Duc de Guise," he being the candidate for that honour who would please them best. Nevertheless, all was to be left to Philip's decision. The Salic law, they promised, for once should be set at naught, the Council of Trent be published, and Isabella Clara Eugenia bring with her to France the Spanish Inquisition.

The projects of the "sixteen," together with the murder of the magistrates, of which Mayenne heard at about the same time, and while at Laon, at first greatly disconcerted him. He feared to return to Paris, believing that he no longer possessed sufficient power to impose restrictions

* L'Estoile, *Journal de Henri IV.*

on his sole authority on those desperate assassins. The Spanish ambassador, Diego d'Ibarra, urged him, of course, in Philip's interests, to refrain from returning to Paris, as it would be at the risk of his life. The Duchesses de Montpensier and Nemours — his sister and mother — with the secretaries Villeroy and Jeannin, advised him otherwise.

Accordingly he left Laon, accompanied by a strong detachment of troops. His nephew he adroitly despatched to Guise to confer in his stead with the Duke of Parma. It had been proposed to close the gates of Paris against Mayenne, or to stab him on his entry. Nothing of the sort occurred, but, on the contrary, a considerable number of the League faction went to salute him on his arrival in Paris at the Faubourg Saint-Antoine. Requests, demands, and petitions immediately flowed in upon him, which he neither granted nor refused; as also he announced neither pardon nor vengeance with reference to what had passed. Very secretly he employed three days in making his preparations, and taking precautions against any failure in the plan he proposed to carry out.

Unexpectedly the assassins of Brisson and his colleagues were arrested at midnight and conducted to an underground chamber of the Louvre, where they were immediately hanged. On the following morning their bodies were hanging on the Place de Grève, on the same gibbets they had themselves employed for exposing those of the victims of their own murderous deed. The enforcement in this instance of the *lex talionis* was approved by many of the Catholic nobility and *bourgeoisie*, while the rest of the "sixteen" were startled with fear on finding the usually indolent and timidly prudent lieutenant-general acting with so much decision and promptitude.

Bussy-Leclerc was also driven from the Bastille. He had sworn, when called on to evacuate that fortress, that he would rather be buried beneath its ruins than obey the command. Troops immediately surrounded it, and cannon were pointed; but before the first was fired Bussy capitulated, bargaining for his life and the worldly wealth he had stored up there. But the troops pillaged his ill-gotten treasure, and Bussy, with several of the "sixteen," escaped to Belgium. Less fortunate than others, who seem to have carried their plunder with them, Bussy was compelled to resume for a living his old profession of *maître d'armes*.

The priests and the Spaniards were furious against Mayenne for the course he had adopted towards "good Catholics," — martyrs, who were animated only by their zeal for religion. Mayenne replied that an example was necessary, and the measures he had taken requisite for the reëstablishment of order and obedience; "good Catholics," he said, had nothing to fear. The factious Council of Sixteen was, indeed, at an end, and no efforts of fanatical priests and Spaniards succeeded in reviving it, though two or three of its least ardent members yet remained in Paris. They appear to have silently accepted defeat, and to have regarded the influence of the "sixteen" as buried under the gibbets of the Place de Grève.

Mayenne, however, improved the opportunity recent events afforded him, and omitted nothing that tended to the consolidation of his power. The States General were ready to assemble in the early part of the following year. New oaths of obedience to him were taken by the officers and the *bourgeoisie* generally. Until the election of a king he was to be supreme in his authority, and no nomination of a candidate for the throne was to be favourably entertained until his approbation had been given.

The candidate he especially desired to thwart was his nephew, whose chances of election were greater than any of the would-be kings of France. Truly he had done nothing to acquire popularity, but it was conferred on him in the expectation that another idol of the populace would shortly reappear in the person of the son of their late "grand Guise."

While these preparations were going on for depriving the gallant Henri of Navarre of his legitimate rights, he, whose aim was to prevent the election of any one of those claimants as leading to further troubles and discord in France, was,

on his part, assembling his troops, and those sent
by his allies to assist him in overcoming and dispersing the hungry host, who, if they could not
have each the whole of France, at least hoped to
have it sliced up and divided amongst them.

CHAPTER X.

Turenne's Expedition so Successful that the King, to Reward
Him, Arranges His Marriage with the Heiress of Sedan and
Bouillon. — Turenne's Expression of His Gratitude. — Henri
Hastens from the Marriage *Fêtes* to the Siege of Rouen. —
Biron Thwarts the King's Projects. — Villars's Manœuvres
Embarrassing. — The Entrenchments Carried. — Biron's Advice
Leads the King into Error. — Parma Recalled to France and
Guise Defeated. — Chicot Killed by His Prisoner. — The
King Demands a Heavy Ransom.

HE Vicomte de Turenne had been travel-
ling in Germany, Holland, and England,
for several months, soliciting aid from
the Protestant princes to enable Henri IV. to continue the war.   He succeeded so well that he
returned towards the end of the year at the head
of 8,000 German infantry, 4,000 cavalry following,
commanded by the Prince of Anhalt.   Seven
thousand troops were also promised by Queen
Elizabeth, and shortly after arrived — the Earl of
Essex commanding.   At first she had pressed for
the restitution of Calais in return for her aid, but
eventually yielded to Turenne's representations
that Henri in his actual position could not venture
to cede any part of the territory of France without
incurring the resentment and the opposition of his

subjects.   Some ammunition was also sent from
England, and a sum of money — not a large one;
but a similar sum, it was hinted, would be forthcoming by and by if needed.   The queen likewise
partly guaranteed the pay of 2,000 Dutch troops,
whom Prince Maurice of Nassau spared from his
own small army to aid the cause of the heretic
king.

To receive the English and German reinforcements Henri went in person to Mézières, returning thence to Sedan.   With his own troops and a
corps of 6,000 Swiss, he had now an army 40,000
strong, — a larger force than any he had yet commanded.   With a part of this army Biron invested
Rouen, Henri proposing to follow immediately
with another detachment.   But considering that
he was greatly indebted to Turenne for his exertions on his behalf, he had prepared at Sedan —
besides the marshal's baton already promised him,
in spite of the clamour of the Catholics — a fitting
reward, as it seemed to him, for his services.   It
was the hand of Charlotte de La Marck, sole
heiress of the principality of Sedan and duchy of
Bouillon.

She was prohibited from marrying a Catholic
by the testament of her brother, Robert de La
Marck, Duc de Bouillon, who died at Geneva in
1587 of excessive grief and fatigue.*   Charlotte

* His death, as well as that of several of the Huguenot
nobility, resulted from extreme suffering undergone during that

had many suitors among both Catholic and Protestant princes and the nobility, but Henri thought
none so suitable a match for the young princess
as the Vicomte de Turenne. The Duc de Montpensier would have preferred that she should
marry his son, the Prince de Dombes, and called
the king's attention to the disparity in the ages of
the princess and the viscount. She was seventeen,
Turenne was thirty-six, but esteemed one of the
most elegant cavaliers of that day. He was distinguished also for his dauntless courage, his
gallantry and bravery.

Though Charlotte knew Turenne only by repute,
that was so much in his favour that she was willing
to accept the husband the king had provided for
her, and on whose behalf he so ably and eloquently
pleaded. Apparently her expectations were not
disappointed when the hero himself appeared to
plead his cause in person. The marriage took
place shortly after Turenne's arrival, the necessities
of the war not permitting a longer delay.* The
king paid a hasty visit to Gabrielle, then returned
to Sedan to be present at the nuptials, and to play

terrible retreat of the remnant of the Protestant army that escaped the massacre of Auneau, where they were so cruelly
betrayed and slaughtered by the bloodthirsty Henri Duc de
Guise and the Duc de Pont, eldest son of the Duc de Lorraine.
Of the many crimes and atrocious deeds committed during the
so-called " religious wars " of France, few exceed in revolting
barbarity the " affair of Auneau " (1587).

* Peyran, *Histoire de l'ancienne principauté de Sedan.*

the part of father to Charlotte. It was then decided that Turenne should assume the title of Duc
de Bouillon, Sovereign Prince of Sedan.

The Duc de Montpensier was consoled for his
son's loss of so eligible a bride by Henri's assurance that he would not neglect the Prince de
Dombes's matrimonial interests. Already he had
a princess in view for him.

The new prince was anxious to present the king
before he left Sedan with some token of his gratitude, but no suitable offering readily suggested
itself to him. However, after giving the subject
much thought, it occurred to Turenne that the
old Leaguer, the Duc de Lorraine, held possession
of the adjacent town of Stenay, which, with the
assistance of the three hundred gentlemen of his
suite, he believed might be taken at night by surprise, and restored to the king. The idea was
original, also appropriate, as the gift of a soldier
to a soldier, and pleased him none the less, probably, because if he succeeded the frontier of his
new domain would be freed from a troublesome
neighbour.

Immediately he communicated with his cavaliers,
who joyfully consented to join in the adventure,
and to hold themselves secretly in readiness to
start for Stenay shortly before the ball and marriage festivities were ended. Peyran states that
Turenne contrived to slip away unperceived, armed
cap-à-pie, to meet his companions ; also that neither

the king, the bride, the wedding guests, nor any member of his household had been informed of his project. Great, therefore, was the consternation when his absence was perceived. But when hours passed away, and still he came not, and tidings of him were sought in vain, it was concluded that either fanatical Leaguers or indignant and envious Catholics had maliciously chosen the moment of the noble Huguenot's auspicious nuptials to lay a snare to take him captive.

From other accounts it would appear that, although Turenne made a mystery of the nature of the adventure he was compelled, he said, to engage in that night, he did not keep the secret of his departure so profoundly as Peyran states (at least, not from the young duchess and his royal guest). But whichever version of the story be correct, Turenne's real motive for absenting himself was revealed in the early morning; for at daybreak a clarion is sounded, announcing the arrival of several hundred armed cavaliers, riding at full speed towards the château. The first to alight is the newly elected Prince of Sedan. The king is there to receive and probably reprove him, but he, falling on one knee, presents to his sovereign the keys of the town of Stenay in a silver dish. He and his followers have taken Stenay in the king's name, and he now begs him to regard that town as a pledge of his gratitude for the signal favours conferred on him.

" *Ventre Saint-Gris!* " exclaimed the king, raising Turenne, and embracing him ; "if every new
married couple would present me with a similar
wedding gift, I should soon be master of my kingdom." Charlotte smilingly expressed her approval
of her husband's happy idea and its gallant
achievement, and he, again bending the knee,
imprinted a kiss on her hand.

It was not, however, solely, or even chiefly,
with the view of recompensing him for raising
a body of troops that Henri was solicitous to
arrange Turenne's marriage with the heiress of
Sedan. It was rather considered a master-stroke
of policy on his part. The duchy of Bouillon
had played a considerable part in the political and
religious wars of the sixteenth century, and it was
important to Henri's interests that this small
independent frontier State should not fall into the
hands of any prince of the house of Austria or
of Lorraine. By conferring the hand of the
heiress, together with the joint sovereignty of the
duchy, on Turenne, he secured it to the Protestants, and with it the further advantage of creat-
ing new interests for the restless and ambitious
Turenne, which Henri hoped would keep him at a
distance from the South, where he was desirous
of being declared the head of the Protestants of
France.*

---

*The Duc de Bouillon's gratitude was rather short-lived. He
was the cause of considerable trouble to his benefactor, and of

From the marriage festivities of Sedan, Henri hastened to Darnetal, his headquarters being there established, in order to press the siege of Rouen with more vigor than was displayed by Biron, who began the investment of the city early in November. It was then December, and the weather unusually severe, when Henri arrived at his camp with the rest of the royal forces. The inclemency of the season made no change in his plans, for his constitution was of iron, like Rosny's and that of many other of his leading officers ; and glory, he thought, might be reaped in winter as well as in summer. He distributed his troops on both banks of the Seine, around the city and the strongly fortified mountain of Sainte-Catherine.

Before beginning the attack Henri sent a written address to the inhabitants, exhorting them "not to believe the calumnies of the King of Spain, who accused him of a design to abolish the Catholic religion, while it was well known that in the cities and towns reduced to his allegiance the religion of the people was in no way interfered with." He then urged them "to acknowledge their legitimate king, without compelling him to take up arms against them, as he would otherwise

much discord, jealousy and dissension in his camp. Yet Henri supported his pretension to the duchy, as the heir of Charlotte de La Marck, who died about two years after their marriage, and left it to him by will. Her right to do so was disputed by the collateral branches of the family. The Catholics murmured, but the duke was not dispossessed.

be unable to prevent the sack and pillage of the town." Very haughtily the mayor and corporation, representing the people, replied that they "awaited the result of his menaces, and would die rather than acknowledge a heretic as King of France."

The siege of Rouen, which lasted six months, was in some respects a second siege of Paris, though both besiegers and besieged carefully sought to avoid the errors committed during the latter. The people did not suffer the horrors of famine to so great an extent; but the attacks and repulses were more savage and sanguinary. The League was powerful at Rouen, and the defence of the city was in the hands of a man of great energy and resource, Villars-Brancas, Governor of Normandy, distinguished no less for his military capacity than his bravery. He had long foreseen the siege of Rouen, and had abundantly provisioned the city, and considerably reinforced the garrison. Suspected persons were expelled, and the rest of the inhabitants enrolled as soldiers, or employed in the work of thoroughly fortifying the city.

Maréchal de Biron, it is asserted, might have greatly obstructed the completion of these works, and especially the elaborate batteries constructed on Mount Sainte-Catherine, had he cared to do so. A rumor ran through the camp that the marshal before the siege began asked the king for the government of Normandy, should Rouen be taken, and that the king, in reply, named another officer to whom he would feel himself more particularly bound to give it. Annoyed at this, Biron secretly determined to thwart the king's projects, and, while prolonging the siege, allow him to derive no benefit from it. His advice in the Council as to the manner of beginning the attack was calculated, as he well knew, to render all the efforts of the king and his army to take Rouen useless.

The marshal, naturally of violent temper and arrogant manner, yielded to no one's opinion when differing from his own, but expected that all should yield to his. As he was a general of ability and experience, he was probably often in the right, when his private interests were not concerned. On the occasion in question he advised the first attack to be made on the château, where Villars was strongest. Rosny ventured to differ from him, recommending an attack first on the town. "The city taken," he said, "the château surrenders." Biron was fond of repeating this in a mocking, contemptuous manner. Several officers agreed with Rosny, but the marshal's advice prevailed.

The king soon became aware that he had entered on a work of no small difficulty. Villars not only defended the château from within, but made a sortie and cut a long and deep entrenchment communicating at one end with the château, and placed six or seven hundred men there to

guard it. As this exposed the besiegers to be
attacked in the rear, while the garrison of the
château was in front of them, the king resolved
that he would render this entrenchment useless.
He chose the night for his purpose, taking with
him three hundred gentlemen fully armed.*
Rosny was of the party. Besides their ordinary
arms, each carried a halberd in his hand, and two
pistols in his waist - belt. To this troop of cavaliers were added four hundred musketeers or
pikemen.

It was midnight when the party set out ; the
cold was extreme, and the ground deeply covered
with snow. The entrenchment was attacked in
several places, and for half an hour the action was
kept up with equal obstinacy and animosity on
both sides. Great efforts, several times vigorously repulsed, were made by the assailants to
reach the bank. Rosny was twice thrown down,
his halberd broken, and his pistols lost. But at
length the entrenchment was carried by sheer
force, and cleared of fifty or sixty of the besieged,
dead or dying, who were thrown over the steep
of the mountain. The entrenchment was exposed
to the fire of the cannon of the fort, but the king
having taken the precaution of ordering a quantity
of gabions, barrels, and pieces of wood to be
brought, a shelter was formed for the English,
who were left to guard it.

* *Mémoires de Sully ;* D'Aubigné, *Histoire universelle.*

Villars was far from expecting to see this out-work carried so promptly. When he heard that the king in person had conducted this enterprise, "*Par dieu!*" he exclaimed, "this prince by his valour deserves a thousand crowns! I am sorry he does not adopt a better creed, and thus give us as great a desire to conquer other crowns for him, as by the heresy he clings to he gives us cause to dispute his right to the one he claims. But it shall not be said that I have failed to attempt in person what a great king has personally effected."

That same night Villars, at the head of four hundred fully armed men — the same number, he was told, that accompanied the king — and eight hundred of his best pikemen, attacked the English and dislodged them. Henri, irritated by Villars's vanity, determined on a second attack. The English hearing this, and fearing to be reproached (which they certainly did not deserve) with having too promptly given way before the enemy, re-quested the king to add a hundred English cavaliers to his troop, and to allow only English foot-soldiers to accompany him. Further, they asked to be permitted to begin the attack, which being granted, they behaved so valorously that, in spite of the resolute resistance of the enemy, the entrenchment was retaken, — the English by their unflagging vigilance maintaining possession of it.

So much fighting and fatigue being needed for

the taking of a mere outwork, it was easy to per-
ceive that the siege must be long and laborious ;
for it was not simply a blockade he proposed, but
regular siege operations, pushed forward with as
much vigour as the inclemency of a severe mid-
winter permitted.   The king felt keenly that it
was an enterprise almost hopeless in its chances
of success, owing to the error he had fallen into
from adopting Biron's opinion as to the best point
of attack.   Little zeal, too, was evinced by his
officers in carrying out his directions, so great
was the jealousy existing between Catholics and
Protestants.   The former, not at all caring to
conceal their sentiments, openly declared that so
long as the king was not of their religion he could
expect from them no great devotion to his cause
or sympathy with his views.*

Prodigies of valour on the part of the king
availed only to convince the people that if his
project failed it was due to no fault of his.   But
his efforts were not seconded, half the officers of
his army fearing, almost as much as his enemies,
a success which would put an end to the campaign,
and probably to the war.

The rough labour of the trenches, rendered
more trying by heavy snow-storms, intense frosts,
insufficient clothing, and scant rations, greatly
fatigued the infantry of the Royalist auxiliaries.
The English, it appears, though acknowledged to

* *Mémoires de Sully.*

be very brave soldiers, bore up with difficulty against these hardships ; many, indeed, succumbed to them ; others suffered severely from frost-bite.

Henri, desirous of sending these troops to their homes, despatched Du Plessis-Mornay to England to ask the queen for further aid, — a reinforcement and some money. Elizabeth, vexed at the absence of Essex for a longer time than she had expected or had given him leave to remain in France, received the Huguenot negotiator very ungraciously, though professing great esteem for him as a man of eminent learning and sincere piety. She, however, positively refused to give further assistance to Henri, but relented on the return of Essex, when she sent the king word that he did wrong to place his life so recklessly in danger, and begged him to take better care of it.

The siege of Rouen had continued four months when Mayenne thought it expedient to urge the return of the Duke of Parma to afford aid to that town. Yet Villars had assured him he could hold out some time longer ; and while Mayenne and the unwilling Parma — who was decidedly averse to Philip's views on France — discussed the question of ceding La Fère to the Spaniards, as a military magazine for Philip's army, the Governor of Rouen acted. Leaving the defence of the town and the forts to the *bourgeois* militia, Villars made a sortie with the whole of his garrison, 2,500 men, swept the besiegers' trenches, and killed all they

found there ; overthrew their gabions and stock-
ades, burnt their lodgments, and seized five pieces
of cannon.   It was only after the lapse of two
hours that Biron appeared on the scene, returning
in haste from Darnetal.   He succeeded, however,
in driving back the Leaguers into the city, but,
being wounded, did not recover the guns, which
were drawn in triumph into the beleaguered town.

Henri — of whose absence Villars had taken
advantage — having been wrongly informed that
the French troops, the Lorrainers of the League,
the Spaniards of the Netherlands, and the remnant
of the dissolute papal army, had left La Fère and
thence were slowly advancing towards Picardy,
under the conduct of the Dukes of Parma, Mayenne and Guise, the Comte de Chaligny, etc.,
resolved to avoid the error he had fallen into in
1590.   He believed that he could both carry on
the siege and check the progress of the army of
relief.   All his infantry — diminished in number,
harassed, and fatigued — he left in his camp before
Rouen, with a portion of his cavalry, under Biron's
orders, and took with him 2,000 German *reïtres*,
2,000 French, and 2,000 mounted arquebusiers.*
With this small but brilliant troop (the finest
cavalry he had yet possessed) he advanced to the
entrance of Picardy to watch the approach of the
enemy, and to disquiet him on his march.

* It was at this time that these arquebusiers, who dismounted
when they were about to fight, were first named dragoons.

But the enemy was long in coming. The allied army was still at La Fère, and its chiefs negotiating, when news reached them of Villars's brilliant sortie. Parma was anxious to march at once and complete the victory which the Leaguers had partly achieved. But Mayenne and his partisans, believing that Rouen was really saved — the people having thanked and fêted La Dame de Lorette for their deliverance — were satisfied with what Villars had already done, and dreaded a more decisive victory achieved by Parma, which would make them subjects of Philip of Spain.

However, siege operations being resumed by the Royalists, the Spaniards, with the intention of reinforcing Villars, began their march to Picardy, by Amiens and Ponthieu. The young Duc de Guise commanded the Spanish duke's vanguard, and was at the head of a corps of cavalry. Henri, informed of this, resolved to attack him, and, with 1,200 *reîtres* and 1,000 mounted arquebusiers, he killed or put to flight the greater part of the vanguard. The duke's baggage was pillaged, and the green standard of the Guises taken, the duke himself escaping capture only by the great fleetness of his horse.

A prince of the house of Lorraine, the Comte de Chaligny, half-brother of the widowed Queen of France, was taken prisoner in this attack by a Gascon gentleman named Chicot, whose eccentric manners and language, and his familiarities with

the king, whom he was accustomed to " *tutoyer*,"
had gained him in the camp the sobriquet of "the
king's buffoon." He was very wealthy, and his
devotion to the royal cause led him to follow
Henri IV. in all his enterprises. On the occasion
in question he had fought with great bravery, and
having secured this prince as his captive, he took
him to the king, to whom he presented him, saying:
" *Tiens*, Henriot, I have brought thee a prisoner of
mine own, and I give him to thee." The count
had not the honour of knowing M. de Chicot, but
as soon as he became aware from the laughter and
remarks of those around him of the kind of man
to whom he, who commanded a detachment, had
surrendered, and who affected to treat him also
with extreme contempt, his indignation so over-
came him that he struck his captor a heavy blow
on the head, which rendered him insensible.
Some few days after poor Chicot died.

Such acts were common enough in those days,
but the king required of Chaligny a heavy ransom,
as he had a singular regard for Chicot, in spite of
his eccentricities. He made no use of the money
for his own needs, but sent it to the Duchesse de
Longueville, to compensate her for the thirty
thousand crowns the Leaguers had compelled her
to pay as ransom when, at the beginning of the
campaign, they arrested her in Picardy.

CHAPTER XI.

The Spanish Armies Advancing in Order of Battle, 25,000 Strong. — The King Rides Out with 100 Cavaliers to Meet Them. — Sixty of His Cavaliers Killed, and the King Wounded. — His Fame as a Dauntless Soldier Spread throughout Europe. — Parma Avoids Giving Battle. — Biron's Treachery. — Parma's Retreat. — Officers Refuse to Pursue. — Sterile Glory. — Ill-will, Want of Money. — The Army Disbanded. — Death of Parma. — War Suspended.

AFTER his successful attack on the enemy's vanguard, the king advanced with his 6,000 horsemen in the direction of Aumale. Givry was sent forward with a small escort to reconnoitre. He soon returned with the report that the Spanish armies, about 25,000 strong (as he thought, for a mist prevailed), were advancing directly upon him towards the plain. So near were they that their drums and trumpets might be distinctly heard. On ascending the hill of Aumale, to take a rapid survey himself of the situation, the king beheld, as the mist dispersed, an army of from 16,000 to 17,000 infantry, and from 7,000 to 8,000 cavalry — the infantry marching in the middle, the cavalry divided on the two flanks.*

* An order of battle of which the armies of the Prince of Parma appear to have given the first examples, and which for nearly a century remained unchanged. — J. SERVAN, Notes to *Guerres des Français.*

He at once perceived that, with a corps of
6,000 cavalry only, he could not face an army in
order of battle, and that simply for a skirmish the
corps was far too numerous.   He therefore sent
off the greater part of them to Neuchâtel, retain-
ing but 400 with him, of whom 300 were to halt
on the slope of the hill, to aid him in case of need.
For himself, he did not merely propose to wait
the approach of the enemy, but, with his hundred
cavaliers, to ride out to meet him.

"We listened," says Rosny, "in silence while he
gave his orders and made such disposition as
seemed to us calculated only to result in certain
death to the king and probably the whole troop.
In utter astonishment we gazed at each other
— none daring to speak, all unwilling to remain
silent.   At last, I was deputed to represent to the
king how unprecedented was the peril he was
about to expose himself to.

" 'That,' he replied, 'is the language of people
who are afraid.   I should never have expected to
hear it from any of you.'

" 'We *are* afraid, Sire,' I rejoined; 'but our
fear is for your Majesty's safety.   Give us any
orders you please; we will strive to execute them,
provided you retire.' "

These words, as Henri afterwards acknowledged,
sensibly affected him.   "He had no doubts," he
said, "of the courage or the fidelity of his officers;
but he would also have them believe that he was

Duke of Parma.

Photo-Etching. — From an old Portrait.

ALEXANDER FARNESE,
HARTOGH VAN PARMA EN PLAISANCE.
GOUVERNEUR GENERAEL EN VELD'TOVERSTE
IN DE SPAENSCHE NEDERLANDEN.

not so utterly reckless as they seemed to imagine ; that he cared to keep his skin whole as much as any of them, and that he should retire the moment he perceived that any inconvenience or difficulty of action was likely to occur." There was an end of the matter, as his manner seemed to say, and he and his hundred cavaliers forthwith advanced to meet the Spanish army.

This audacious manœuvre was regarded by their prudent general as a snare to draw his cavalry into the open country, where he supposed the king's to be concealed, and superior in numbers to his own. Accordingly a halt was made, Parma remaining at his post in the centre of the army, seated in an open chariot and unarmed. That a hundred men should have the audacity to brave an army of 26,000 greatly raised the ire of the Spanish soldiers, who, when their general — assured that, within sight at least, there was really but one hundred of them — ordered a detachment of cavalry to attack the Royalists, rushed so furiously upon them that they were driven with exceeding force, *pêle-mêle*, towards the valley. In this direction, which the king's movements led them to take, he was thrust nearer to the bridge of Aumale, over which he proposed to retreat. "Charge !" exclaimed the king, in order to check the pursuit ; and, as he foresaw, the enemy, suspecting an ambuscade, immediately halted. But when fifty or sixty pistol-shots alone

responded, the onset was renewed, and with re-
doubled impetus.

The 300 arquebusiers, who were to assist the
king and his cavaliers at this point, if needed, had
taken up another position, and were of no assistance whatever. Pursuing their point, the Spaniards became mingled with the Royalists, of whom
sixty perished in the *mêlée*. If the enemy, continues the narrator, had then surrounded the forty
remaining cavaliers and their leader, Henri IV.
and France had been lost that day. But the
Spanish duke was not then aware that the king
was the leader of that handful of reckless men,
whose temerity so amazed him and his officers,
and against whom his troops fought with the one
disadvantage to which Henri and his troop owed
their escape, — the constant expectation of a surprise. Separating himself and his Royalists from
the general fray, he overthrew, with incredible
force and rapidity, all who opposed his passage,
and succeeded in placing himself with the utmost
coolness at the rear of the remnant of his troop,
defiling with them towards the bridge of Aumale,
which was reached and crossed without confusion.
The last to cross was the king — determined to
protect his soldiers, not to be protected by them,
and thus effecting this remarkable retreat in perfect order.

A small detachment pursued for a short distance,
their ardour greatly restrained by the fear, of which

they could not divest themselves, of falling into an ambuscade. Suddenly they raised the cry, " Henri de Navarre!" The king was recognised, but happily for him too late for Spanish vengeance; the pursuit ceased, for the 300 cavaliers now made their appearance, which favoured the enemy's idea of a surprise. A parting shot was fired at the king, and a ball from an arquebuse pierced his saddle-bow and wounded him in the loins.*

This "chivalric action," as Henri's more than rash act has been called, cost sixty brave men their lives, many of them his most devoted friends. It had no motive but the vain one of being able to boast that with one hundred men he had attacked an army of between 20,000 and 30,000, and that, after slaying with his own hand more men than he lost, and being reduced to forty followers, he had effected his retreat safely and in good order under the eyes of the Spanish general, — a retreat of far greater difficulty than that general's own famous retreat, so much and so often lauded by the military men of that day. Henri, however, was fain to confess on reflection that his great exploit was not one he could glory in, but simply an error, and so he named it always, referring to this combat as " The Error of Aumale."

" Heroic error!" exclaims his ever faithful friend

* This was the only wound the hero of so many fights ever received.

and admirer, the Baron de Rosny.   And as an act
of astonishing heroism it was generally regarded.
The fame of Henri IV. spread far and wide, and
the appellation "the greatest soldier in Europe"
was freely and unanimously accorded him.   Queen
Elizabeth, while complimenting him on his valour,
for the second time entreated him to avoid endan-
gering his life so recklessly.   Du Plessis-Mornay
also wrote :

> SIRE: You have played the part of Alexander long
> enough; it is now time that you adopt that of Augustus.
> It is for us to die for you, and in that is our glory; it is for
> you to live for France, and I venture to say that is your
> duty.

The Duke of Parma, vexed that so favourable
an opportunity of effectually putting an end to the
war, and of capturing or killing the heretic Henri
of Navarre, had escaped him, justified himself
(remissness being imputed to him by zealous Leaguers) by saying that he "had thought he was
opposed to a general, not to a carabineer, who
came to fire his pistol in his lines."   An act of
humanity very foreign to his nature was, however,
accredited to him by his partisans, in the recall of
the pursuers of the forty hardly pressed men,
whose daring attack on him he could not under-
stand, but whose valour he nevertheless admired.

The king, though wounded at the combat of
Aumale, rode on with his forty heroic companions
and the 300 arquebusiers.   On arriving at Neu-

châtel he was assisted to dismount, feeling stiff and in pain. This occasioned the greatest disquietude — a veritable panic in the camp. But as soon as the surgeon had examined and dressed the wound he reassured the anxious inquirers. The king's wound was neither dangerous nor likely to inconvenience him very long. The officers in camp then assembled around his bed, and the combat of Aumale was fought over again for their benefit.

Great as was the dissension in his camp, and scant the confidence he could repose in the chief captains of his army, several of whom forsook or returned to his standard as his fortunes fluctuated or private interests influenced them, yet they liked the Béarnais personally, as a comrade-in-arms and joyous companion. If they cared little or naught for his rights, they admired his dauntless courage, and enjoyed his Gascon wit, that kept the camp lively, composing and singing also in his honour that old Royalist chant:

> "Vive Henri quatre,
> Vive ce roi vaillant,
> Ce diable à quatre
> Qui a le triple talent
> De boire et de battre
> Et d'être vert galant."

At Neuchâtel the king first heard of Villars's successful sortie. Biron's culpable negligence alone, he felt convinced, had afforded Villars this advantage ; but although he considered the fault

irreparable, he refrained from allowing his dissatisfaction with the marshal to appear. The
siege, he perceived, must be raised as soon as a
plausible pretext could be found for diminishing
the disgrace of it, as well as for directing on the
common enemy the fury of the two parties (Protestants and Catholics) composing his army.

At once he set out for Rouen, putting off, as
he said, the healing of his wound until a more
convenient season. On arrival he heard with
satisfaction that the Duke of Parma, reinforced
by Mayenne's army and the papal troops, was
advancing to give him battle. The army was
also joined on its march by the cardinal legate,
Bishop of Placentia, despatched by Innocent IX.
to convey his benediction to the generals of the
League and all ranks of their army when in
presence of the heretic enemy.* Hastily reas-
sembling his troops, dispersed in various garrisons, Henri awaited his foes for a whole day,
drawn up in order of battle, at Bans, three leagues
from Rouen.

But Parma had no intention of fighting and
risking his great reputation in a conflict with so
reckless and dauntless an adversary as the King

* Gregory XIV. died about six weeks previously, having
occupied the papal throne long enough to squander on the
Leaguers and their armies the treasure amassed by Sixtus V.
for the embellishment of Rome. Innocent IX. reigned but
two months, and was succeeded by Clement VIII., Cardinal
Hyppolito Aldobrandini.

of Navarre. Taking advantage, therefore, of the
mountainous nature of the district, he contrived,
by a skilful manœuvre, to avoid the Royalist army
and to reach Rouen April 22d, then beginning
to suffer from a scarcity of provisions. Biron on
the preceding evening, while the king was at
Dieppe, being unable to defend his lines, evacuated
the camp and began his retreat. This emboldened
the Leaguers, who prevailed on the Spanish general
to lay siege to Caudebec, where the Royalists had
stored a quantity of wheat.

He was rather opposed to the scheme, being
then without information of Henri's movements,
but yielding to Mayenne's advice, he reconnoitred
the place, and while doing so was wounded in the
right arm by a ball from an arquebuse. But
Caudebec was besieged, and two days after surrendered ; Yvetot also. This, it appears, was an
error which the duke was led into by Mayenne's
supposed greater knowledge of the country,
and Henri quickly availed himself of it. Hastening from Pont-de-l'Arche, in the Pays de Caux, he
fell suddenly on the enemy's vanguard, retook
Yvetot, forced an entrenched wood, and was
pushing his successes still further, when Parma,
who had been confined to his bed by fever, the
pain of his wound, and general bad health, succeeded, after much fighting and the loss of 3,000
men, in arresting his further progress.

Master of all the defiles in the country between

Caudebec and Rouen, Henri thought his enemy so effectually shut up between the Seine and the sea that his position was become desperate.

" *Vive dieu !*" he exclaimed, with his usual gaiety. " If I lose the kingdom of France, I am at least in possession of the kingdom of Yvetot."*

He proposed on the morrow to attack the Spanish camp, but whether from being too confident in having entrapped the Spaniard into a position from which he could not release himself, fertile in resource though he was known to be, or that the Royalist scouts neglected to keep the king informed of the enemy's movements, when dawn appeared the camp was empty. " Scarcely," Rosny remarks, " could the king and his army believe their eyes. Was it," they exclaimed, " a reality or an illusion ?"

The great Spanish general had for some days been preparing for such an emergency. Pontoons, rafts, and towing boats were constructed for him at Rouen, which the reflux of the tide brought rapidly down to Caudebec, whose position favoured a secret embarkation. From the events of the day the

---

*The allodial lands or freehold estate (the only one north of the Loire) which, from the fourteenth to the seventeenth century, was proverbially renowned as the kingdom of Yvetot, owed the appellation to the exceptional condition of the lords or owners of the estates possessing them in full sovereignty, exempt from service of any kind, and rendering neither fealty nor homage even to the king — as distinguished from feudal lords ; hence they were sometimes called kings.

duke seemed to divine Henri's purpose of attacking his camp on the morrow, and, notwithstanding
his sufferings from wounds and ill-health, he
determined to save his army from falling into the
hands of the probable victors. A bridge was
rapidly put together, protected on either bank by
an earthwork and a party of cavalry, and before
morning dawned the whole of his army, with the
baggage and guns, was, under his immediate orders,
transported to the opposite bank of the Seine, not
a man being left behind.

This escape of his enemy was naturally very
mortifying to Henri IV., yet the perfect order
and ability with which it had been effected drew
from him and his officers many expressions of
admiration. It, however, appears to have been
doubtful that it would have fully assured the
safety of the Spanish army if Henri's project of at
once proceeding to Pont-de-l'Arche, and there, or
at Vernon, crossing the Seine, sending on before
him his light cavalry to destroy the bridges on the
Eure, over which the Spaniards must pass, had
been immediately, as he proposed, adopted.

A council of war was held, and some few of the
officers, Rosny being one of them, supported
the king's proposal; but the greater number
vehemently opposed it, as though it were the most
unreasonable and wildest of projects. Catholics,
Protestants, and foreigners vied with each other
in raising up obstacles against it, and in affecting

to regard it as utterly chimerical and delusive.
Irritated by the intention he perceived in their
objections rather than the objections themselves,
the king replied with some harshness that " all
these obstacles were insurmountable only to those
in whom failure of courage and fear of labour made
them appear so." Thus thwarted by his officers,
Henri was compelled to renounce the hope of
vanquishing the Duke of Parma and taking the city
of Rouen.

The Spanish army arrived at Saint-Cloud by
forced marches in four days, and reached the
Netherlands by way of Brie and Champagne without further impediment. While passing the
capital a detachment of troops — 1,500 Walloons —
was sent by the duke into Paris as a reinforcement of the army of the League, with the promise
also to return before the end of the winter with a
considerable force to lend support to the States
General, who were then, after many delays, to
assemble and to proceed to the election of a king.
He was, however, in almost a dying state when he
arrived at the baths of Spa, where he learned that
the Dutch, as he had anticipated, had deprived
his government of several fortified towns.

Twice had this reputed great general snatched
victory from the hands of Henri IV., and delayed
the end of the crisis. For, with all his heroism,
the king had conquered naught but sterile glory,
and was now after two years of strenuous effort

in a no better position than on the morrow of Ivry.
The League, however, was tottering towards its
fall, and thus was working for him.

The ill will and spirit of revolt so startlingly
displayed in his council and his army, together
with a generally expressed weariness of the war
and a longing for repose, which seemed to presage
the fulfilment of the threat of the Catholics to
abandon his cause, induced the king to spare himself further humiliation by assenting with the best
grace possible to their several wishes and demands.
Though profoundly grieved and disappointed, he
concealed his feelings, expressing neither chagrin
nor anger. A part of the army was at once disbanded, and a *congé* granted to all who sought it.

The foreign auxiliaries who desired to return to
their home, and, of course, to receive the arrears
of pay due to them, had permission to retire, their
demands also being satisfied so far as the king's
general insufficiency of means for his own or his
soldiers' needs permitted. For the rest he thanked
them most graciously for their services, and gave
them much praise for their valour. There were
officers in his camp, both Catholic and Protestant,
of whose zeal for his cause and fidelity to him
there was no question, but who, after the fatigues
of a long and harassing campaign, desired a short
interval of repose. To them he granted leave to
retire for a space with their worn and weary
troops into the various garrisons.

Henri reserved for his own command a *corps d'élite* of 6,000 infantry and 3,000 cavalry, for though the army of the League had abandoned Normandy after the retreat of the Spaniards, war still continued, but with little vigour. The king retook Caudebec, while " Crillon the brave," and Bellegarde, *grand-écuyer*, effectually resisted Villars, who laid seige to Quilleboeuf.

The last military event of the year was the siege of Épernay, invested by Maréchal de Biron after raising the siege of Rouen. The garrison and the inhabitants made a valiant resistance. Henri was present and eventually Épernay was taken ; but it cost the marshal his life, his head being blown off by a cannon-ball. Great sorrow was expressed by the king for the loss of so distinguished a general, though, as was commonly believed, he had played the part of traitor towards him, and prevented the taking of both Paris and Rouen. L'Estoile, in his *"Journal de Hénri IV.,"* speaks of Biron as " a great captain, serving the king for his own convenience, thwarting in every possible way his designs for making peace, as one who desired the continuance of war for his own ambitious purposes and private profit, which he ever preferred to the public welfare and good of the people."

He is said to have been a man of some culture, and as well versed in *les belles-lettres* as in the art of war ; but his great qualities were obscured by

Maréchal de Biron.

Photo-Etching. — From an old Portrait.

ARMAND DE GONTAULT,

De Biron Marechal de France

Tué au Siege d'Epernai agé de 68 ans.

his arrogance and culpable egotism. His son, Charles de Biron, who with less genius inherited his valour and also his vices, was appointed by the king to the post of Admiral of France, resigned at that time by the Duc d'Épernon.*

The war continued, but with little energy on either side, except in the Southeast, where the great Dauphiny captain, the Huguenot Duc de Lesdiguières, with his second in command, Bernard de La Valette, was carrying all before him.† The duke's remarkable military genius and astonishing activity imparted a grander character to the events of the war in that part of France than in the North, where it was languishing, — Mayenne being ill at Rouen, and Henri in absolute penury. He was induced therefore to disband a part of his troops, and to send the rest to various garrisons, until money came in from some quarter, and he could compel Parma — whom Philip had ordered to risk everything, and even to make peace with

---

* The marshal is supposed to have left military memoirs, the loss of which, from his experience and capacity, is to be regretted. It is singular that the son of such a man should have received so little education that his greatest effort with the pen was signing his name, which with difficulty he accomplished.

† La Valette, the brother of the Duc d'Épernon, was killed at the siege of a town in Provence after a second time defeating Charles Emanuel, Duke of Savoy, who had invaded France. Lesdiguières did not allow the Savoyard to profit by the death of that brave officer, but drove him back from place to place as far as Nice.

the Dutch for the sake of accomplishing his views
on France — to accept battle.

It was by no means certain that the States
General, though convoked to assemble in Paris on
the 17th of January, would really hold their session in that city, — Parma, in Philip's name,
opposing it, and naming Rheims as a more suitable and convenient locality. Though exceedingly
ill, he made known, as a sort of menace, that he
was preparing to redeem his promise of returning
to France, accompanied by a larger army than
heretofore. Already several thousand Spanish,
Italian, and Walloon troops were on the frontier,
and others arriving to join them. It was a moment
of extreme anxiety to all parties; but great was
the consternation when, instead of the expected
intelligence that the general had begun his march,
a courier arrived with the news that he had
breathed his last at Arras on the 5th of December, in his forty-sixth year.

The renowned Alexandro Farnese, Prince of
Parma, succumbed to a malady that had long
afflicted him, and which his endeavours to bear
up against until he had succeeded in carrying
out Philip's views on France served but to increase, and to hasten the fatal end. His death
was a great political event, changing the face of
affairs in France, and menacing a speedy end
to the expiring League. To Spain it was a
blow almost as calamitous as the disaster of the

Armada. It, however, led to the suspension of the war for awhile, and gave the king a little leisure to solace himself for his many disappointments and useless feats of heroism in the society of his belle Gabrielle ; also to confer with his *fidus Achates,* Rosny, on the subject of his abjuration ; * for "thousands of voices now rang incessantly in his ears that the struggle he was engaged in could end only in the ruin of France or a compromise." †

* Rosny was suffering from the reopening of some of his wounds, — especially that in the nape of his neck, which affected his articulation. Again he resolved to withdraw from camps and the tented field and to devote himself henceforth to the cultivation and improvement of his estates. He was destined, however, again to change his mind.

† *Mémoires de Sully ;* Mathieu ; D'Aubigné ; L'Estoile.

CHAPTER XII.

THE interval between the temporary dis-
bandment of the Royalist army and the
assembling of the States General was
passed by Henri IV. at Mantes, and chiefly in the
society of the Marquise de Monceaux, to whom he
daily became more devoted and more passionately
attached. Her liveliness and amiability of temper,
together with the sympathy she evinced in all his
undertakings in the arduous struggle for the attain-
ment of his legitimate rights, endeared her to him,
as he himself declared, far more than her brilliant
beauty. He confided his perplexities to her, and
as she was not wanting in ability, courage, and
firmness, her suggestions — though she did not, it
appears, presume to advise, but merely played the

woman's part of consoler — are said to have been frequently very judicious.

Henri's position was then a most difficult one. Many of his stanchest adherents, in view of the troubles with which unfortunate France was still further threatened, called on him to name the council, general or national, to whose instruction in Catholicism he would be willing to submit, and thus carry into effect the promise that led them to espouse his cause. He had named, when that promise was given, a delay of six months for its realisation; but nearly three years had elapsed and it yet remained unfulfilled.

Henri had long resisted this pressure, making the continuance of war his excuse, for it was wounding to his dignity and sentiments rather than to his positive religious belief. He would have preferred to conquer his kingdom as a Protestant, and afterwards, as a concession voluntarily made to his subjects, to adopt the dominant religion. Partly, that kingdom was already conquered, but much yet remained to be done ere victory could be considered complete. Those Catholics and "politiques" who recognised him as the legitimate sovereign of France, and hitherto, though murmuringly, had borne with his prolonged delay to receive instruction, now plainly menaced him with their intention to join the third party, which lately had become formidable, — its aim being to exclude the foreign pretenders and elect the Cardinal de Bourbon king, unless Henri without delay abjured his heresy and returned to the true faith.

From recent events of the late campaign, it was sufficiently clear that not alone on the battle-field would the great question then agitating France be finally decided. It might have been otherwise if money had been profusely forthcoming ; for almost every influential man of that day had his price. But Henri was reduced almost to penury. The famous *poule au pot,* which some day, he hoped, would be within the means of every peasant family in France, was then a *rara avis* even in the *ménage* of the soldier-king, who was reduced to share the meals of his comrades of the camp — his purveyor having represented to him that "his payments being six months in arrears, he could supply him no longer without money in advance." His shirts, as he said, were in rags, his doublet out at elbows, and he had not a horse in his stable worthy to carry so valiant a knight.

How Gabrielle fared, who was fond of rich dresses and jewels rare, we are not told. She probably looked to the future for the wealth and state her royal lover had not then the power to give her,— sharing with a light heart meanwhile his temporary destitution. She was supposed by the Catholics to have a leaning towards the Huguenot heresy, from the fact of the king being an excommunicated relapsed heretic appearing to be a matter of indifference to her, though professedly a Catholic. On the other hand, the Huguenots suspected that, using her influence over the king from interested motives, she was gradually bringing him to regard the required recantation with less repugnance. "Her ambition," D'Aubigné said, "led her to cherish the hope of becoming Queen of France should Henri abjure Calvinism, and as a Catholic obtain a divorce from Marguerite."

To some extent, probably, the Huguenots were right; but Rosny's arguments in favour of abjuration doubtless greatly outweighed in such a matter the tender persuasion of Gabrielle. "Considerations also of interest and policy very strongly combated the moral sentiment that rebelled in the king's breast against confessing with his lips what in his heart he disbelieved." His Calvinism, indeed, had little of the seriousness which distinguished that of the chief men of "the religion." It sat very lightly upon him, though no doubt he had in some degree an affection for it, if only for the sake of the men who had sacrificed so much for him and his cause; who had shed their blood and exhausted their means to enable him, so far, to carry on the struggle for his crown.

Naturally, then, he shrank from raising, as it were, a barrier between him and the devoted followers who had looked up to him as their prince and chief, from the day when the energetic and

noble-minded Jeanne d'Albret brought him and his
cousin of Condé to the Huguenot camp, to present
them to Admiral de Coligny as his youthful
lieutenants and future heads of the Protestant
party.

While Henri was still wavering — now assuring
the Huguenot chiefs that he " would live and die
in their religion," now using every means to obtain
from the most influential of them their sanction to
the policy, at least, of the change he had almost
prevailed on himself to make — the date was
finally fixed for the assembling of the States General in Paris.   They were authorised by the lately
issued bull of Clement VIII. simply to elect a
Catholic King of France.   But on the publication
of this bull, the legate, in concert with the Spanish
ambassador, proposed that on the opening of the
States an oath should be taken by the deputies to
the effect that they would never treat with the
King of Navarre under any pretence whatever,
even should he renounce his heresy and declare
himself a Catholic.

The Archbishop of Lyons, however, with Villeroy and one or two others of the council, positively
refused to countenance so rash an engagement,
the archbishop adding that to declare the King
of Navarre's reconciliation with the Church impossible was to anticipate the judgment of the
Pope and to entrench on his authority, — an argu-
ment that at once silenced the legate.

Mayenne had already exhorted the Royalist Catholics ("*le parti contraire*," as he termed them) "to separate themselves from heretics, and send deputies to Paris to take part with the Holy Union in a discussion touching the safety of the Church and state." Meanwhile the seven or eight pretenders to the throne were scheming and intriguing on all sides ; and as the deputies arrived in Paris, the agents of these would-be kings of France — lying in wait day and night for their prey — followed them to their houses or hôtels, to solicit their votes in favour of the election of this or that royal candidate.*

These pretenders were at the same time severally and secretly, not excepting even the King of Spain, making proposals to Henri IV. to assist him in securing his crown, on condition of certain provinces being ceded to them in return for the aid afforded. He was, in fact, to slice up France among them, and, to secure his crown, make them a present of his kingdom. Mayenne's pretensions exceeded even those of Philip II., being simply impossible to comply with.

These overtures being rejected, it was determined by the king and his council to endeavour to come to an understanding with Clement VIII. respecting the king's instruction, and the questions relating thereto. Cardinal de Gondy, hitherto neutral, now joined the Royalist party, and with

* L'Estoile, *Journal de Henri IV.*

the Marquis de Pisani set out for Rome, the Venetians having undertaken to open the matter to his holiness. But the Spaniards and the Leaguers had forestalled them, and so greatly misrepresented the object of the "heretic mission" that the king's envoys, though good Catholics, were termed "abettors of the Prince of Béarn," and prohibited entering Rome.

On the 26th of January the opening session of the States General took place in the grand upper *salon* of the Louvre. This was usually an imposing spectacle; but they who had seen the grand gatherings of 1576 and 1588 declared the one now in question, as compared with them, to be but their merest shadow. Yet Mayenne sat under the royal canopy, representing absent majesty, and, as he told them, the object for which they were assembled was one of highest interest and importance — to elect a sovereign ruler of France, "the first nation of Christendom."

Sixty deputies only were present of the clergy and *Tiers État.* The seats assigned to the nobility were entirely vacant, not one representative of their order being present. The smallness of the attendance was attributed partly to the terrible weather then prevailing in France, the dangerous condition of the roads at that season, and the perils which threatened travellers from distant provinces from bands of desperate starving men — many of them disbanded soldiers and ruined peasantry — who infested the principal routes, and to obtain relief for their own necessities attacked unarmed or unescorted wayfarers. Such was the state to which the fanaticism of religious warfare had reduced fair France.

At the second and third assembling of the States, the deputies appeared in greater force, but on no occasion did their number exceed one hundred and thirty to a hundred and fifty. It was chiefly on the *Tiers État* that Mayenne and the Spaniards relied for the success of their projects ; the former had nominated the greater part, the latter had paid them. The ardent zeal of the Leaguers had latterly greatly abated, in the provinces especially. Generally, too, the *Tiers État* were much dismayed by the powers of sovereignty conferred on them ; courage failed them at first, and they welcomed the intervention of the Parliament of Paris as a support rather than a derogation of their power.

That great judicial body having by a decree rejected as ineligible all the seven or eight foreign candidates for the throne, announced that "the States General were assembled in order to declare and establish a *French* Catholic prince only, and to proclaim the nearest heir to the throne, according to the laws of the kingdom, not excepting Henri of Navarre, should he change his religion in time." The Parliament also claimed the right to verify the decrees of the States, consequently

to control their decisions and refuse them regis-
tration.   This display of renewed vigour on the
part of the Parliament had the excellent effect
of reviving the zeal of all good patriots in favour
of their legitimate sovereign.

On the 29th of January, a trumpeter from the
king's army appeared at the Porte Saint-Honoré
and requested permission to enter, being the bearer
of letters from the Catholic princes and nobility
assembled at Chartres to the lieutenant - general,
"Monseigneur le Duc de Mayenne." "The
people," says L'Estoile, "soon crowded around
the messenger and anxiously questioned him.   He
answered that he was the bearer of good news."
This good news was supposed to mean peace,
therefore gave general satisfaction ; for amongst
the poorer classes there was much suffering from
a dearth of provisions, the small towns in the
faubourgs held by the king being forbidden to
send supplies to the capital.

Escorted by an anxious crowd, the trumpeter
was conducted to Mayenne, who received the
despatches in the presence of his council, hastily
assembled to hear them read, and to advise on
their contents.   They were a double reply to
Mayenne's exhortation to the Royalist Catholics
— or "*parti contraire*" — to separate themselves
from heretics, etc.   The first was to the effect
that "the principal Catholic prelates, princes, and
nobility then with the king, convinced of his sin-

cere and holy intentions, and after having received his majesty's promise to seek religious instruction without delay, now offered to enter into conference and communication, by their appointed deputies, with deputies from the three estates, in whatever neutral place or town between Paris and Saint-Denis they should name as most convenient, — promising themselves, with the assistance of God, the Author of peace and Preserver of the French monarchy, that there would be found in this conference a remedy for the misfortunes of the state, and for the peace and repose of all well-meaning people. — Chartres, January 29, 1593."

The king's message — in the form of a royal declaration — replied to the principle advanced by Mayenne in his exhortation addressed to the Royalist Catholic nobility then with the king, that "the only fundamental law of the kingdom was the Salic law; holy, immutable, and established by Divine ordinance." Further, he declared "null and void all the acts and decrees of the assembly of the States in Paris, and those who took any part in them guilty of high treason." For the rest, he said "he was willing to receive instruction."

Scarcely could the legate — the fiery Bishop of Placentia — restrain his rage during the reading of those heretical documents. When it was concluded, he rose from his seat, and, in a voice almost choked by fury and passionate vehemence, exclaimed that "the assembly itself would be guilty of heresy should it give any heed to propositions issuing from the hands of heretics." He therefore proposed that those offensive communications be forthwith destroyed.

Villeroy, Jeannin, and other members of the council, informed his eminence that the rules and regulations of the States General forbade the destruction or suppression of any letters or other documents addressed to them. The lieutenant-general, being appealed to, admitted that such was the rule, and that they must be submitted to the States for discussion at their next meeting.

The next session of the States took place on the 4th of February. It was rather more numerously attended, military escorts, of which several of the deputies availed themselves, having been sent to Champagne and Burgundy. Villars, Governor of Normandy, with some of the members from that district, also made his appearance.* The legate, too, was present for the purpose of bestowing the pontifical benediction on the assembly in the name of Clement VIII. Objection was made

---

* The lieutenant-general had lately conferred on Villars the post of Admiral of France; probably with the intention of offering an affront to the king, who but a few weeks earlier, on the Duc d'Épernon's resignation of it, appointed the Baron de Biron to the office, or rather sinecure, — the Admiral of France being then more destitute of a French navy to command than even one or two of his predecessors in the earlier part of the sixteenth century.

to receiving him, several deputies representing that it was contrary to the constitution of France to admit foreigners to take part in their discussions. He might give them the holy father's benediction, but only " on the clearly expressed understanding that his delegation ended there, — he having no voice, either deliberative or conclusive, in that assembly." They, however, allowed him on this occasion — the séance not being a political, but a religious one — to occupy the seat of honour under the royal canopy, on the right of the lieutenant-general, the temporary representative of majesty ; but as his eminence was not permitted to rave, and rage, and oppose all that was contrary to the designs of Spain, he withdrew from the assembly in disgust.

Strengthened in numbers, the deputies appear to have better comprehended the dignity of their office, and to have determined to uphold it. That the *Tiers État* and nobility declined to yield to priestly influence was evident, while certain innovations, proposed by the lieutenant-general, in the conduct of the assembly's proceedings, were resisted with equal firmness. On the letters from Henri and his partisans being submitted by Mayenne to the assembly, the old Cardinal de Pellevé, deputy from the clergy of Rheims, proposed to refer them to the Sorbonne. The assembly, however, rejected the cardinal's proposition, and decided on duly considering the advisableness or otherwise of consenting to the suggested conference.

Some few days after, the lieutenant-general left Paris for Soissons, to receive the Duc de Feria, grandee of Spain, and "ambassador extraordinary from the Catholic king, accredited to the very reverend, illustrious, magnificent, and well-beloved assembly of the States General of France." Before leaving Paris, Mayenne received the assurance of the States that nothing decisive on the great question of the royal election should take place in his absence. But the *Tiers État* urged his speedy return, that the object of assembling them might be accomplished without delay, many of the deputies being poor men, anxious to get back to their homes and business affairs.

The letters from Chartres were then discussed, the three orders deliberating separately, but arriving at the same conclusion, viz., the acceptance of the conference with the Catholics of the "*parti contraire*," concerning the preservation of the true religion and the welfare of the state. The *Tiers État* were prepared to go still further, and to discuss the claims of the King of Navarre to the throne of his ancestors. Their advice or opinion on this head was overruled, but a conciliatory tone was carefully observed in the general reply, lest, otherwise, the "politiques," or "*parti contraire*," towards whom popular favour began to incline, should take offence, and the request for a conference be withdrawn.

The village of Suresne was chosen by common consent as the place of meeting. " On the 29th of April, crowds assembled on the ramparts to witness the departure of the commissioners, twelve in number, selected by the League to represent the lieutenant-general and his council, and the three orders of the States. As the party rode off, the people exclaimed, ' Peace! bring us back peace!' the cry being often and vigorously repeated long after these messengers of peace — as it was hoped, at least by the people, they would prove to be — were out of sight and hearing " (L'Estoile).

Henri a few days earlier had announced to the Baron François d'O his determination to assemble the French prelates at Mantes within the next three months, for the purpose of receiving religious instruction from them.* The king's promise was transmitted by the Seigneur d'O to the Archbishop of Bourges, who received it at the moment of his setting out for Suresne with the other Royalist commissioners. A suspension of arms then took place, but extending only to a radius of four leagues around Paris.

The "satire of satires, the Satire *Ménippée*," was

---

* "Strange mediator in a religious matter!" exclaimed the historian, H. Martin, — François d'O being one of the most dissolute of men, but full of holy zeal for religion.

then beginning to be privately circulated from hand to hand in Paris. Its lively sarcasm and piquant irony had wonderful influence on the affairs of the period. The extreme ridicule it threw on the League and the "coalition of would-be kings," its pungent wit and fervid eloquence, are believed to have tended more effectually to overthrow the pretensions of Philip II. and the infanta, Mayenne, and the rest of them, than all that Henri's partisans, his own good sword, his valour and renunciation of heresy, achieved for him in support of his cause and its ultimate success. In vain the already shattered party of the fanatical "sixteen" strove again to raise itself into notice, and, supported by Spanish gold, to influence the people and incite them to acts of religious frenzy, to the prejudice of their legitimate ruler. A stinging blow from *Ménippée* proved, happily, their *coup-de-grâce*.*

* The "*Satire Ménippée ou Catholicon d'Espagne*," is a serio-comic epic in prose and verse after the manner of the cynical Grecian philosopher Menippus, whose name its authors gave it. It is in three parts: the first relates to two quacks, a Spaniard and a Lorrainer, who have brought to Paris a new "Catholicon," "an electuary of greater virtues than the philosopher's stone," also "*un fin galimatias*, or confused but witty form of words, composed expressly for the cure of the king's evil." The second part consists of long harangues spoken in a fantastic magic palace, called the *Salle des États*, whither the chiefs of the League were summoned by a herald to make their confession, and being under a spell, they all, unconsciously, say the very things they wish to conceal. The third part is the reply to these harangues, supposed to be made by the

Tiers État. It is a discourse of great eloquence , brave and loyal language ; frank, natural, and pathetic, falling on the ear as an echo from the ancient Forum. The *Ménippée* was the production of a genial party of friends — witty, spiritual, erudite — who abhorred the League, and, while smiling contemptuously on the assumption of power and importance by "the sixteen knaves who wanted to sell the crown of France to Spain," could not forgive them the evils they had brought on France. This party of friends, accustomed to sup together weekly at the hospitable board of the Canon Pierre le Roy, consisted of the facetious rhymer, Gilles Durand; the councillor Jacques Gillot; Florent Chrestien, formerly preceptor to Henri IV.; the Provost Nicolas Rapin ; the councillor Pierre Pithou, and Passerat, the poet and distinguished Hellenist. The weekly repast was not one that would have satisfied a Lucullus ; it was rather " a feast of reason and the flow of soul." For the vigilance of the small Royalist garrisons around Paris kept the inhabitants on a decidedly short allowance of provisions. The agitating questions of the day were naturally very freely discussed at this weekly reunion of wits — the tricks and artifices of Rome, Spain, and Lorraine, and their representatives, calling forth many an epigrammatic remark, both lively and severe. The idea of the satire first occurred to the host of the party — Canon le Roy ; but each had a part of it assigned him suited to his peculiar talent. All were sworn to secrecy and in due time the *Ménippée* appeared, worth, as invariably asserted, a *coup-d'état* to Henri IV., clearing away the obstacles that lay between him and the throne. — GUSTAVE MERLET, Notes to *Origines de la Littérature Française.*

CHAPTER XIII.

Arrival of a Spanish Grandee to Urge the Claims of the Infanta
to the Throne of France, but Bringing with Him Few Troops
and No Money. — Mayenne, Displeased, Continues the War,
Conjointly with the Comte de Mansfeldt. — Conference of
Suresne. — Liberal Promises of Philip II. if the Infanta Be
Declared Queen of France, and the Archduke Ernest Be
Elected King. — Convocation at Mantes. — After Much Hesi-
tation Henri's Scruples Are Overcome. — He Confesses with
His Lips What in His Heart He Disbelieves, and Takes the
Perilous Leap.

BEFORE repairing to Paris, the Duc de
Feria spent a fortnight at Soissons with
the lieutenant-general of the League.
The latter determined to regulate the course he
would take in the matter that brought an ambas-
sador-extraordinary from Spain to the States
General of France according to the result of his
private conferences with him. The ambassador
probably had made a similar determination; but
the only result arrived at was mutual dissatisfaction.

According to L'Estoile,* "the Spanish grandee
was too haughty, too ceremonious, too confident
of the infanta's rightful claim to the throne of

*Journal de Henri IV.

France, in spite of the Salic law." But, above all, the number of doubloons he brought in further- ance of his master's schemes was so small — as far as he allowed Mayenne to know — that he might be said to have arrived almost empty-handed. The army, too, that Mayenne was expecting with which to menace the refractory States, if showing a leaning towards the views of the " politique " party, was but a small corps of 5,000 Walloons, com- manded by the Comte de Mansfeldt. True, there was no lack of promises ; but Philip, who, as his ambassador declared, had already spent millions on the French, desired some real service rendered before making further payments. Besides, just then, he had neither money nor troops to spare, having for the second time become bankrupt and repudiated his debts ; while revolt in Aragon, as well as in his distant provinces, necessitated the keeping of a large reserve of troops at home.

From Soissons, Feria proceeded to Paris, which city he entered with a very brilliant retinue. Mayenne, with the much diminished army of the League, joined Mansfeldt and his Walloons, taking with him the young Duc de Guise, of whom he was exceedingly jealous, and who, on his part, was flattering himself with the prospect of wearing the crown and marrying the infanta. He, however, received a friendly warning from Maréchal La Chastre to beware of placing much reliance on that hope; to which the young duke appears to

have given due heed. For, shortly after, being
addressed as "sire" by one who desired to flatter
the possible sovereign-elect of France, the duke
flew into a rage, and declared that "if any one
dared again thus to address him, he would stab
him to the heart."

As for Mayenne, instead of returning to Paris,
as the *Tiers État* were calling on him to do, he
announced, to the despair of the people, his intention of continuing the war. He had decided
on besieging Noyon, as Mansfeldt cared neither
to go far from the frontier, nor with so small a
force to encounter Biron, who was greatly harassing Rheims, to the assistance of which city
Mayenne had at first proposed to hasten. Henri
being at Compiègne visiting his marquise, the
small garrison of Noyon, after a desperate resistance, capitulated. Mansfeldt's army was greatly
reduced by this siege, and the difficulty of obtaining provisions led to many desertions. This,
together with the want of discipline prevailing in
the ranks of the few troops that remained with
him, and the report that Henri was advancing,
induced their commander to withdraw to the
frontier.

The conference of Suresne dragged on from
week to week, the sittings being frequently suspended because of Mayenne's continued absence
from Paris. He was again engaged in secret
negotiations with Henri, yet, at the same time, to

avoid a rupture with the Spaniards, " he swore on the Gospel, in the hands of the legate, never to make peace with the King of Navarre, whatever acts of Catholicism he might see fit to perform or to assent to." Mayenne returned to Paris on the 10th of May, and announced officially to the States General that the Spanish ambassador had a special communication to make to them.

A commission was appointed, and the conference held at the legate's residence. The Duc de Feria then, in the name of his Catholic majesty, proposed to the League to send to France, within two months of that date, an army of 14,000 foreign troops, to be wholly provided for at the king's cost for one year ; also a sum of 2,200,000 crowns for the purpose of raising a detachment of French troops, for whose support during the following year a similar sum was guaranteed, on condition, of course, that the Infanta Isabella Clara Eugenia should be declared Queen of France. No sooner were the words uttered than, to the surprise of all present, that furious Leaguer, Guillaume Roze, Bishop of Senlis, hastily rising from his seat, exclaimed in his harshest tones : " I now fully recognise that the ' politique ' party spoke the truth when they publicly declared that interest and ambition had a far larger part in this war than zeal for religion. If the Duc de Feria does not desist from putting forth such preposterous pretensions, I, too, shall become a ' politique.' Abrogate the Salic law!" he cried; "you ask for the ruin of the kingdom!" *

The Spaniard listened to this outburst with unmoved gravity, then demanded that his proposition should be referred to the three orders of the States in full assembly.   On the 29th the second audience took place, the Parliament meanwhile having declared "null, and of no effect, whatever decision the States might arrive at, if it tended to the detriment of the inviolable Salic law, or other fundamental law of the kingdom."   The *Tiers État* on this occasion refused to allow the place of honour to be taken by the ambassador, as suggested by the clergy.   Also, they would not permit the assembly to rise on his entrance, and, as it appears was expected, remain standing while he was present.   But in spite of the arrogance with which the clergy replied to the *Tiers État*, the latter firmly maintained their own and the national dignity.   Nothing daunted, the ambassador then introduced Inigo Mendoza, a Spanish doctor of law, and requested of the assembly a hearing for him.   This learned doctor, in the course of a long and dreary Latin harangue, found no difficulty in explaining away the inviolability ascribed by the French to their Salic law.   In conclusion, he denounced as "usurpers all those kings who had ascended the throne of France to the prejudice of the female branches of the royal line."

* L'Estoile, *Journal de Henri IV.*

This harangue was listened to with silent indifference, and drew forth no reply. The Spanish
duke then reverted to his former proposal, but
increased the number of troops then promised
from 14,000 to 20,000, paid by Spain for two
years. He again reminded the assembly of the
millions of gold his Catholic majesty had spent on
France, and "claimed the crown for the infanta by
right, both of the law of nature and the law
Divine." Being asked to whom Philip II. proposed to marry his daughter, the question was not
immediately answered; but on the 13th of June,
the ambassador having sent to Spain, fearful of
committing himself, for fresh, or rather more
positive instructions, it was announced that "if
the States were resolved not to yield with regard
to the Salic law, the Archduke Ernest should be
elected King of France, and afterwards marry the
infanta." He further advised them to lose no
time in proceeding to the election of a king who
was inflamed with so ardent a zeal for the Catholic
religion.

This announcement was a fatal blow to Philip's
hopes, but a great gain to the "*parti politique,*"
whose numbers became doubled when it was
known that Feria proposed, as an alternative to
the abrogation of the Salic law, the election of an
Austrian archduke to the throne of France. The
preachers, both Leaguers and "politiques," harangued the Parisians from their pulpits in lan-

guage of extraordinary violence. Great excitement among the people resulted from these appeals; but the one great boon for which they clamoured was peace, "peace that would once more bring repose and the necessaries of life."

The "heretic king," they were aware, had proposed a truce, to continue until the council of prelates, convoked for the 15th of July for his religious instruction, should terminate their conference. Mayenne, whose policy was that of continual delay or adjournment, for the purpose, as he said, of reflection, which seems never to have brought him nearer to a decision, had not yet either consented to or refused the proposed suspension of hostilities.

The legate meanwhile was pronouncing anathemas on all who should even speak of a truce. "He entreated, yea, he commanded," the three estates to withdraw from all communication with the Catholics of the "*parti contraire*" who refused to leave the King of Navarre. "They were," he said, "regarded but as bastards in the kingdom of heaven, but the Leaguers as the legitimate children of God.

Neither the States nor the people were intimidated by his invectives. "The latter declared they would seize the legate and behead him on the Place de Grève." * Rushing tumultuously to the Hôtel de Ville, they insisted that the provost

* L'Estoile, *Journal de Henri IV.*

should instantly seek the lieutenant-general, and demand his consent to the truce. The nobility and *Tiers État* had already declared for it, and Mayenne at last agreed that it was indispensable. It, indeed, would enable him to adjourn the election of a king, to embarrass the Spaniards, and, while obtaining a truce, avert a peace, by impelling the States to some important attempt against the rights of Henri IV.

Feria was already informed that "it was contrary to the laws and customs of the great French nation to elect a foreign prince as king." But Philip had urged persistence; he was determined to annex France to Spain if in any way possible. Again, therefore, his ambassador appears before the States in full assembly. "His gracious master is now willing to confer the hand of the infanta on a French prince, he and the princess to be declared conjointly kings proprietary (*rois propriétaires*) of the crown, — the prince whom Philip would select for his son-in-law to be named within the next two months." This the duke announced as his Catholic majesty's final offer — his last word. It was warmly approved and supported by the legate, but met with no favourable reception from the *noblesse* and *Tiers État.* The clergy followed the lead of the legate; but "when leaving the Louvre, both duke and legate were hissed and hooted by the people, who threatened them with a bath in the Seine."

The mention of a French prince as the possible King of France and husband-elect of the infanta revived the hopes of the Cardinal de Bourbon and the friends of the third party. Great promises were made to Mayenne for his support should an election take place, and the cardinal, released from his vows, be the chosen happy man to wed the infanta. The lieutenant-general of the kingdom was to retain his post, and all other lucrative offices, governorships, etc., which, for the welfare of the state, he had conferred on himself, and generally was to rule as King of France, wanting only the name. Of that alone the cardinal appeared to be ambitious. His incapacity for governing was his highest recommendation in the eyes of his unscrupulous partisans, who for their own personal advantage — so intensely corrupt was the spirit of the times — sought to promote his views.

Of the cardinal himself, it was asserted that he was less in love with the crown than inflamed with holy zeal for the Roman religion, the strict observance of which, as king, he proposed firmly to enforce. From Gregory XIV. he had received but scant encouragement when seeking aid from Rome; but the indignity with which the heretic Henri's embassy had lately been received gave him hopes that Clement VIII. would yield a more favourable ear to the wishes of a son of the true Church, — one of "God's legitimate children."

The cardinal's hopes were fated to be but of short duration, for the ambassador, a few days after the announcement of his royal master's "last word," followed it up by a second and very last word. On the 10th of July, he informed the lieu-tenant-general in council that "as it was necessary for the salvation of France and her holy religion, his Catholic majesty consented to give his daughter to the Duc de Guise." To secure the probable acceptance of this proposal, it should have been the very first word instead of the last. Though the name of Guise then awakened less enthusiasm than of old, yet had the partisans of the young duke availed themselves of it to excite the feelings of the people in his favour, the son of the murdered popular hero and his Spanish bride would, not improbably, have been elected King and Queen of France, and thus have rendered Henri's position more difficult.

But the political aspect of affairs had greatly changed during the four months in which the Spaniards had been striving and intriguing to obtain the crown of France. The prelates were to assemble on the 15th of July for the religious instruction of their legitimate king. This was a mere formality, to precede his abjuration, for he had already expressed his firm resolve to be convinced. To zealous Catholics and furious Leaguers this was not satisfactory. But the larger number of the Catholic nobility, military men and others, had, on their part, resolved, as it fell in with their worldly interests, to be content with the manner of the king's return to the true faith (his Huguenot ministers called it turning from God to idols) and for awhile to dispense with the Pope's absolulution and blessing.

In reply to Philip's latest proposal, the lieutenant-general required the ambassador to produce his letters of authority. Contrary to his expectation, the request was immediately complied with, when, to conceal his mortification, he affected to feel very deeply the Spanish monarch's condescension in conferring so great an honour on his family. He, would, however, have felt it even more deeply had it been conferred on his own son, the Duc d'Aiguillon. As it was, he closely scanned the conditions and discussed them with considerable warmth, demanding for himself, his family, and the members of his government the most extravagant advantages.

The Duc de Feria vainly insisted, as a first step towards the recognition of the new arrangement, that the marriage of Guise and the infanta should be officially communicated to the States. But Mayenne, a few days previously, had suggested to the three orders the expediency of deferring the election of a king until means could be raised to establish him on the throne, and an army provided for his defence. The *noblesse* and *Tiers État* assented, and, after much expostulation, the clergy also. Their decision was then made known to the ambassador, who disregarded it, believing that the long-withheld proposal would be eagerly accepted. Perceiving, however, that Mayenne clung tenaciously to the power he was invested with, he entreated that, if it were really determined to postpone the election of a king, there might at least be no question of treating with heretics for a truce.

The Royalists, not without reason, regarded this successful manœuvre for thwarting his nephew's ambition, and prolonging the interregnum for his own personal advantage, as a victory gained by Mayenne for the benefit of Henri IV. But peace was demanded more imperatively than before, in spite of the ravings of legate and priests, the intrigues of the Spaniards, and the desperate efforts of the fast-expiring League to retain its hold on the remaining shred of its former influence. For Henri was besieging Dreux, to the consternation of the people, who dreaded another famine, — the already diminished supplies of the capital being chiefly drawn from that city.

The siege was undertaken at Rosny's suggestion, during one of those frequent private and confidential conversations with Henri IV., which drew upon him so much jealous ill-feeling from both Catholics and Protestants.* The baron was of opinion that a military expedition would hasten

* *Mémoires de Sully.*

Mayenne's and the States' decision with regard to
the truce, as well as help to sustain the king's
martial renown with the people.   Money only was
wanting.   With Rosny's assistance, a considerable
loan was negotiated at Mantes.   Biron was ordered
to immediately invest Dreux, and Rosny to prepare
and conduct the artillery.

The town offered but slight resistance.   The
château-fort held out, relying on the strength of
its famous gray cannon-proof tower.   But Rosny
promised to destroy the tower if the king would
give him the four English and Scotch miners who
were in his army, and thirty-six labourers.   The
king doubted his success, but acceded to his
request.   Rosny and his pioneers then began
their labours under the rays of a burning July sun,
having first constructed a shelter from the fire of
the garrison and the various missiles showered
upon them by the people who had sought safety in
the impregnable tower.

So laborious was the task undertaken, so intense
the heat, that the men, who worked in parties of
four, were relieved every ten minutes, the work
being thus continued incessantly for the space of
six days — Rosny being wholly unmoved by the
sneers and sarcastic remarks of the lookers-on.
An opening of six or seven feet square being
made in the wall at the foot of the tower, Rosny
stowed away in it "three or four hundred pounds
of," as he says, "very excellent gunpowder,"

which he enclosed with "good stones, bound together with plaster." He then laid his train, con-
necting it with the tower by a roll of dry leather
filled with "good powder."

Thus far he had succeeded in his object, notwithstanding the efforts of the soldiers and people
in the tower to prevent the progress of the work,
and to injure the miners engaged in it. On the
match being applied to the train, the Royalist
officers assembled in gleeful anticipation of witnessing Rosny's confusion and failure. The
effect was not speedy; a dull rumbling sound
only was first heard, followed by a little smoke.
Many sarcastic remarks were made, and much
raillery expended on Rosny's experiments in
mining.

Presently he, says he, had his revenge. All
was jest and laughter, when suddenly a column of
thick black smoke rose high in the air (the jesters
fled), and, with a report like the roar of artillery,
the famous gray tower of Dreux parted precisely
in the middle, one half falling to the ground, and
burying in its ruins men, women, and children
who had sought refuge within it. The half that
remained standing was also full of people, who,
terrified at the danger with which they were
threatened and the firing of the soldiers upon
them, uttered piercing cries and lamentations.
As soon as the king became aware of this, he
ordered the firing on these defenceless men and

women to cease, and assistance to be given to
relieve them from their perilous position, and to
each of them he also gave a crown. The château
at once surrendered.*

From the conquest of Dreux, Henri hastened
to Mantes. He was anxious to transfer thence to
Saint-Denis the assembly of prelates convoked
for his instruction. For the Calvinists, from
whom he desired to separate with as little pain
as possible, both to them and himself, were in
great force at Mantes, and held their religious
services there. The chief men of " the religion "
were invited by Henri to attend the conference,
at which the nature of the schism between the reformed and Catholic religions was to be explained.
A serious discussion they would have attended;
but to prearranged arguments for the defeat of
the truth they declined to listen.

The Calvinist minister, Gabriel d'Amours, wrote
to the king recommending that " he should rather
listen to his minister Gabriel d'Amours than to
Gabrielle, his *amoureuse*. We are told," he says,
" in these regions " (Geneva), " that you are about
to imitate Solomon, who turned aside to idolatry, —
women being the cause of it; also," he continues,
" that you desire to be instructed by the bishops
of the Romish Church. But you are a king who
has no need of instruction. You are a greater
theologian than I, your minister, and have no lack

* *Mémoires de Sully.*

of knowledge, though you have a little lack of conscience.''

Similar protests came from Théodore de Bèze, Jean de l'Espine, and others at Saint-Jean-d'Angély. Henri's sister, Catherine of Navarre, an unwavering Protestant herself, in a letter to Du Plessis-Mornay, sorrowfully expressed her regret at the step Henri was taking. He had a strong affection for his sister, but was not likely to be in any way influenced by her wishes or entreaties with regard to the question of his so-called conversion.

Yet it seems evident that to abjure the errors of Calvinism in order to embrace the errors of Romanism was wholly repugnant to him, from the fact that for four years, in spite of the pressure continually put upon him, he evaded seeking the needed preliminary "religious enlightenment" from the Roman Catholic clergy. To the very last he had scruples which the unscrupulous Abbé du Perron, with his eloquent sophistry, easily, though but for a time, dispelled.*

Rosny confesses that for more than two years he had endeavoured to persuade the king to adopt the Roman religion, and had sought by degrees to prepare him for the sacrifice required of him. He knew, he says, that it would displease the

* This learned, subtle and atheistical *abbé* — a Calvinist before it answered his purpose to become a Catholic — was soon to be rewarded with the bishopric of Evreux.

Protestant princes who were near neighbours of France, also the French Calvinists. But with distracted France restored to peace and prosperity under her legitimate and *Catholic* king, there would be no need of foreign aid, while, as regarded the Huguenots, Henri was under such important obligations to them that he relied on his gratitude to grant them essential advantages that would induce them to look on the change of religion without murmuring. He appears to have been under the fullest conviction that abjuration was his best, or rather only, course to save the kingdom from ruin, and to avert crime. For he states that not only the crown, but the king's life was in danger ; that his nearest relatives, his intimate counsellors, and the officers of his army, were caballing against him and plotting assassination.

Henri, though brave to rashness, was not a Coligny ; the unbending will, the firmness of purpose to carry on the struggle to the end, were wanting in him. His life thus far had been one of hardship, trial and persecution, which only a man of his joyous and genial temperament, and so hopeful and humane as he, could so long have borne up against. But, as Rosny urged on him, peace and repose were now absolutely needed, both for the unhappy country and for the king himself. "Must the woes of France never cease," he exclaimed, "and a prince who so well deserves happiness consume his whole life in the midst of the horrors of warfare?" Again, then, he recommended him to adopt the only means of putting an end to the vexations, anxieties, and difficulties that beset him in this world; but he added, laughingly, "I answer not for the next."

However, at a subsequent interview he bade him not despair of salvation.* He assured him that, although a Protestant, he held it as infallible that a man dying in the *observance of the Decalogue* and belief of the Apostles' Creed; in the love of God and his neighbour; with the hope also, by the Divine mercy, to obtain salvation through the death, the merits, and the justice of Jesus Christ, could not fail of being saved. "If your majesty should be pleased to adopt this opinion," he continued, "not only shall I have no doubt of your salvation, whatever outward profession you may make of the Catholic religion or observance of its rites, but shall also feel fully persuaded that, not regarding us Protestants as an execrable people doomed to damnation, you will never undertake to injure or extirpate us."

Henri declared that he certainly would not. "He was too heavily indebted to his Huguenots

---

* Henri was accustomed to send a confidential domestic to bring the Baron de Rosny to him at break of day to discuss these matters without interruption, — using these precautions because of the great jealousy of both Catholics and Protestants of the intimate friendly relations existing between the baron and the king.

for their devotion to him and his cause, and loved them far too much to attempt to do them wrong. On the contrary, he desired that they would seriously reflect how he could best serve and protect them." Rosny thanked him for himself and his coreligionists generally. Their conference being ended, Henri repaired to Saint-Denis.

It was the 15th of July. Four priests from Paris were already arrived, having braved the legate's prohibition and menaces of excommunication. One of them was the fluent pulpit orator and fanatical denouncer of heresy, "the terrible Lincestre," as he had been named from his violence. To every one's surprise, he had latterly been preaching peace and concord, and now attended the congress of Catholic theologians and prelates at the king's invitation. If this "pillar of the League," it was prophesied, were about to be withdrawn from it, then its speedy downfall might surely be reckoned on. The 22d was appointed for the assembling of the archbishops, bishops, doctors of theology, and general clergy.

Henri meanwhile took leave of the Calvinist ministers at Mantes, and attended their service for the last time. "*If,*" he still told them, "*if* he should determine on the change, there need be no alarm on their part. If he should enter 'the house,' it would be to purify it, not to dwell there." Oppress them he never would, and as his treatment of them ever had been, so it would continue. He would not listen to their reproaches; but being much affected, said in a faltering voice : " Rather pray to God for me, my friends, and preserve your friendship for me, and I shall love you for it." Doubtless it cost him a severe pang thus to separate himself from them.

On the 22d he appeared before his instructors, amongst whom was the Cardinal de Bourbon. The latter, notwithstanding the advice strongly inculcated by his faithless confidant, the bishop-elect of Evreux, to hold his peace and give no offence to the illustrious catechumen, yet was so much annoyed at the vanishing of his dream of a crown and an infanta, that he rose in the assembly to express a doubt of the competence of the French prelates to anticipate the decision of the Pope by receiving the king into the bosom of the Church. The majority declared him in error. The bishops, they affirmed, were competent to judge in cases of heresy, and that the bulls of excommunication launched against the King of Navarre by Sixtus V. and Gregory XIV. (on which the cardinal founded his objections) were contrary to the laws of the kingdom and the liberties of the Gallican Church. For this affront to the king the cardinal was excluded from the conference on the following day, Friday, the 23d of July.

At an early hour the Archbishop of Bourges, with the Bishops of Nantes, Chartres, Mans, and Evreux, awaited the king's arrival. Soon after he

appeared, and the discussion of the points of faith
in controversy between the Church of Rome and
the Calvinists was then entered upon. Henri's
replies to the arguments of the prelates, together
with his embarrassing questions concerning many
of the dogmas of the Church — to show the fallacy
of which he very aptly quoted Scripture — quite
bore out the assertion of the Calvinist minister
that he was too good a theologian to need instruction. The learned prelates were astonished, and
unable to give him the satisfactory reasons he
asked of them. It seemed as though, instead of
converting, they were about to be converted.

The formula prepared for his acceptance and
signature, to be afterwards forwarded to the Pope,
had been drawn up by some over-zealous priest or
priests. It included not only the essential points
of difference to which he was expected to assent,
but a list of minute observances to which he was
required to conform, as well as certain puerilities
as articles of belief. The king remonstrated, and
the contention it occasioned appeared likely to
bring the whole affair to an abrupt conclusion. A
compromise was, however, arrived at, and it was
conceded that all that was useless should be
omitted. Henri had determined to be convinced,
but was far from being so, and the prelates who
had determined to believe that they had convinced
him were not a little disconcerted by the ill success
of their teaching. But, in order to bring the

conference to a conclusion, the king, with much earnestness, said :

"You have not satisfied me on this point" (the adoration of the Host, which had been long under discussion), "nor have I been generally so well pleased with your instruction as I had hoped to be. Nevertheless, I this day place my soul in your hands. I pray you, guard it well, for where you now compel me to enter, there, until my death, I shall remain — that I solemnly swear and protest to you." Overcome by emotion, tears filled his eyes.* A very detailed confession of faith, including all the Roman dogmas, was placed before him for signature. He resisted, and would only sign the simplified formula, from which was effaced as far as possible what was repugnant to him.†

The abjuration was fixed for Sunday, the 25th. On the 23d the king wrote to Gabrielle :

"On Sunday I take the perilous leap. Now while I write to you a hundred importunate people surround me and make me hate Saint-Denis even as you hate Mantes."

It was truly a very perilous leap. His abjuration disappointed so many hopes, that caballing and intriguing and attempts at assassination became more frequent than before. Very early on

---

* L'Estoile, *Journal de Henri IV.*

† The first and fullest confession of faith which he rejected was said to be the one sent to the Pope — Henri's signature being imitated by M. de Lorraine.— *Mém. de Du Plessis-Mornay.*

the morning of the 25th, Henri had a long private conversation with the Calvinist minister, La Faye, whom he two or three times embraced on taking leave of him. Afterwards, at about eight o'clock, wearing a white satin doublet and long black mantle, he left his hôtel on foot, followed by the princes of the blood, officers of the crown, and a numerous *cortège* of noblemen and gentlemen. The French, Scotch, and Swiss guards, with the drummers and twelve trumpeters, preceded him.

Tapestry decorated the fronts of the houses; the streets were strewed with flowers, and large bouquets were in every window. Yet Henri was subdued in manner far more than was customary with him. The crowd was immense. People had flocked in from surrounding villages, eager to see the novel sight of a king renouncing heresy, and that king the hero of a hundred fights. Long and loud were the cries of " *Vive le roi !* " the women adding " God bless him ! and may we soon see him at Notre-Dame." The Parisians were also there in great force, though the legate had prohibited all Catholics, whether clergy or laity, from going to Saint-Denis or taking any part in that day's proceedings.

To enforce this prohibition the gates of Paris were closed by order of the lieutenant-general; but the people presented themselves in such numbers and so menacingly demanded egress, that in order to avert a threatened tumult the gates were opened to them. Either from curiosity or real pleasure occasioned by the event, few who could get to Saint-Denis remained in Paris, and none, it was remarked, were louder in their acclamations than the Parisians. The air resounded with their vivas.

Slowly continuing his march (for the people pressed upon him and impeded his progress in their anxiety to see him), he and his *cortège* arrived at the grand entrance of the abbey. It was closed ; but after the king had knocked the doors were thrown open. Under the porch stood the Archbishop of Bourges, officiating priest, surrounded by seven bishops, several *abbés*, all the priests and monks of Saint-Denis — bearing the cross, the books of the Gospel, and the holy water ; the deans of Paris and Beauvais were there, and the four curés of Paris, one of whom was Lincestre. The Cardinal de Bourbon also attended. but full of envy, bad feeling, and ill-humour. In reply to the archbishop's questions, Henri announced that he was the king, and desired to be received within the pale of the Catholic, Apostolic, and Roman Church. He then knelt and made the following profession of faith :

" I protest and swear before God Almighty to live and die in the holy Catholic religion ; to protect and defend it against all and every one at the peril of my blood and my life, renouncing all heresies contrary to the aforesaid holy religion."

"The form of his profession," signed by him, was afterwards handed to the archbishop, whose ring was presented to him to kiss. The kneeling penitent then received absolution and benediction, "sacred words of reconciliation with Heaven and his people," exclaims Mathieu, "which were listened to in profoundest silence by the vast concourse of priests and laymen who filled every part of the ancient basilica." Again kneeling before the grand altar, the king repeated his oath and profession of faith on the Gospel, and was afterwards conducted to a confessional placed under a canopy. While engaged there with the archbishop, the choir assembled and sang a *Te Deum* expressive of the Church's joy at receiving the stray sheep into the fold of the faithful.

But the ceremony was not yet ended. A *prie-dieu*, draped with blue velvet embroidered with *fleurs-de-lys* in gold, was placed for the king, and high mass was celebrated in the presence of the Court, the people, and the Royalist magistrates, who arrived in a body from Tours to be present at the ceremony. At its conclusion the Cardinal de Bourbon again held the Gospel before the king, who kissed it, after which he laid his offering on the altar, and was then reconducted by the archbishop and the rest of the clergy to the grand porch of the cathedral. Thence he returned to his quarters on foot, joyous thousands accompanying him, to whose enthusiastic acclamations were added the roar of cannon, the pealing of church bells, the blast of trumpets, and volleys of artillery.

A quantity of silver money, coined for the occasion, was thrown amongst the people, and the scramble for it appears to have amused the king and raised his spirits after the depressing ordeal he had gone through. "The people," he said, "seemed famishing for the sight of a king." * In the afternoon the archbishop preached the sermon at Saint-Denis, the king attending. He was again present at vespers. Writing to Gabrielle of the events of the day, he tells her :

"While at church, an old woman of eighty played me an amusing trick which I was not the only one or the first to laugh at. In her joy at my conversion she came close to me, and, taking me by the head, kissed me heartily. You will have to make me amends for this to-morrow." (*Lettres de Henri IV.*)

As night drew on the people of Saint-Denis and neighbouring villages made bonfires in the streets and illuminated their houses, in celebration of the auspicious event, from which the return of peace and prosperity to afflicted France was hopefully looked forward to by many.

Five days after, a three months' truce was signed between Mayenne and Henri IV., as "chiefs of the two parties, Royalists and Leaguers." The fanatical legate, unable to prevent it, resigned himself to the inevitable. But that the truce might

* L'Estoile.

not be followed by a peace, he required the lieutenant-general, the Ducs de Guise, de Nemours,
d'Aumale, and others, with the principal officers of
the army of the League, to swear on the cross and
on the Gospels never to recognise the King of
Navarre as King of France, even should there be
added to his right of birth a sincere abjuration.

CHAPTER XIV.

IMMEDIATELY after the ceremony at
Saint-Denis, an autograph letter from
Henri IV. to Clement VIII. announced
his abjuration; also the early departure of a
solemn embassy to solicit, on the part of the king,
the holy pontiff's ratification of the absolution and
benediction bestowed on him by the Archbishop
of Bourges and assisting prelates. This missive,
expressive of the king's filial devotion to his holiness, was entrusted to La Clielle, Henry's *maître
d'hôtel.* The ambassador shortly to follow was the
Duc de Nevers, and to accompany him the king
named the Bishop of Mans and the Dean of Paris.

Henri then hastened to Compiègne, where the

congratulations of la belle Gabrielle awaited him, which probably allayed some prickings of conscience occasioned by the partial renunciation of Protestantism with which his lenient Catholic instructors were fain to be content. But would Clement VIII. be disposed to ratify their reception of this wandering sheep again into the fold of the faithful? Very recently he had declared that " unless angels were sent from heaven to whisper the fact in his ears, he would never believe in the conversion of the King of Navarre." In this, though without intending it, he certainly attributed a steadfastness to Henri which, unfortunately, as some thought, he did not deserve.

However, great anxiety prevailed, both amongst Catholics and Protestants, respecting the holy father's decision. The people, who had suffered so greatly from unceasing warfare, were grateful to Henri for granting a truce, though but for three months; and very heartily they prayed for his success at Rome, in order that the truce might become a peace. The lieutenant-general was far from sympathising in this wish. Peace to him meant the loss of that power to which he the more tenaciously clung now that threatening events seemed hastening on to deprive him of it. He not only desired that the necessary papal authority and approbation might never be accorded to the recent ceremony at Saint - Denis, but secretly sent envoys to Rome, charged to employ every means likely to strengthen Clement's already declared inflexibility to the king's appeal for absolution.

The opportunity of throwing another obstacle in Henri's path was afforded Mayenne by the demand of the States General for their dismissal. They had no power, they asserted, to regulate the succession to the throne, and there being no further question for their discussion, they were anxious — the *Tiers État* especially — to return to their homes and their avocations. Many were in great distress, owing to their long sojourn in the capital. But Mayenne was bound by oath to the Spaniards to " keep the States sitting until a king approved by Philip should be elected," the needy deputies of the *Tiers État* being paid by Spain.

Mayenne, therefore, so far yielded to the request of the assembly as to grant a *congé* of three months to the greater part of those who came from distant provinces. But before permitting their departure he urged on them the acceptance of the Council of Trent, of which the *Tiers État* and *noblesse* had constantly adjourned the deliberation, in spite of the persistence of the clergy. Without a particle of zeal for the Church, but anxious only for release from their irksome duties, the provincial deputies at once accepted the Council of Trent. The *noblesse* a few days after followed the example of the *Tiers État*, the deputies of Paris and the Île-de-France in both instances opposing.

Thus were the clergy reinstated in the privileges and powers they enjoyed in the Middle Ages.

A *Te Deum* was sung on the occasion at Saint-Germain l'Auxerrois. The fanatical legate was jubilant, and announced that he had received letters from the Pope, authorising him to prolong his stay in Paris. He had threatened the inhabitants that he would withdraw the light of his countenance from them; but in his satisfaction with the lieutenant-general for so fully and acceptably repaying him for his toleration of the truce, he resolved to spare the Parisians the infliction with which he had menaced them. Mayenne was fully aware that neither Henri nor the clergy of the Gallican Church would accept the discipline of the Council of Trent, so often proposed and always rejected. The Parliament, too, would refuse to register this decree of the States; yet it would serve to embarrass Henri in his negotiation with the Pope, and further embitter Clement's feeling against him.

The Huguenots generally were not less anxious than the Catholics concerning the result of the mission to Rome. For with the exception of Rosny and a few others who, like him, regarded the loss of their chief with the patriotic feeling that the interests of the kingdom were served by his adoption of the dominant religion, a hope certainly prevailed that his rejection at Rome might be the means of "rescuing him from the service of idols, and sending him back, a penitent, to God."

Some among them did, indeed, think so ill of him as to believe that if he could obtain pardon from Spain and the Pope by no other means, he would be willing to turn his arms against his former friends, and seek their extirpation. Even Du Plessis-Mornay was not wholly free from these sad forebodings. Henri, so far as the jealousy of the Catholics permitted, sought to reassure the Huguenots. "Nothing in the world," he told them, "would induce him to serve as an instrument for their oppression in the hands of their persecutors." He bade them hold a general assembly at Mantes, and consider what they required of him for their security. They replied with their accustomed sombre enthusiasm, solemnity, and energy. "Sire," they wrote, "your subjects of the reformed religion thank God and you also that their enemies who have separated you from them, as regards external profession, have not yet deprived them of the sincere affection of which you have given new proofs and assurances to our deputies." They then set forth in affecting terms what he and they had suffered together, which they believe can never be effaced from his memory, but must rise up before him and interrupt his most important affairs and ardent pleasures ; following it up by protesting that they will not fail to defend themselves against the enemies

of Jesus Christ, should they not agree to the peace
desired by the king. " If they boast that, because
they have made themselves masters of your body,
you belong to them, we will boast that we have
your mind, your heart, which being free are always
with us. We will demand of them eye for eye,
tooth for tooth. If they banish Jesus Christ from
those cities where they are strongest, we will
banish their idols from those where we are in
greater force. Let them hope no more for patience from us! If you do not restrain them,
if you fail in justice towards us, we will have
recourse to God, who will without delay grant
it to us." *

The Huguenots, however, took courage from
the reports that came from Rome of Clement's
reception of the agents despatched by Henri IV.
to inform him, with all dutiful expressions, of his
reunion to the Church, and praying that this act
of submission and repentance might meet with
the holy pontiff's approval and favour. But on
Henri's messenger, La Clielle, announcing himself the bearer of a letter from Henri IV. to his
holiness, and requesting an audience to deliver it,
as charged, into the pontiff's own hands, he was
informed that he could be received only in secret
audience as a private person, not publicly as agent
of the King of Navarre, whom his holiness would

* *Manuscrits de Colbert* — quoted by Capefigue, *Histoire de la
Ligue.*

not receive. La Clielle was of course compelled to submit; but when, introduced into the pontifical presence, he, with all customary humility, presented his sovereign's letter, Clement, with an air of angry indignation, refused to take it. Cardinal Toleto, the pontiff's confidant, and Father Seraphin Olivieri were present at this interview. A sign from one of them led La Clielle to venture to lay his rejected missive on a table near his holiness, who condescended to allow it to remain there.

Father Seraphin then, addressing Clement, as though replying to his announced determination to receive neither the letter nor its sender, and knowing probably that his anger was rather assumed than real, said: "Holy father, if even the devil should ask an audience of you, and there should be hope of converting him, you could not conscientiously refuse to grant it." So extreme a case suggested in Henri's favour disturbed the indignant pontiff's gravity. He could scarcely repress a laugh, but was none the more gracious to the royal convert's appeal. La Clielle, however, did not leave Rome without a word of encouragement for his master. The cardinal bade him tell Henri "not to despair. His holiness desired only to prove the sincerity of his conversion." He desired, in fact, to be more abjectly entreated, and not for absolution alone.

For the first time, probably, Huguenots and Leaguers found themselves rejoicing over the same event, — the disappointed hopes of Henri IV. at

Rome.   The promised embassy was, however, on
its way to the Holy See, and might yet achieve
its object.   The three months' truce was drawing
to a close, when, at the Baron de Rosny's suggestion, it was further prolonged for two months.
Henri at first refused to accede to Mayenne's
request, but Rosny perceiving that it was advantageous also to the Royalist cause, he consented.
The sword had indeed been sheathed, but the war
of pens had been, and still continued, violent and
incessant.   On the one side scandalous libels, on
the other scathing ridicule ; a parody of the States
General of the League with the *"Satire Ménippée"* circulated among the people, playing a great
part ; while the account of the lieutenant-general's
confessions, the decrees of the poverty-stricken
deputies, the schemes of the Spaniards and their
"divine infanta," everywhere drew forth peals of
laughter.

Nevertheless, Mayenne had been endeavouring
to resuscitate the iniquitous council of sixteen,
whose power he so recently had effectually crushed.
But the rage of those fanatics, already discredited
in the eyes of the public, availed little, — the
general anxiety being to obtain an extension of
the truce.   The Sorbonnists declared that the Pope
himself could not absolve a " relapsed heretic "
except at the point of death, while, with their full
approval, the preachers from their pulpits demanded
if there was not among the people a Jehu or a

Jacques Clément who would do a deed most pleasing in the sight of God, and thus secure for himself a distinguished place among the saints in
glory.*

An unexpected change in the route the king
proposed to take in a recent journey had occasioned,
it appears, the failure of an attempt on his life,
planned by the curé Pelletier. But shortly after
this disappointment a new candidate appeared for
the promised heavenly honours awaiting the regi-
cide. As regarded the king, he harboured no ill-
feeling towards him, and hitherto his career had
been marked by no crime. This poor youth,
named Pierre Barrière, was then suffering from
the pangs of unrequited love. Under such an
infliction what was this world or its pleasures to
him? In his despair he strolled into one of the
churches of Lyons and became fascinated by the
fanatical discourse of the preacher, and the crime
he by no means obscurely suggested. To Barrière's
distorted fancy it seemed that his was the hand
destined to do the deed that would elevate him to
glory and send the heretic to perdition.

This project he made known to an Italian
Dominican, and to two or three priests of Lyons.
The latter, while approving his zeal, advised
Barrière to go to Paris, where he saw the rector of
the Jesuits, Father Varade, who encouraged him
in his delusion. While the wretched youth was

* Boucher's " Nine Sermons "; Garin's " Harangues."

following the king and nerving himself for his
infamous design — which, when it came to the
point, courage failed him to carry into effect —
the *Veni Creator* was sung by the people in the
churches where Varade and other Jesuits preached,
"for an object," it was announced, "of great benefit to Christendom."

But the Italian Dominican in the meantime
informed the king and his ministers of the pro-
jected assassination.   Barrière was arrested at
Melun, where the meditated blow was to be struck,
and was judged on the spot by a special commission hastily assembled.   Sentence of death was
passed on him, and the unfortunate victim of fanatical priests was immediately broken alive on the
wheel, — his torture ending in death that same
night.

This project to assassinate the king was but one
of many then fostered by the expiring League,
whose rage against the "converted heretic" was
far greater than it had ever been against the "relapsed heretic."   His conversion, whether real or
simulated, had already won to his allegiance the
inhabitants of many cities and towns, in spite of
the outrageous violence of the pamphleteers and
the diatribes of pulpit orators, to whom, indeed,
his own champions had responded vigorously,
refuting many of their calumnies.

The news from Rome was, however, unfavourable.   Clement refused to receive the Duc de

Nevers in an official character. "He did not," he said, "believe Navarre was a Catholic, and would never grant him absolution." Being asked if there were any means open to the king of convincing him of his sincerity, his holiness refused to enter into the subject, and declined to state his refusal in writing. But he required that the two ecclesiastics who accompanied the duke should "purge themselves before the grand inquisitor," for having taken part in this unholy matter, and that the duke should limit his stay in Rome to ten days. He was further prohibited from visiting the cardinals.

The Duc de Nevers, indignant at Clement's strange conduct, with great energy represented to him the fatal consequences which his refusal would inevitably draw down, both on France and Rome. The holy father was inflexible, and the duke then withdrew, but did not leave Rome immediately. He imagined that the Pope might be influenced by some of his cardinals, several of whom were favourable to Henri, and induced to change his resolve. He, however, waited in vain. Patience being exhausted, he left his hôtel, which had been respected, and no attempt made either to force him from it or to secure the persons of his ecclesiastical colleagues. He, however, announced on his departure from Rome that "he would kill any apparitor who, in the name of the holy office, should dare to lay his hand on either the Bishop of Mans or the Dean of Paris."

Clement VIII., it appears, was by no means disinclined to grant the absolution asked of him by
the King of France.   His object in refusing it
was the hope that Henri would acknowledge, in a
further appeal, that "the Pope having deprived
him of his temporal rights, he alone could restore
them."   In this he was disappointed, the greater
part of the French Catholics determining to dispense with the Pope's intervention, foreign authority counting for nothing in the reconciliation of
the two parties so long opposed to each other.*
Mayenne thought to turn Clement's refusal to
account for maturing his own plans, therefore
again sought an extension of the truce.   Henri
refused, and on the 27th of December published a
general citation to all his subjects, then separated
from him, to place themselves within a month
again under his authority.

After years of almost incessant fighting, the
peace enjoyed during the five months' truce had
proved so acceptable to the people that the prospect of a return to the horrors of civil war filled
them with despair.   The cities of the League
turned their anger on Mayenne, who, refusing
(being secretly bound by oath to the Spaniards) to

* A very able treatise on the " Liberties of the Gallican
Church," written by one of the authors of the " *Satire Ménippée*,"
was published at this time, and greatly served the Royalist cause.
Montaigne's Essays, also then very generally read, influenced the
more reasonable part of the community, though Montaigne was
not a decided partisan of either cause.

treat with Henri for the League in a body, impelled them, which he was far from expecting, severally to treat for themselves. The Comte de Vitry, Governor of Meaux, and hitherto a zealous Leaguer, having summoned the municipal council, delivered into their hands the keys of the city. He then informed them that he had no intention of resuming the war against Henri IV., but on the contrary proposed to join him, as he had embraced Catholicism. A general assembly was afterwards convened by the mayor, when the authorities, with the consent of the inhabitants, resolved to follow the governor's example. A royal edict of reconciliation was the result, with many advantages to Vitry, and the suppression of some burdensome taxes in acknowledgment of the people's voluntary surrender.

A few days after, the important city of Lyons hoisted the white standard. The people had revolted against the despotism of their governor, Mayenne's brother, the Duc de Nemours, whom they seized and confined in the fortified château of Pierre-Encise. In the unsettled state of the country, the duke, not taking the will of the people into account, thought to carve out for himself of Lyons and its surrounding dependencies a small but flourishing and independent principality. He began his reign rather tyrannically, but the citizens determined that they would not have the duke to reign over them. The Archbishop of

Lyons — a Leaguer and a friend of Mayenne, to whose care the city was temporarily confided — was unable to resist the demand of the Lyonnais that both château and prisoner be surrendered to Henri IV.   Great rejoicings followed.   The arms of the League and of Spain were burnt in the market-place, and white scarfs and white plumes took the place of the green ones of Lorraine. The burning of the League, represented by the effigy of a hideous old woman, terminated the proceedings, amidst enthusiastic cries of *" Vive la liberté française !"* and the joyous chant of *"Vive Henri Quatre !"* etc.

The cities of Péronne, Montdidier, Orléans, and Bourges followed the lead of Meaux and Lyons in quick succession.   The partisans of Mayenne, and that remnant of the League which the lieutenant-general now vainly strove to reinvest with a semblance of the power he, for his own aims, had deprived it of, began to display much alarm.   Royalism was certainly spreading, and the king watched the development of this feeling amongst the Parisians with intense anxiety.   He thought the time had arrived for his coronation. Many well-wishers of his cause scarcely regarded him as king so long as he remained uncrowned, while the zeal and the hopes of some discouraged partisans were likely to be fortified by the event, and the submission of Paris accelerated.

Rheims being in the possession of the young

Duc de Guise, the ceremony of the *sacre* could not take place in that grand old edifice, its cathedral. Yet a very small military force would have placed Rheims in Henri's power. The inhabitants, being desirous of surrendering to the king, were with difficulty restrained by Guise, who shortly after made a merit of necessity, and delivered the city to the king, fearing to lose the substantial advantages to be derived from treating with him. But this did not occur early enough for the king to be crowned at Rheims.

Henri, having consulted the most learned and best informed prelates on the subject, was assured that, although the kings of France were usually crowned at Rheims, the ceremony might be performed, as it had been before, in another church or cathedral of France. The king then chose the abbey of Chartres, where Louis VI. was crowned early in the twelfth century. The 17th of February was named for the celebration of the rite.*

---

* Louis, in some respects, resembled Henri in his habits and character. According to the early historians, he was " a prince of wonderful activity, notwithstanding his bulky person and surname of ' Le Gros.' Always on horseback, lance in hand, he was continually fighting the feudal nobility, who disturbed the peace of the country and by their unceasing wars oppressed the poor and destroyed the churches."

CHAPTER XV.

IT had been usual to keep the old Carlovingian crown, so long used at the coronation of the kings of France, at the abbey of Saint-Denis, with the rest of the royal treasure. But when the profligate Chevalier d'Aumale made a night attack on the town, in order to plunder the abbey, as already he had plundered that of Saint-Antoine, the first things he proposed to lay his sacrilegious hands upon were the crown and the ornaments of the regalia. The governor, the valiant Captain Dominique de Vicq — in spite of the disadvantage of a wooden leg, having lost his own in battle — at once, with great activity, assembled the gendarmerie and confronted

D'Aumale and his troop. A sharp skirmish followed, in which the chevalier was killed ; but the
crown and the rest of the regalia fell into the
hands of his party, and so great was the dearth
of money that they were melted down for coin.*
As a crown was indispensable for the approaching
ceremony, a new one was ordered,— to be paid for,
by and by, like the pensions, and millions in cash
for the surrendered provinces, when the crown
should be firmly fixed on Henri's head. For of
cash in hand he had none. He was the poorest
gentleman in his kingdom. Promises and pleasant
jests were all he had then to give, and of them
there was of course no stint.

The friendly Archbishop of Bourges, so lenient
on the occasion of the penitent heretic's abjuration,
had expected, as representative of the Archbishop
of Rheims and grand almoner, to place the crown
on the new monarch's head. But in the interim
Henri had presented the archbishop to a see of
greater importance, that of Sens ; he was, therefore, the metropolitan of Chartres. But the
canons of the Church prohibited an archbishop
from officiating in the diocese of his suffragan;
consequently the Bishop of Chartres, Nicolas de

* No great amount was obtained from such sources ; but what
was coined bore the effigy of " Charles X." until 1595. The coin
in general circulation in Paris and the chief towns of France was
the Spanish pistole, so vast were the sums that Philip had lav-
ished on the League and its armies in the vain attempt to reduce
France to the rank of a province of Spain.

Thou (brother of the historian), claimed the honour of crowning Henri IV. — a claim which the archbishop regretfully allowed.

The custom of draping the cathedral with velvet hangings and gold embroidery, of displaying the royal jewels and the most precious treasures of the Church, and of incurring in other ways vast and needless expense on the occasion of the coronation of a king of France, was in the present instance necessarily departed from. Yet some preparation, to give effect to the ceremony, was absolutely requisite. A delay of ten days was, therefore, sought and granted, more especially for the completion of the new crown, — of course the most important part of the regalia.

During the interval Henri turned his thoughts towards allaying the asperity of feeling then existing between two members of his family whose absence from the approaching ceremony he greatly desired to prevent. These two royal cousins were the Comte de Soissons and the Prince de Dombes, — the latter, by the recent death of his father, being then Duc de Montpensier. Henri, whose friendly efforts were, it seems, but partially successful, would have preferred that the Baron de Rosny, who had some influence with the princes, should have undertaken their reconciliation. But the baron had asked for a *congé*, having four or five thousand crowns' worth of wheat and other crops to dispose of, and several fine horses of his famous breed — then much sought after. He was then engaged also in giving directions for the building of a château at Rosny, — Madame la Baronne apparently being as diligent as the architect and the builder in superintending its construction.

Rarely had Rosny a short leave of absence but before its expiration he was summoned by the king to return. On the occasion in question Henri was anxiously awaiting him at Mantes, intending thence to return to Chartres, when unexpectedly the widowed Queen Louise sought an interview with him. Henri received her with very great ceremony in the church of Notre-Dame de Mantes, where the *procureur-général* read a rather reproachful statement of the circumstances attending the assassination of Henri III., and complained of the delay in bringing its instigators to justice, and in celebrating that monarch's funeral rites. To this the king replied that "due punishment should certainly be inflicted on all persons of whatever rank found guilty of having participated in that act ; but as to the funeral ceremonies, they must be deferred, he was unwillingly compelled to say, until the wars were ended." The sorrowing Queen Louise was, therefore, constrained to return much disappointed to the seclusion of Chenonceaux, where she passed her life in lamenting a worthless husband and the most worthless of kings, awaiting quieter times for the satisfaction of her pious wishes, — wishes she was destined never to see accomplished.*

Henri was accustomed to put off the late king's funeral from year to year, but less, as L'Estoile states was his opinion, from fear of fatal consequence to himself — as prophesied by an astrologer — than from the inconvenience to one who, like Henri, had so little superfluous cash to spare, of expending a large sum on the pompous obsequies of his far-from-lamented predecessor.

In all haste Rosny obeyed the king's recall to Mantes. He was expecting to be despatched to Rouen to resume the negotiation with Villars (broken off partly because of the exorbitant price at which the Governor of Normandy proposed to sell himself, and his demand for the restitution of Fécamp). But to his extreme vexation, he found that Henri had hastened his return merely that he might complete that good understanding between his royal cousins which he had failed fully to effect himself. Rosny was but little disposed to undertake the task assigned him, and urged on the king the danger of delaying to come

---

* It is related that, at the conclusion of this visit of great ceremony, " the good princess hearing the *Exaudiat* chanted by the choir, and remembering that it was the custom of the pious *débauché* Henri III. to order it to be chanted every day at mass, she became so violently agitated that she swooned, and for some time could not be restored to consciousness, — to the great alarm of the king, the princes, and others in attendance." — PALMA-CAYET.

to some terms with Villars. He, however, was
deaf to the entreaties of his bosom friend, who
soon perceived that there was no escape from the
unpleasant office about to be thrust upon him.

With the view of lightening his task, Henri
allowed him the assistance of Du Perron, the wily
Bishop of Evreux, " who alone," he thought,
" would scarcely succeed in so delicate a mission."
Rosny was on friendly terms with both princes,
whose ill-feeling towards each other originated
in a contention regarding their respective preroga-
tives as princes of the blood. Unfriendliness had
since grown into enmity, from the circumstance —
whether by chance or design — of their aspiring
to the same offices in the state, the same governments, etc., and, above-all, to the good graces
of the same lady, so that the king found it
impossible to keep on terms of friendship with
either.

His leaning was towards Montpensier, who was
immensely rich, disposed to be faithful to the
Royalist cause, courteous in manners, brave but
unassuming, and " could appear in the field or on
grand state occasions with a retinue of five hundred gentlemen, all richly equipped and splendidly
mounted." His rival, Charles de Bourbon, Comte
de Soissons and Dreux, was the youngest of the
princes of the branch of Condé, and a more dazzling personage than his worthy cousin of Montpensier. He was handsome in person, of great

bravery, — of which he had given conspicuous proof at Coutras and the siege of Rouen, — of distinguished manners, and very skilful in the warlike games and exercises then the favourite pastime of the cavaliers of that day. He had fine estates at Nogent and Blandy, but was much less wealthy than the duke, and his retinue of gentle-men not nearly so numerous.

In his attachment to this or that party he was less to be relied on than Montpensier, being some-times professedly devoted to Henri IV., at others secretly favouring the intrigues of his brother, the young Cardinal de Bourbon, and the plots of the third party. One advantage, however, Soissons decidedly had over the duke as regarded their rivalry as lovers : he possessed the lady's heart, and Catherine de Bourbon was as immovably true to her lover as to her religion.

Long and difficult proved the task which the king had deputed the Huguenot baron and the Catholic bishop to bring to a happy conclusion, — the count being less amenable to reason and less yielding than the duke. But after many prayers and much patience, they succeeded in persuading the princes to consent to see each other, and finally to embrace and be friends. Rosny adds that he would not guarantee that the heart had any large share in this reconciliation.* Yet he was well satisfied to have so far succeeded with-

* *Mémoires de Sully.*

out touching on the subject of love and marriage. He looked upon that as an absolutely insurmountable obstacle, which, remaining undecided, still left between the rivals a chief cause of variance.

There was nothing now to prevent the baron — at least, so he thought — from proceeding at once on his diplomatic mission to Rouen ; but when he required of Henri his instructions and full powers to treat with Villars, he learned, to his dismay, that the good understanding between the two princes, so much desired by the king, was, in fact, but the first step to another arrangement he even more anxiously desired. Rosny "shuddered," he says, when informed that "to him alone could the king entrust this most delicate and most unpleasant mission" — that of prevailing on Madame Catherine to give up the mutual promise of marriage signed by her and the Comte de Soissons some three or four years back, the fulfilment of which had been retarded only by the troubled and disastrous state of the country.

Once in possession of this document, Henri proposed to gratify the Duc de Montpensier by giving him Madame Catherine in marriage, using his authority, if needful, to compel her to accept him. But whether she resisted or not, he would at least be freed from the constant dread of her marriage with Soissons secretly taking place ; for although clandestine, it yet would embarrass him greatly, he said, "that the Comte de Soissons should make himself his heir in spite of him." *

In silent embarrassment Rosny listened to the king's statement of his wishes and intentions. Anxiously desirous of being released from a task so repugnant to him, and, as he foresaw, so difficult, he endeavoured to bring the king to consider how contrary to his interests was the delay in continuing the negotiations with Villars, who, supposing all arrangements with him were at an end, would not fail to close at once with the proposals of his enemies. Not a moment, he declared, should be lost; and when Normandy had become Royalist, he could then, with less anxiety concerning the king's cause, visit Madame Catherine. But Henri was so intent on his project that Normandy and the arrogant Villars seemed of but little moment to him; and Rosny's urgent request to be allowed to set out that very minute for Rouen he would not even listen to, but desired him, without loss of time, to take the road to Chartres.

* Henri had promised to give his sister in marriage to Soissons after he had fought so valiantly for him at Coutras, and, as Catherine expressed it, " she and the count had conceived a great friendship for each other." But Rosny, already strongly prejudiced against Soissons, informed the king that it was reported that the count wished to marry the King of Navarre's sister for the sake of the large estates she would be entitled to. For this there appears to have been no better foundation than for another report, — that he was connected with evil spirits, and had obtained the princess's affection by sorcery.

The baron was then left to his own reflections, and he confesses that the more he reflected on the commission imposed on him, the more embarrassing it appeared. He was well assured, from his knowledge of the character and temper of Madame Catherine, that no human eloquence would avail to gain her approval of the king's views, — that to please him she should renounce the man she loved, and who returned her love, to marry one whom she detested. The document to be obtained from her Rosny regarded as really, for Henri's purposes, a valueless one, as it could be renewed at the lovers' pleasure. To give it value a statement must be added to it, recognising that the fulfilment of the promise was conditional — depending on the king's consent.

This increased the difficulty. Henri had left to the baron's decision the means to be taken for carrying out his project. "Artifice," he said, "if necessary; force, if it must be;" and this, with a promise not to interfere, whatever course Rosny might take, was all the instruction or assistance Henri promised in the matter, of which he proposed, should any reference be made to it in his presence, to feign himself wholly uninformed. The princess was residing at Chartres in much retirement, associating almost entirely with the families of the Huguenot nobility, — the Catholics, the ladies especially, looking upon her with some suspicion, surprised that she, too, like her brother, a " *hérétique relaps*," had not followed his example and forsworn her errors.*

Her most intimate friend, and the confidante both of the count and the princess, was the Comtesse de Guiche.   They met at her house, and when Soissons was absent or with the armies, their correspondence passed through her hands.   Henri probably did not forbid this intimacy with his sister, owing to some slight trace of tenderness still lingering in his feelings towards the once " belle Corisande," though she had grown too fat and florid for beauty.   Yet he did not approve it, for the lady was very resentful, and the Baron de Rosny dreaded encountering her opposition in the part he was about to play.

Though Henri had said " force, if it must be," naturally the baron perceived that force was out of the question.   Artifice alone remained ; and hateful though it was to him, yet, as his sovereign commanded, artifice must be used.   Rosny had very extreme ideas of the duty a subject owes the king.   His conscience, however, gave him some

* Henri abjured for his sister at the time of the Saint-Bartholomew massacre, when he and the Prince de Condé were called upon by Charles IX. to renounce their Protestantism, — to choose as he said, between death and the mass.   Catherine was then a delicate child of eleven years, sorrowing deeply for the loss of her mother.   She never embraced Catholicism, and while at the Louvre, happily for her perhaps, she lived, almost forgotten, remote from the royal apartments, and with a lady friend of her mother who had taken charge of her and her education.

very sharp twinges, to which he replied by very specious arguments, that did not, in fact, quite command his own approval, but compelled him to acknowledge, at least by his conscience, that he was about to act a deceitful part, unworthy of one who bore the reputation of a man of strict honour.

He began by telling Du Perron — "his own bishop," as he terms him — and his younger brother that he had heard the king intended shortly to celebrate the marriage of his sister, Madame Catherine, with the Comte de Soissons.* Their mutual attachment, he said, was well known to the king, while other reasons led him to regard their union as suitable and desirable. Probably he would have no legitimate issue, in which case it would please him that his sister's children should succeed as the heirs of his separate kingdom of Navarre.†

This was supposed to be a confidential communication, but as the brothers Du Perron were intimate with Soissons and his family, and were,

---

*The Abbé du Perron was appointed to the bishropic of Evreux at the suggestion and through the influence of the Baron de Rosny. As unscrupulous as he was learned and eloquent, no more suitable person could have been selected to aid the baron in removing all lingering hesitation from Henri's mind at the time of his pretended conversion.

† Henri had intended to retain his kingdom of Navarre as his private property, but this was found to be contrary to the decrees of the French constitution, by which the private possessions of the kings of France became on their accession the property of the crown. Navarre was thus united to France.

besides, far from remarkable for reticence, Rosny
felt assured that his secret would soon be known ;
at least, to all whom it concerned.   Two days he
allowed for the news of the happiness in store for
them to reach the ears of Madame Catherine and
the count.   He had seen very little of the former
since, by her brother's command, she left Béarn,
whither Soissons, secretly leaving the army, went
with the hope of persuading Palma-Cayet to marry
them unknown to the king.   Cayet's refusal
thwarted this hope; also Soissons's project of
carrying off the princess from Béarn — she being
by no means unwilling to assent to it — was prevented by the information despatched by Henri to
his minister, the Baron Pangeas.

Rosny, however, determined on paying Madame
Catherine a visit, as if to take leave of her on
setting out on his diplomatic mission.   They had
known each other from childhood, and had danced
and practised their parts in the ballets together at
the then gay little court of Nérac.   He was therefore graciously received, and none, he testifies,
could be more gracious, more dignified, than the
Princesse Catherine de Navarre.   He would have
preferred to find her alone rather than with the
Comtesse de Guiche, and still better would he
have been pleased had M. de Soissons been absent.
It was, however, evident from their reception of
him that the Du Perrons, as he expected, had not
failed to unburden themselves of their secret.

After a little ordinary conversation, Madame de Guiche, perceiving that Rosny was not likely to introduce the subject all were thinking of, at once brought it on the tapis. Rising from her seat, "in a transport of friendliness" she embraced M. le Baron; then addressing Soissons and the princess, she said : "This is the man whose influence, more than any other, can greatly promote your wishes." Madame, in reply, said to the baron very calmly that "he was, of course, well aware that both she and M. le Comte had always felt a great esteem for him, and would now be very greatly obliged if he would aid them in recovering the favour of the king, her brother." She said no more, M. de Rosny informs us, but by her amiable and engaging manners allowed him to see her kindly disposition towards him.

He affected, he says, to be gained over to their views, and to be desirous of promoting them. If he were certain that secrecy would be observed he could give, he said, some information of considerable interest to them. Of course they promised not to betray him ; but apparently he had not quite concocted his story, for he gave them only a few hints, and asked for a delay of three days before imparting all he knew. They willingly consented, but as the baron had intended — or rather pretended — simply to pay his respects to the princess on the eve of departure for Rouen, it was necessary to invent a pretext for his delay

in setting out. In this the princess aided him by
inviting him to a further conference three days
later on.

Henri was much amused when told of the
progress of Rosny's stratagem. Punctually — the
three days being elapsed — he paid his next visit,
yet still required much pressing before he would
speak freely. He then repeated what he had told
the Du Perrons, but adding that the king had felt
especially aggrieved by M. de Soissons and Madame
Catherine seeking to set him at defiance, and to
marry without his consent. The three friends (the
countess being included in this reproach) acknowledged that it would have been better, perhaps, to
have shown more confidence in the king's good
feeling towards them.

The baron replied that his majesty, as they
were aware, was naturally disposed to forgive and
forget, and that by pursuing henceforth a contrary
course of conduct, the result they desired would be
effected. The fullest reliance must now be placed
in him; the engagements they had signed must be
given up, with a further declaration, signed and
sealed, to the effect that they entirely renounced
the idea of marriage unless with the king's full
consent to their union. The written engagement
they consented to give up. It was in the possession of Madame de Guiche, who had left it, she
said, at Béarn, but would send for it immediately.

It was, however, with great difficulty the baron

obtained from Soissons and the princess the written renunciation of their hopes of marriage, whether Henri gave or withheld his consent. "How," he said, "could the king have faith in their promises if they refused to give them in writing? How could he be persuaded of their obedience if they declined to afford him this proof of their sincerity?" His arguments seemed to have little weight with them. They thought the king required of them more than he had a right to expect; and here the discussion seemed likely to end.

But as a final effort on Rosny's part, he proposed that the declaration should be given into his hands, as though made to him, on the understanding — he pledging his word of honour to that effect — that on no pretence should it ever pass into the king's possession. After considerable hesitation this was agreed to; Rosny assuring them that he believed they would find, before the expiration of the next three months, the king himself anxious to anticipate their wishes and to "cement their union."*

Henri was the more delighted with Rosny's success, as he had scarcely ventured to hope for it; but he required the lovers' declaration to renounce each other to be given him. Rosny firmly refused to part with it, — to quiet his conscience probably for the deceitful part he had been playing; but he says it was to prove to the

* *Mémoires de Sully.*

king that he placed the observance of his word of
honour before even the obedience he owed his
sovereign.

As no realisation of the hopes held out to the
count and the princess followed the concessions
they had made, it may be easily imagined that
they did not readily pardon the deception practised
on them by M. de Rosny at Henri's instigation.
The baron declares, in his Memoirs, that his
thoughts never recurred to it without occasioning
him some very uncomfortable sensations.   Yet
he is of opinion — considering the repugnance he
evinced when urged to undertake such a mission
— that he ought to have been spared all the
vexations he afterwards experienced in consequence of it.*

However, for the time being, his mission was
ended, and so far the king was satisfied with its
result ; though it did not enable him to combine,
as he wished, the event of his coronation with the
fulfilment of his promise to the late Duc de
Montpensier, to give his sister in marriage to
his son, the Prince de Dombes.   This promise
was given to compensate the duke for his disappointment when Henri, in preference to the
Prince de Dombes, favoured the marriage of the
heiress of Sedan with the Vicomte de Turenne, to
whom he was under great obligations, and whose
pretensions were strengthened by the fact of his

* *Mémoires de Sully.*

Protestantism — Charlotte de la Marck, by her brother's will, being precluded from marrying a Catholic.

The question of inducing Madame Catherine to transfer her affections from Soissons to Montpensier by persuasive measures, or by an act of royal authority compelling her to accept the duke's proposals, was reserved for future consideration. The 27th of February had arrived, and any further delay in crowning Henri IV. was deemed by himself and his friends inexpedient.

Though wanting the splendour of church decoration customary on an occurrence so important, yet the coronation of the first king of the Bourbon dynasty was a ceremony of exceeding interest, dignity, and solemnity. Far more effective was the unconcealed architectural beauty of the fine old abbey of Chartres than any velvet hangings or embroidery could make it. The *coup-d'œil* was especially grand, when the king, kneeling in front of the high altar — surrounded by the princes of the blood, the peers of the realm, the ecclesiastical peers, the *haute noblesse*, the marshals of France, officers of various grades, and soldiers of the royal army, all ranks being there represented — received from the hands of the Bishop of Chartres the crown which was his by a threefold right : first, by right of inheritance ; secondly, of valour with which, under every disadvantage, he had persistently fought for it ; and thirdly, of

purchase,— vast sums and extravagant pensions
having yet to be paid to rebel subjects for the
peaceable cession of almost every province of
his kingdom.

The holy oil of Saint-Remi of Rheims not being
obtainable for the anointing of the king, a vial of
oil of similar miraculous holiness, sent from heaven
to Saint-Martin de Tours by angels, was brought to
Chartres by the monks of the abbey of Marmoûtier,
under the conduct of the Governor of Tours.

It was a subject of regret with many persons
that this great soldier-king, perhaps the greatest
of warrior monarchs, — for with dauntless bravery
he combined the rarer quality of great clemency,
— had not the moral courage to omit from the
antiquated coronation oath of the Middle Ages
the words that bound him to exterminate with
the utmost rigour that portion of his subjects
denounced by the Church as heretics. At the
time of his abjuration many dogmas of the Romish
Church were set before him as articles of faith, to
several of which he took objection, " treating them
as puerilities," and concluding the course of instruction to which he submitted with the jesting
remark, " I am not yet dead, so let us say nothing
of the requiem." In like manner that part of his
oath binding him to persecute and exterminate he
is said to have regarded as a mere formula, which,
while repeating with his lips, he was mentally
making oath never to observe. Yet it has been

Henri IV.

Photo-Etching. — From an old Portrait.

HENRY IV.

remarked that " by that oath the Edict of Nantes was revoked in spirit before it was granted."*

" There is now a King of France ! " was the glad exclamation of the people, who, despite the ravings of the legate, the menaces of the fanatical preachers, and the revived " sixteen," flocked to Chartres to witness the ceremony, to take part in the festivities of the city, and to swell the loud chorus of " Long live the King ! Long live Henri IV. ! "

On the day following his coronation, Henri was invested by the Bishop of Chartres with the collar of the Order of the Holy Ghost. He afterwards declared himself Grand Master of that Order.

* Henri Martin, *Histoire de France.*

CHAPTER XVI.

Mayenne Refuses the Peace Proposed by Henri IV., He Being Unabsolved by His Holiness. — Governor of Paris, Count Bélin, Required to Resign. — Is Replaced by Cossé-Brissac, Who Makes Terms with the King for Opening the Gates of Paris to Him. — Entry into Paris. — Exit of Spanish and Italian Garrisons, Legate, etc. — Henri in High Spirits. — He Dines at the Louvre. — *Bonjour* to the Heroines of the League. — Surrender of Bastille. — *Fête* in Perpetuity. — Jesuits Refuse to Pray for the King. — Erasing the Past. — Charles X.'s Decrees Annulled.

THE news of the king's coronation was received throughout France by the people with a feeling of general satisfaction. In Paris — where the plague, which then so frequently ravaged that most unwholesome of cities, had but recently abated in rigour — it was especially welcomed, being regarded as a promised cessation of that long series of civil wars by which the kingdom had been everywhere in a measure depopulated, and given up to pillage, strife, and crime. Mayenne, on the contrary, viewed the performance of that solemn rite, and the growing inclination of the people towards their legitimate sovereign, with considerable alarm. To the popular mind Henri had removed the only real obstacle to his possession of the throne by his renunciation

of Protestantism, his rights being further confirmed
— as was considered — by his coronation ; while,
from his well-known clemency, it was generally
believed that he would be far more inclined to
pardon those who had hitherto opposed him than,
when possessed of power, to retaliate with undue
severity.

But Mayenne flattered himself that he could
still compel the *bourgeoisie* to refrain from their
attempts of publicly rejoicing and kindling bonfires to celebrate the auspicious event that had
just taken place at Chartres, and at which many
Parisians, braving the lieutenant-general's prohibition, had been present.   The anathemas of the
legate, the ravings of the fanatical preachers of
the League, the arbitrary power exercised by the
resuscitated " sixteen," together with the Spanish
garrison and the *minotiers*, were, he believed, all
sufficient to overawe the people and suppress any
rising of the "politique party" in the capital.*
Several influential men of that party were ordered
to leave the city, and Comte Bélin, the Governor
of Paris — suspected of favouring the Royalist
cause — was required to resign his post, the Comte
de Cossé-Brissac being named to succeed him.
The Parliament remonstrated ; but Mayenne per-

---

* The *minotiers* were the very dregs of the populace, whom
the Spaniards had enrolled to the number of about 4,000, and to
whom they gave forty-five sous each weekly, and the ancient
measure of a *minot* of wheat.

sisted in his arrangements, and allowed all complaints to pass unnoticed.   A Parliamentary decree
was therefore drawn up, ordering the foreign garrisons to quit Paris, and opposing the removal of
Bélin.   As the issuing of this decree would have
occasioned a sanguinary struggle in Paris itself,
Mayenne found it necessary to protest that "in no
sense was he a Spaniard, and that none desired
an honourable peace more than he."   An arrangement was then come to; the decree was withdrawn, and Brissac accepted as temporary governor.

Very advantageous conditions of peace were
proposed at this time by Henri IV. to the lieutenant-general, but were declined by him, though
strongly urged by the secretaries of state, Villeroy
and Jeannin, to close with the king's offer at once.
He, however, seemed to insinuate that "it would
be a reproach to him to enter into a treaty with
the King of Navarre before his holiness had seen
fit to grant him absolution."   His agents at Rome
meanwhile were doing all in their power to persuade the Pope entirely to withhold it.

Another and perhaps stronger reason for declining to avail himself of the king's proposals
was that Philip II. — though much discouraged
by his unsuccessful endeavours to secure the
crown of France for the infanta — had, as a last
effort in that direction, promised to aid Mayenne
with a small sum of money and a few thousand
troops under Count Mansfeldt, who already had

arrived on the frontier. With them and his own diminished forces Mayenne proposed to attempt some military operations on his own account.

Philip had not sent the effective aid the lieuten-ant-general had looked for; nevertheless, having, as he seemed to believe, placed the capital in a state of defence against the probable attack on it by the newly crowned King of France, he hoped, with this reinforcement, to create at least some trouble for him elsewhere, by compelling him to march his army in another direction to protect those cities that had acknowledged him, and which Mayenne proposed to threaten or to besiege. Like Philip II., Mayenne had almost relinquished his hopes of obtaining the crown of France for him-self. A province or two secured to him as an independent principality was now the extent of his expectations, if not of his ambition; while the Spanish monarch was fain to be content with Marseilles and one or two other cities of impor-tance, conveniently near his own domains. For the realisation of these modest views rather than for the furtherance of Mayenne's plans, the troops under Mansfeldt had been sent to France, with as many doubloons as could well be spared from Philip's now almost empty exchequer.

On the 6th of March, having previously assem-bled the captains of the several quarters of Paris, and enjoined on them the necessity of absolute fidelity and obedience to the governor, Mayenne

announced his departure to join a reinforcement
of the army, promising a speedy return, and adding
that he left with them as a pledge those who were
dearest to him in the world, — his wife and children. He, however, appears to have afterwards
changed his mind in this respect, and to have
thought it better that those who were dearest to
him should accompany him to his government
in Burgundy. His departure left Brissac entirely
master of Paris.

The "sixteen" had welcomed Brissac as an
ally; the Parliament received him as an opponent.
Mayenne and the Spanish garrison believed that
Paris, watched over by the vigilant eye of the new
governor, who was an officer of distinction, was
fully secured from any surprise by which Henri
IV. might attempt to obtain possession of his capital. But all, as was soon discovered, were in error.
Though Brissac in 1591 had protested against
Mayenne's arbitrary act of sending four of the
"sixteen" to be hanged on the Place de Grève,
little or no inquiry being made respecting the
offences with which they were charged, he nevertheless was not one of their partisans, but rather
inclined to the views of the "politique party," who
would have expelled him.

He had, in fact, a fanciful scheme of his own,
which his post of governor he imagined would
enable him to carry out with some facility. He
proposed to change the form of government in

France ; to establish a republic on the Roman model, of which Paris should be the capital. This project he made known to several friends, whom he expected readily to join him in giving effect to it. It did not meet with the favour he anticipated, but was coldly listened to and generally regarded as an idle dream.* At once, however, he abandoned his republican ideas, and scrupled not to listen to a more feasible scheme, — the surrender of Paris to the king. It was proposed to him by the Baron de Saint - Luc, a Huguenot nobleman who had married Brissac's sister, and was commissioned by Henri to negotiate for him, — Rosny being engaged at Rouen in arranging terms with Villars.

The republican general fixed his price at a very high figure, as, indeed, with very few exceptions, did all those patriotic Frenchmen who sold the country to their king after he had so bravely fought for and well - nigh conquered it. But Henri bargained not ; he knew there was an enormous bill to pay, but as he had nothing at the moment wherewith to pay it, he deemed a few thousands more or less of little consequence. He bought Paris of Brissac for a marshal's baton, the governments of Mantes and Corbeil, 200,000 crowns once paid, and a pension of 20,000.

* Brissac is said to have been "a man of culture, and to have devoted much time to the study of ancient history, from which he had derived a sort of classic republicanism."

There were others, of course, in the secret —
members of the "politique party" in the Parliament, and the chiefs of the municipality who had
rejected the Roman republic, but joined, without
hesitation, and generally from disinterested motives, in opening the gates of Paris to the king.
Brissac, determined that nothing should intervene
from any fault of his to break off his bargain with
the king, acted with the utmost celerity, prudence,
secrecy, and discretion.   Henri, at the request of
Brissac and the magistracy, readily promised that
the legate, the Spanish ambassadors, and foreign
troops should be permitted to leave Paris safe
and sound — the latter with the honours of war.*
He also guaranteed to the Parisians the maintenance of their privileges, the abolition of the past,
and the interdiction of the Protestant form of
worship within a radius of ten leagues around
Paris.

Wildly boisterous weather prevailed when, at
about 4 A. M. on the 22d of March, the first sovereign of the Bourbon dynasty stealthily entered
the capital of his kingdom.   The raging wind,
and torrents of driving rain and sleet, rendering
the roads almost impassable, had greatly impeded
his march, and compelled him to halt for awhile at

* The lieutenant-general of the kingdom had invited the
Spaniards to enter Paris as allies, and the "politiques" were
therefore unwilling treacherously to place them in the power of
their enemy.

Saint-Denis, and thus to retard for more than an hour his arrival with his troops at the gates of Paris. This delay, instead of being fraught with the danger he feared to the success of his enterprise, proved to have been the means of preventing its probable failure.

Some members of the Council of Sixteen are said, for a day or two previously, to have "scented treason in the air," and to have communicated to the Spanish general, Feria, that they suspected the governor. The Spaniard made known these suspicions to Brissac, without informing him that he was the suspected traitor, but proposing to make the round of the ramparts with him, accompanied by two or three of his soldiers, in the course of the evening and night (21st and 22d). Brissac made no objection; his plans were well laid and complete, and the fidelity of the guard on duty assured by a liberal expenditure of Spanish pistoles and promises of more. The Spaniards, keenly observant, had twice made the tour of the ramparts, prepared with poniards to stab the faithless governor to the heart on the slightest appearance of treachery.

Two o'clock, the hour at about which the king was expected, had passed, ere Brissac, who dared not show the slightest sign of impatience, was free from the companions of his rounds. He and L'Huillier, provost of the merchants, then hastened to the Porte Neuve, where Henri IV. was to

be received.   The sheriffs L'Anglet and Néret
established themselves at the Portes Saint-Denis
and Saint-Honoré to admit the troops under Vitry
and Saint-Luc, others in the plot taking up their
position at different points of the city.   The garrisons of Corbeil and Melun descended the river in
boats as far as La Rapée, and were welcomed with
open arms by the "politiques" of the *bourgeois*
militia, who took them to the arsenal.

Though all these arrangements, so ably planned,
were carried out as silently as possible, yet the
howling wind and beating rain greatly favoured
the designs of the conspirators: for as three
o'clock struck, Don Diego Ibarra (second in command of the Spaniards), wrapped closely in his
cloak, passed with measured footsteps near the
Porte Neuve, making a solitary and final tour of
the ramparts.   At the foot of the wall, and but a
few yards below him, clinging close to the gate,
and concealed in its dark shadow, stood Brissac
and L'Huillier, listening with beating hearts and
bated breath to the Spanish officer's slowly advancing footsteps.   Suddenly they cease!   An
anxious moment that must have been, both for
governor and provost, seeing that a sanguinary
conflict must have inevitably followed detection.
Happily, however, it was but a violent gust of
wind, driving straight before it a blinding deluge
of rain, that had brought Ibarra to a standstill;
his receding steps being soon after heard, he

probably thought, as he returned to his quarters
believing "all was well," that even treason
would scarcely venture abroad on such a night
as that.

Another anxious hour was passed by the
watchers at the Porte Neuve ere any indications
of Henri's approach were perceived. It is not
surprising that Brissac began to be uneasy, and
to doubt whether he was not himself betrayed.
Henri IV. had, indeed, been warned that no faith
should be placed in Brissac, who was supposed to
be so much enamoured of his Roman republic that
he would not hesitate to disregard his promise
given if he saw, or fancied he saw, a chance of
establishing that form of government. But the
king resolved to act with a full and unreserved
confidence in him. Otherwise, he must, without
any sufficient pretext, put an end to an enterprise
thoroughly well concerted, and the success of
which was to him of the highest importance. He
must trust Brissac, he said, and leave the issue in
the hands of Providence.

At length Henri IV. and his four or five thousand troops made their appearance. They were
in a terrible plight; but nothing daunted, they
silently defiled along the boulevards and quays,
and, joining the other detachments, took up the
positions assigned them. Brissac and L'Huillier
received the king, who embraced both of them,
and throwing over the former his own white scarf,

saluted him as Marshal of France.*   L'Huillier
presented the keys of the city gates, and Maréchal
de Cossé-Brissac, who six years before had closed
the Porte Neuve on Henri III., the last of the
Valois, flying from his capital, now opened it wide
for Henri IV., the first of the Bourbons, to enter
and take possession of it.

It was not without a feeling of hesitancy that
Henri entered that labyrinth of narrow lanes,
crooked streets, and suspicious "no thorough-
fares," that formed the heart of grand old Paris,
the scene of so many deeds of blood, and where
then, as of old, traitors and assassins often lurked.
He is said to have personally assured himself
before leaving the Port Neuve for the still dark
recesses and obscure and winding byways of the
city, that his own troops, with General Matignon,
kept guard there.   Twenty years had nearly
elapsed since, roused by the warnings and coun-
sels of D'Aubigné, he fled from that city from the
perils that threatened him, and from the deteriorat-
ing influence of the gross pleasures of a dissolute
court, with which Catherine de' Medici, for her
own aims, sought to enfeeble the natural energy

---

* Brissac was one of several officers whom Mayenne, shortly
before, had elevated to that highest grade of military rank —
Marshal of France — which, with other distinctions conferred by
the lieutenant-general when playing the sovereign, Henri allowed
to be retained after receiving their confirmation from him.   This
the wits of the day termed the legitimisation of Mayenne's
bastards. — L'ESTOILE.

of his character, and to obliterate all that was noble and honourable in it. Doubtless his moral nature suffered from degrading association with vice in those earlier years, but it is matter for wonder that so much of good was retained.

Henri's return to Paris as King of France to take possession of his capital was accomplished without resorting to sack or bloodshed. Resistance on the part of dissatisfied Leaguers and priests was felt to be vain, as the king's troops or his partisans held the principal posts and places in the city. A few German lansquenets, not in the secret, refused to lay down their arms, which led to a skirmish with a party of Royalists, when, unfortunately, three or four of the former were killed or wounded, — a mischance that Henri much regretted, it having been his wish that Paris should be taken without loss of life or harm to any one.

The first feeling of the Parisians on being roused from their slumbers at break of day by the ringing of bells, the thunder of cannon, the shouts of " *Vivent le roi et la paix !*" mingled with the soldiers' favourite chant, " *Vive Henri Quatre !*" etc., was extreme amazement. That the king was in his capital and joyously received was evident ; but that such an event had been so thoroughly planned and successfully carried out in spite of the Spanish garrison, while Paris slept and the elements raged, seemed to many little less than a miracle.

The Spaniards were, indeed, rather perplexed what course to take in this unexpected state of affairs and change of masters. They, however, assembled their troops to the number of 3,000, in the Place d'Antoine, prepared for resistance should they be attacked. But Henri, in compliance with his promise to Brissac, deputed the Comte de Saint-Pôl to inform the Duc de Feria that, although he held the city with a force greatly outnumbering his, he had no design of taking either their lives or their property. He required only that they should evacuate Paris without delay. A safe-conduct was to be granted them and permission to march out with the honours of war. The king's message was doubtless a welcome relief. His request was readily assented to, and his offers accepted. The Spanish general, after musing for awhile, seemed struck by Henri's magnanimity. "The Béarnais," he exclaimed, "is a great king — a very great king." Philip would certainly not have done likewise had the troops of "the Béarnais" been in his power.

About four in the afternoon, drums beating, colours flying, the Spaniards marched out of Paris. Sixty or more rabid Leaguers and priests, amongst whom were several of the "sixteen," finding their occupation gone, availed themselves of the opportunity afforded them to quit the city with the foreigners. From the window above the Porte Saint-Denis Henri witnessed their departure. The Duc de Feria and his officers saluted him as they passed, but did not lower their colours to the "Prince of Béarn." He, however, returned their courtesy, and called to them, "Gentlemen, commend me to your master; but let him not send you hither again!" They were accompanied on their way to Soissons, as far as Le Bourget-Drancy, by the Barons de Saint-Luc and de Solignac and a detachment of troops.

An hour later the Pope's Italian regiment followed, and similar courtesies were exchanged. With the Italians the legate left Paris, having refused either to visit or to receive the king. The state of excitement he had lived in during the last year or two had affected his health, and he died from the fatigue of the journey ere he reached Rome.

Paris was at last free from foreign soldiers, to the great delight of king and people, both of whom now repaired to Notre-Dame, where a *Te Deum* was chanted as a thanksgiving. The clergy, carrying the cross, awaited Henri IV. under the grand portal, and the nave and galleries were crowded as on a grand fête-day. He afterwards dined at the Louvre in public, and was in his gayest humour. Business, for that day, he declared, he could not attend to; for to find himself in the ancient palace of the French kings, listening to the joyous acclamations of the people who recently

had anathematised him and sworn never to acknowledge him, seemed more like a dream than a
reality.   But in order to dispel all anxiety and
doubt as to his ultimate intentions — for a man of
less noble nature might have found gratification
in vengeance — a general amnesty was announced,
from the benefit of which none who had borne
arms against him, not even the infamous "sixteen,"
were to be excluded.   The governor, the provost,
the sheriffs, and the rest of the municipality, in full
force, crossed the bridges, preceded by a herald
and trumpeters, proclaiming the good news in all
parts of the city.

When the "heroines of the League" were informed that the Béarnais had triumphantly entered
Paris, the Duchesse de Montpensier is said to have
exclaimed in an agony of terror, "I am lost! Have
I no friend here who has a poniard and will plunge
it in my breast?"   But L'Estoile, a contemporary,
and likely to have been better informed than Mé-
zeray and Péréfixe, says she flew into a rage and
behaved like a mad woman, exclaiming with passionate vehemence: "Is there no one in Paris
who has a poniard, and with it the courage to
plunge it in *his* heart?"   She then inveighed
against Brissac, of whose cowardice she said she
had long since had proofs; but she knew not until
that morning that he was a traitor as well as a
coward.

"The duchess had scarcely begun," continues

L'Estoile, "to recover her senses a little when M. de Saint-Pôl appeared, deputed on the king's behalf to bid the ladies *bonjour,* and to assure them that neither to themselves would any offence be offered, nor to their hôtels and property any injury done; for he had taken them under his own especial protection and safeguard. This unexpected act of gallantry rather discomfited the ladies, but especially Madame de Montpensier, who had found difficulty in calling to mind terms sufficiently opprobrious and insulting to apply to "the Béarnais." Yet she contrived to conceal her vexation and to thank him for his courtesy with the best grace she could assume on the spur of an inopportune moment.

Later in the day she and the Duchesse de Nemours presented themselves at the Louvre to compliment the king. Perhaps it was curiosity; yet he received them very graciously, and conversed with so much freedom and liveliness that he seemed anxious to set them at ease, and to spare them any confusion they might be supposed to feel in their interview with one whom Madame de Nemours professed to dislike and Madame de Montpensier to hate with intensest hatred. In the course of their conversation she said she could have wished that it had devolved on her brother, the Duc de Mayenne, to lower the drawbridge for his majesty to enter his capital. " *Ventre Saint-Gris !* " said the king, " I should probably have had

a long time to wait there, and should not have
entered at so early an hour."

On the following day Henri returned the " heroines' " visit, when in appearance at least they had
resigned themselves to the triumph of the Béarnais, and in the evening played a game of cards
with him at the Louvre. The old Cardinal de
Pellevé, called the patriarch of the League, was
seized with a violent fit of ungovernable anger at
the events of the 22d, and his rage increasing
when he saw that no effectual opposition was made
to the proceedings of the " heretic pretender," he
took to his bed, and died on the 26th. On the
same day Dubourg, governor of the Bastille, and
Beaulieu, captain of the Château de Vincennes,
surrendered to the king, — the smallness of the
garrisons and an insufficiency of ammunition preventing them from sustaining a siege. With these
two fortresses in his power, Henri IV. was actually
in possession of his capital. The great work of
the 22d was therefore considered complete, and
the perpetual solemnisation of the day ordered,
" as a thanksgiving to God for the happy deliverance of the city from the oppression of the League
and its subjugation to the legitimate king.*

In the course of the following month, both the
University and the Sorbonne had taken the oath
of allegiance to Henri IV. — the Faculty of
Theology deciding that "contrary to the doubts

---

* Its celebration was discontinued only at the Revolution.

expressed by certain persons of sinister opinions, Henri of Bourbon was the true and legitimate heir to the throne of France, consequently entitled to the full obedience of all classes of his subjects. Although the Holy Father — misled by the false representations of factious enemies of the state — had not yet publicly recognised him as the eldest son of the Church, this, they declared, did not depend on the king. Power," the Faculty continued, " came, as Saint-Paul said, from God, and he who resisted the power *incurred damnation."* *

Those magistrates of the Royalist Parliament who had refused to remain in Paris while the city was in the hands of the Leaguers, but who had held their sittings at Tours or Châlons, were now scarcely willing to rejoin those members of the sovereign court who had continued to reside in the capital. Yet all were not Leaguers. The inveterate ones of that faction had decamped with the Spaniards. A few were Royalists, and many were of the " politique party " — for instance, De Belloy and Edouard Molé, with whom the king had been in secret correspondence. It was, however, his wish that there should be complete oblivion of the past.† Of the sovereign court of Parliament

---

* Saint-Paul's Epistle to the Romans, xiii., 1, 2.

† " Private crimes," of course were excepted ; for the assassination of Henri III. had by and by to be inquired into, and Queen Louise would have had the king give to that inquiry precedence of all other affairs of his kingdom.

he exacted only that on the assembling of the reinstated sections of Paris the oath of allegiance should be taken by all the members.

Having sworn fidelity to Henri IV., the Parliament seemed to vie with the king in their anxiety to throw a veil over the past, especially in matters most nearly concerning themselves, and in which some had played a conspicuous part. Their first act was to declare the reception of the decrees of the Council of Trent contrary to the liberties of the Gallican Church ; therefore implicitly annulled, together with all other acts and decrees of the recent illegally convened States of the League. It was resolved also to blot out from the public records of the kingdom all that had taken place while the government was in the hands of the League. The name of the "pretended King Charles X." was, by order of the Parliament, erased from all minutes, despatches, and decrees whatsoever.

Already two celebrated lawyers — Pierre Pithou (one of the authors of the *"Ménippée"*) and Antoine Loisel, charged *ad interim* with the functions of procurator-general and advocate-general — had received instructions from the chancellor to take from the public registers, as well those of the Parliament as of other official bodies, all they discovered in them opposed to the dignity of the reigning king and his predecessor, and contrary to the laws of the realm. They were also to

remove from public places all pictures, inscriptions, etc., tending to preserve the memory of what had occurred in Paris while it was in the power of the League.*

The Parliament itself annulled all oaths, ordinances and decrees, whether freely given or extorted by violence, since the 29th of December, 1588, to the prejudice of the authority of the kings and the laws of the realm. Inquiry was also to be made "into the circumstances of that terrible parricide, the assassination of Henri III.;" while, under the pains and penalties of high treason, all persons were prohibited from recognising the Duc de Mayenne in the quality of lieutenant-general of the kingdom,—he and the princes of his house being also enjoined under the same penalties to "acknowledge the King Henri IV. as their lawful sovereign, and forthwith to withdraw from the pretended party of the Union."† Thus, so far as was possible, the Parliament strove to undo all that had been done in Paris and elsewhere in France during the last five years, and to render that period almost a blank in the political history of the capital and other chief towns.‡

The Jesuits did not follow the example set

---

* L'Estoile, *Journal de Henri IV.*   † Mathieu; L'Estoile.

‡ It appears from M. Bernard's introduction to the State Papers of 1593, quoted by H. Martin, that "Pithou, as a bibliophilist and historian, preserved the documents which, as a political

them by the Sorbonne in their apostasy to the League. By the oath of allegiance to Henri IV., and subsequent public assertion of his legitimate right to the throne, independent of the Pope's intervention, that learned body was said to have anathematised itself. The Jesuits were more consistent, and would neither take the oath nor afford the king the benefit of their prayers until his holiness should give the word of command. None the less the grand affair of the League had come to an end.

The Sorbonne had given it the *coup-de-grace* when at its last gasp, overwhelmed by the ridicule heaped on it by the " *Satire Ménippée*," no longer furtively circulated in manuscript (though its authors and printers still prudently chose to remain *incognito*). It was now printed and published, and in every one's hands, convulsing the inhabitants of the good city of Paris with laughter at the harangues and proceedings of the foreign quacks, their famous " Catholicon, Sovereign Electuary," and "*fin galimatias*, prepared for the cure of the king's evil." The puerile superstitions, absurd exaggerations, — all, indeed, that lent itself to ridicule in the League, — were seized with pitiless sagacity, its blows being so

---

functionary, he was charged to destroy. Those removed by him from the Parliamentary registers have, however, been recovered and restored to their place in the judicial archives of the period."

well aimed, and hitting so hard, that for two
centuries the League was scarcely viewed in any
other light than that in which it is represented by
the " *Satire Ménippée.*"*

* De Thou, *Littérature Française du IXᵉ au XVIIᵉ Siècle;*
Gustave Merlet.

CHAPTER XVII.

Want of Funds for the Burial of the League. — Aid Sought
from Elizabeth and the German Princes. — The Treaty of
Governor Villars with Henri IV. — Rouen Becomes Royal. —
Clement VIII. Withholds the Absolution. — Henri's Irrev-
erent Devotions. — An Army Assembling for a Fresh Cam-
paign. — Spaniards Take La Capelle. — Prince Balagny. —
Henri Marches on Laon. — Mayenne's Flight to Brussels. —
Death of Cardinal de Bourbon. — Death of François d'O.
— Christening of César, Monsieur.

F the League was dead, it had yet to be
buried, and royally, too, under a mountain of gold. But where — in the then
plundered and ruined condition of France, its
commerce, its manufactures, — its former agricul-
tural abundance, and all other sources of wealth
dried up, — was the gold to be obtained to meet
all those onerous engagements the king had entered
into for rewarding the fidelity of friends, and
satisfying the rapacious demands put ·forth by
rebels as the price of submission? The great
soldier, who was then " studying the part of King
of France in the palace of the Louvre," was at
times much disturbed by these thoughts. Many
of the once well-to-do *bourgeoisie* were almost
ruined by the civil wars, and the people, who were

reduced to much poverty — relying on the king's reputation for clemency and sympathy with them — looked for a partial release from the burden of past years rather than increased taxation.

The infamous François d'O had hastened to Paris on learning Henri's successful entry into that city, and was reinstated in the offices he held under Henri III. — of Governor of Paris and the Île de France, with the superintendence of the finances. D'O was eager to seize whatever sum, large or small, might then perchance be found in the public coffers, — fearing, he said, that it should fall into the hands of the military men or magistrates, who would be likely to retain it for arrears of pay or salary. All classes had indeed suffered during those years of religious strife and civil warfare, and many of the least wealthy of the nobility — Huguenots especially — had sold or mortgaged their estates to supply Henri with the " sinews of war."

The sinews of war still were wanting ; for there were signs that before the sword was finally sheathed another struggle was impending. It was useless to look for supplies from D'O. A very small portion of the revenues of the kingdom ever passed out of his and his colleagues' hands for the use of the king and the necessities of the state, whose much-needed reorganisation Henri was not yet seated firmly enough on his throne to attempt. The king was desirous of levying troops

in readiness for his next campaign, but, to his surprise, found greater difficulty in doing so than
when his fortunes seemed most desperate. There
were cavaliers ready to take the command, but
the troops, with the exception of a few Swiss,
whose only trade was war, were indisposed for
more fighting.

All honours and rewards Henri IV. had hitherto
been able to confer were given to Catholics. The
Huguenots were displeased, held aloof, and were
less ready than formerly to fight for the king who
had abandoned them. His appeal for both money
and troops must again be made to Elizabeth of
England and the Protestant German princes, who
were far from being pleased by his renunciation of
Protestantism. He had justified this change as
best he could by acknowledging that "his motives
were purely political." Elizabeth (with reference
to the perilous leap, as he termed his abjuration
when writing to Gabrielle) wrote to him :

"It is indeed a most perilous thing to do evil that good
may come; but I trust that a more healthy inspiration may
yet be vouchsafed you, and meanwhile I shall unceasingly
give you the foremost place in my devotions. You promise
me still all friendship and fidelity. I confess that I have
merited them. But I shall not repent if you do not change
your Father, otherwise I shall be to you but a bastard
sister on the Father's side. But may God guide you in the
right way!"

The king was then anxiously expecting the
return of the Baron de Rosny, whose part in the

affairs of France was daily becoming more important. The baron was then at Rouen, and was to
bring back the treaty between Villars and the
king. The negotiation had already been once
broken off, the demands of the Governor of
Rouen being too excessive to comply with. A
rough but brave soldier, of rude manners and
violent temper, Villars — though a rebel in arms
— in treating for the peace his sovereign offered
him, assumed the airs of a foreign potentate pre-
scribing terms to a vanquished enemy. This arrogant governor was greatly under the influence of
his *maître d'hôtel,* La Fond, formerly *valet de
chambre* to Rosny, and who, as already related,
by advice and friendly reproof, prevented his
hasty entrance into a matrimonial engagement
which La Fond considered a *mésalliance* for the
young Baron de Béthune Rosny.

Through the intervention of this same influential gentleman, the diplomatic discussion between
Villars and Rosny was resumed. For the possession of Rouen was of considerable importance to
Henri, as with it the whole of Normandy would
at once declare for him. Rosny's instructions,
therefore, were to yield as far as feasible to the
views of this grasping governor, and without further unnecessary delay, as preliminaries had been
signed by the king before his entry into Paris.

While Rosny was corresponding with the king
— for the governor would abate nothing of his

terms — some of Mayenne's partisans persuaded Villars that the baron was plotting his assassination. This so greatly enraged him that when the treaty, its conditions at last agreed to, was prepared and placed before him for signature, he snatched it from Rosny's hands, tore it in pieces, and stamped upon it, to the amazement of the Huguenot ambassador. In terms far from complimentary Villars gave the explanation demanded. But Rosny soon convinced him that he had been led into error. The governor's secretary was his informant, and on being summoned confessed that his report was false. In accordance with the short and ready mode in vogue in those days, of administering justice and striking terror into the hearts of evil-doers, the unfortunate secretary was arrested, and, by the angry governor's command, immediately hanged from a front window of his house.

A day or two after, a new treaty being prepared, Villars signed it, and donned the white scarf which Rosny handed to him. As all Rouen rejoiced at the return of peace, white scarfs were generally worn. A *Te Deum* was chanted, the bells rang, the cannon roared, and bonfires were lighted; several volleys of musketry were fired, and Villars, become enthusiastic, exclaimed, as he stood in the midst of a party of friends whom he had invited to supper, and who approved the part he had adopted: "*Allons! Morbleu!* Let us all

cry, Long live the king." This was readily responded to, and taken up by the crowd outside,
attracted by the illumination of the governor's
house, and perhaps by the spectacle of the suspended secretary. On the following day the governor, "with great civility," requested the Spanish
garrison to march out of Rouen. The Spanish
commandant, the Huguenot ambassador, the trai-
tor-leaguer governor and some of his friends, had
supped together on the previous evening, and with
great hilarity had pledged their respective sovereigns in bumpers of champagne.

"Why should they not," said the Spaniard,
after learning from Rosny the honourable treatment the foreign garrisons of Paris had received
from the king. "His success," he continued,
"may not augur well for us; but our masters
are not enemies, there being no declared war
between them." Villars was in high spirits. He
had sold the city to the king, and himself, as he
said, for life, for 1,200,000 *livres* to pay his debts;
a pension of 60,000; the government, *en chef,* of
Rouen; the grand admiralty of France; the disposal of five or six abbeys; a governorship for his
brother, and a few other minor advantages.* A
service of plate was presented by the city of Rouen
to the Baron de Rosny, who accepted it for the
king. But Henri declined to receive it, and desired his ambassador to retain the offering of the

* *Mémoires de Sully*, Vol. II.

inhabitants of Rouen, which — as he wished it — he would again present to him, joining his own acknowledgments to those of the citizens for the ability with which he had conducted the negotiation with Villars.*

As soon as Rouen and Havre became Royalist cities, Abbeville and Montreuil declared for the king. Beauvais and Amiens were with difficulty restrained by the Duc d'Aumale from doing likewise. The duke held those towns with a Spanish garrison for Philip II., preferring to serve the King of Spain, and to swear allegiance to him, to taking the oath to Henri IV.

Champagne was also anxious to shake off the yoke of the League, and Troyes, one of the strongholds of that faction, expelled its governor, the young Prince de Joinville, Guise's brother, and called on Maréchal de Biron to take possession. At Sens, Auxerre, and Mâcon, the *bourgeoisie* attacked and turned out the foreign garrisons; Dijon and Beaune, from ardent Leaguers, had become enthusiastic Royalists. But the garrisons were stronger, and resisted the efforts of the people, who, becoming excited, hissed and hooted the fanatical preachers when "from the pulpit

---

* It was Rosny's unswerving habit to receive no presents from any one for services connected with the duties of his office. When any present or offering was made to him he accepted it only by a warrant under the king's hand, that it might be publicly known, and registered at the Chamber of Accounts, — an example followed by few.

they threatened them with the vengeance of Heaven for desiring to yield obedience to a relapsed heretic, whom the Pope himself could not absolve except as a penitent on his death-bed."

The mayor and provost of the maritime town of Saint-Malo sent word to the king that they were ready to hoist the royal colours; that they would tolerate no Spaniards in Brittany nor give aid to the chiefs of the Union. All they asked was oblivion of the past, which Henri readily granted, with the confirmation of their ancient franchises and privileges. Every day brought news to the king of the surrender or subjection of some city or province, and every night, in celebration of the happy event, the gloomy streets of old Paris were resplendent with illuminations, and blazing bonfires flickered and flashed at every corner and in every open space.

The Royalist priests were constantly employed in chanting the *Te Deum*, and the king attended mass, vespers, and compline, with much assiduity. Bareheaded, he followed in the streets the processions of monks and the relics of saints; and reviving an ancient custom of the kings of France, he touched several hundred persons for the king's evil. He was afterwards assured, and by Palma-Cayet, too (who had "also turned from God to idols"), that "two or three persons were actually cured."

Yet all this outward compliance with the cere-

monies and usages of Romanism does not appear
to have convinced Clement VIII. of the sincerity
of the royal penitent's conversion, as he continued
to withhold the absolution, which two prelates,
Cardinal d'Ossat and the wily Du Perron, bishop
of Évreux — the former with no declared official
character; the latter in quality of ambassador —
were now despatched to Rome earnestly to solicit
in Henri's name.   The clerical embassy was more
graciously received than the previous one of the
"politique" Duc de Nevers.   Still Clement mused
and lingered, expecting probably that Henri would
by this delay be induced to ask the papal confirmation of his right to the throne.   If so, he waited
in vain.   Neither the king nor the nation would
permit him to interfere in that respect.   But as he
continued to withhold what really was sought
from him, one of his confidential priests, probably
the good Father Seraphin Olivieri (who on a former occasion pleaded for Henri by urging on the
holy pontiff that "he could not conscientiously
decline to receive the devil himself, if there was a
chance of converting him"), reminded his holiness
that "as England had been lost by the too hasty
decision of Clement VII. to launch his bull of
excommunication against its sovereign, so France
might be lost by the too lingering delay of
Clement VIII. to remove the barrier which prevented the penitent monarch from reëntering the
pale of the Church."   (There had been some

question of appointing a patriarch for the Gallican Church if Clement continued obstinate.)

His holiness, however, did not immediately act on this suggestion. He is said to have really so much doubted Henri's sincerity as to believe in the probability of another relapse into Calvinism; still, he encouraged the hope that in due time the royal penitent's prayer would be granted. Certainly the manner in which the king went through his new devotional exercises was both undignified and irreverent. That he had any faith in them as acts of piety is not likely; and his mocking air, which was, indeed, habitual to him, may have tended to convince the Huguenots that his heart, as he always declared, was yet wholly with them.

When Rosny's despatches informed the king of the signing of the treaty with Villars, he was desirous of making a public entry into the capital of Normandy. But the daily arrival of deputations from the inhabitants of surrendered cities and provinces, together with the disquieting news of Mayenne's movements in Burgundy and Philip's views on Marseilles, prevented him for a time from carrying out his purpose. He, therefore, when recalling the baron, added to his despatches a letter for Villars, in which he addressed him as "cousin," and contrived, in the course of a short letter, to name him by all his titles — general, admiral, governor, marshal, etc., concluding with an invitation to court. Villars was much gratified, and declared that he was "heart and soul the servitor of a man so noble, a king so gallant and brave."

Rosny was ordered to return immediately. He could not, therefore, wait for Villars, who required, he said, some time for preparation to appear at court with suitable dignity. Soon after, the admiral, etc., made his appearance at the Louvre, attended by a suite of more than a hundred gentlemen, "of whom some were of the first nobility of France," and whose velvets and satins, plumed hats, gold spurs, and other rich appointments threw the marshals and generals who were with the king quite into the shade. The Court of Henri IV. was, of course, not yet formed, and he and the men of war about him, both Catholics and Huguenots, had for a long time had little money and less leisure to devote to finery. The king, who rather piqued himself on the plainness of his attire (though he did sometimes complain to his *fidus Achates*, the baron, of the slits and patches in his shirts and other garments), was on the occasion in question most conspicuously shabby, "in his old gray doublet and darned trunk-hose with dogskin leggings."

After the astonishment of all present at the magnificence of the gentlemen of Villars's household and the grandeur of his equipages (rare at that period) had subsided, the company are said to have opened their eyes in amazement still wider on unexpectedly witnessing the grasping Villars giving proofs of generosity and modesty of which they thought him incapable.

" He accosted the king," Rosny informs us, " with an air at once noble and submissive, and threw himself on his knees at his majesty's feet. ' Admiral,' exclaimed the king — mortified by this attitude, and promptly raising him — 'such submission is due to God alone.' Then, in order to honour him, as he had so much humbled himself, Henri turned to the assembled courtiers and spoke admiringly of the great bravery of M. de Villars, of the distinguished part he had played in many severe engagements, and this with so much discernment that by his remarks he shed on his many valorous deeds renewed importance.

" The admiral strove to stem this flow of praise by protestations of respect and devotedness, when, perceiving that the Duc de Montpensier was present, he approached him, took his hands and kissed them, addressing him as his superior, and resigning to him, in appropriate terms and with the best grace, the governorship-in-chief of Rouen. This office in his recent treaty Villars insisted on being given to him, though already in the possession of the duke, who, to oblige the king, relinquished it to Villars, lest refusal should occasion another rejection of the treaty. The prince, who at first received his addresses very coldly, was so much touched by his generosity

that he embraced him several times, and thence-
forth regarded him as one of his dearest friends."*

Maréchal de Biron, on hearing of this act of
courtesy, fancied that Villars would feel himself
bound to cede to him the post of grand-admiral,
which the king conferred on him during the unsuccessful siege of Rouen.   It was then — and had
been for some time — held by Villars, while in the
service of the League.   That he should retain it
on swearing allegiance to the king was one of the
stipulations of the treaty, confirmed by Henri, who
compensated Biron by giving him a marshal's baton
and the governorship of two towns.   But Biron, as
usual, was dissatisfied.   He had the vanity to boast
that Henri IV. owed his crown to him, and already
gave indications of that factious spirit which ulti-
mately proved so disastrous to himself and others.

The king continued to negotiate with those
chiefs of the League still in arms against him.
The Duc d'Elbeuf, — Governor of Poitiers and a
prince of Lorraine, — weary of Mayenne's proceedings, declared for Henri IV., if not gratuitously,
at least spontaneously.   When congratulated on
his kingdom being gradually restored to him,
Henri exclaimed : " *Ventre Saint-Gris !* say not
rendu, but *vendu*."   The Spaniards, however, perceived that, whether surrendered or sold, the
interior of the kingdom and their influence in it
were fast slipping away from them.   They deter-

* *Mémoires de Sully.*

mined, therefore, to arrest the progress of royalism by a bold effort, and to lay siege to La
Capelle, in Thiérache.

Henri, though occupied with plans for the
better conducting of public business, resolved on
setting these domestic matters aside for a time, in
order to hasten to the relief of the besieged city.
But so small was his army (the troops sent by
Elizabeth having been despatched to Brittany,
under Maréchal d'Aumont, for the subjugation of
that province), and so slowly were additions made
to it, that some time elapsed ere he could muster
a small corps to precede a larger detachment,
which he left his officers to assemble from various
garrisons and to follow him as speedily as possible.
Henri arrived at La Capelle only to find the siege
far advanced, and Count Mansfeldt, who commanded, so advantageously posted that, with the
feeble corps he had with him, Henri would not
undertake to force him.

The place was strongly fortified. Perhaps the
governor would hold out, and give time for the rest
of the troops to join. But his garrison was small,
and provisions and ammunition were wanting. This
appears to have been in some way turned to advantage by him. Rosny says that he was deeply im-
bued with the spirit of the times, and, like so many
others, was more anxious to turn his position to
account than to discharge its duties. " Relief was
on its way to La Capelle, but the governor sur-

rendered this strong fortress to the Spaniards and was ruined by his avarice."

By way of reprisal, Henri laid siege to the fine old town of Laon, strongly defended by nature, being built on a mountain ridge at a considerable height above the level of the sea. Its elaborate fortifications had been so much strengthened and extended by the Leaguers that the place was considered impregnable. He, it was declared, who should attempt to attack it would speedily repent of his temerity. This was well known to the king, who nevertheless was not deterred by it from carrying out his purpose. He thought it a suitable occasion for sustaining his military reputation, to which he owed much of his success in treating with rebel governors, who for the most part preferred surrender for a pension or other advantage to being besieged by so able and active an enemy.

Mayenne was then at Laon, but fled on hearing of Henri's approach, making his way to Brussels, to entreat the Archduke Ernest to send troops to the aid of the beleaguered city. The Spanish officers urged the archduke to arrest Mayenne as a traitor, the Duc de Feria and Don Diego d'Ibarra having informed Philip that he alone, for his own private aims, had prevented the infanta from being declared queen and marrying Guise. The archduke was then with difficulty defending himself against the Netherlanders; but as Laon was an important town, and Philip was desirous (of which the Spaniards now made no secret) of obtaining possession of as much of France as was possible, he promised to send 7,000 troops to Laon, but for the moment despatched orders only to Count Mansfeldt to join his army to Mayenne's and march to the relief of that city.

Dubourg, one of Mayenne's most experienced officers and attached partisans, was Governor of Laon, — the same who, from want of adequate means of defence, surrendered the Bastille, neither accepting reward nor consenting to join the Royalists, but marching out with as many of the garrison as chose to follow him, wearing the black scarf of the Guises.* Mayenne had left his second son, the Comte de Sommerive, at Laon, at the head of two or three hundred gentlemen and young nobles; also Jeannin, secretary of state, a firm adherent, though not approving the lieutenant-general's policy. His own and Mansfeldt's army amounted together to not more than 10,000 men, who failed in their endeavour to revictual Laon before Henri's reinforcements arrived. Biron, with a corps of 8,000, had already joined him, and as many more as would raise his army to 20,000 were on their march.

Balagny, "the marshal prince of Cambray" (a potentate whom Henri had recently confirmed in his usurpation of sovereignty over the frontier city

---

* Since the assassination of Henri, Duc de Guise, at Blois, the Guise family and the Leaguers generally had adopted the black scarf, both as mourning and the signal of vengeance.

of Cambray, of which he was governor, but who
proved incapable of sustaining the rank he coveted),
brought the king 2,000 arquebusiers and a detachment of 300 cavalry.   A small battery of six
cannon was under the joint charge of De Borne,
an old lieutenant-general of artillery, and the Baron
de Rosny.   This gave great satisfaction to the
latter, who, although he had shown much diplomatic ability since the king had employed him as
his negotiator instead of M. Du Plessis-Mornay,
yet, as an artillery officer, he was far better pleased
when he accompanied his sovereign to the wars
than when engaged in treating with rebel governors, or striving to reconcile rival lovers.

He was destined, however, to leave the Royalist
camp almost as soon as he arrived there, and at
Henri's request to return to Paris to look after his
interests in the capital.   Information had reached
the king that Paris was full of evil-intentioned persons, who, taking advantage of his absence, were
assembling daily at the house of the Sieur d'Entragues, who, with his stepson, the Comte d'Angou-
lême (natural son of Charles IX. and Marie
Touchet, whom Entragues had married), was
plotting and intriguing in the interests of Philip
of Spain, whose agents and spies they were.

The attack of the recently appointed Royalist
rector of the university — the physician Jacques
d'Amboise — and the curés of Paris on the "company of Jesus" was another cause of disquietude

to the king. A lawsuit which for several years had been suspended was revived by the rector, who accused the Jesuits of being the authors of all the misery that had fallen on France during thirty years of civil warfare. He and the Gallican and national party presented a request to the royal Parliament of Paris, urging that "these ministers and agents of foreigners, the company of Jesus, be expelled, not only from the university, but from the kingdom." The Jesuits made every possible effort to defend themselves. Hitherto they had refused to take the oath of allegiance to Henri IV. Like Mayenne, they declared that to do so before the holy father had absolved him would be a traitorous act to their conscience. Nevertheless, they found that if they persisted in their refusal they were lost. Therefore — secretly authorised by the Pope, it was supposed — they resigned themselves to their fate, and acknowledged the rights of the Béarnais.

The charges against them, and their able defence of themselves, were heard with closed doors, at the desire of the Jesuits and by favour of the king. Henri was aware that Clement VIII., especially, if not quite openly, protected those wily priests, and had made several concessions to them.* He

---

* For instance, bestowing a cardinal's hat on the fathers Toleto and Bellarmine, contrary to the constitutions of the order, which expressly forbid the Jesuits to accept ecclesiastical dignities.

was, therefore, unwilling to take any part in the present attack on the Jesuit fathers, lest it should give offence to his holiness and induce him still longer to withhold the much-desired absolution. Consequently Rosny was authorised to inform the council before whom the charges were made that "the king did not regard them as sufficiently important to merit banishment. He had, therefore, determined that the question of their expulsion should be reserved for future consideration; that it might be seen how they would henceforth conduct themselves, both as regarded the state and himself personally. Meanwhile, no proceedings whatever were to be taken against them."

A third reason for Rosny's return to Paris was the illness of the young Cardinal de Bourbon, who, since his dream of marrying the infanta and ascending the throne of France had wholly vanished, had fallen into a state of languor or rapid decline that seemed to threaten a speedy death. He was exceedingly anxious to see the Baron de Rosny, of whom he said that, "although he was a Huguenot, he knew no one he more esteemed, whose conversation pleased him so well, or whose advice he thought more judicious."

Although Rosny would have preferred to remain at Laon in charge of his battery, yet the king's service and that monarch's wishes were ever paramount with him. Henri embraced his faithful servitor, and bade him adieu with many flattering expressions of his regard for and confidence in him — adding, as a further reason for seeking his aid in the still difficult position of affairs, that "he had remarked that whatever he undertook fortune crowned with success."

Arrived in Paris, Rosny discovered that Entragues and his stepson were secretly in communication with Spain, and that their residence was the resort of all who were adverse to the king — their pretext being that "while heretics were admitted to all offices in the government, the maintenance of the Catholic religion was very insufficiently assured to France." * Persons whose vigilance and fidelity could be relied on were charged by the baron to keep diligent watch on the proceedings of this factious party. His mission to the council respecting the Jesuits occasioned general surprise, — less, perhaps, that the king should interfere in their favour than that a Huguenot should have been charged to deliver his sentiments concerning them, and have consented to do so. The proceedings against "the company" were adjourned, which the Jesuits regarded as a victory. The indifference which, as some persons thought, Rosny had evinced in this instance towards his own religion, ably represented, they said, the degree of the king's sincerity towards his new profession.

The young Cardinal de Bourbon, who died soon after Rosny's visit, seemed at first to have nothing

* Mathieu; Mezeray.

to confide to his Huguenot friend but lovers quar-
rels, and his conviction that he was under the
spell of a woman by whose enchantments he was
brought to that state of extreme weakness and
languor in which the baron found him.   This
prince of the Church was not in priests' orders,
yet he was Archbishop of Rouen, and held several
very rich abbeys inherited from his uncle, the late
cardinal " Charles X.," whose illegal possession of
them appears to have occasioned him, when near
his end, many qualms of conscience.   The young
cardinal on his death-bed was disturbed by similar
scruples, and sought the king's permission to resign
his abbeys and to confer them on whom he should
himself select.   Permission was granted, but the
cardinal's rapidly wasting disease allowed him
neither time nor energy to avail himself of it.
He was solicitous respecting the sincerity of the
king's conversion, and urged his Huguenot friend
to impress on him the necessity of more inward
heartfelt zeal and outward devotion.*

The king being, as usual, in much need of
funds, Rosny, though anxious to return to Laon
forthwith, resolved on attempting to obtain from
D'O a few thousand *livres* to take back with him
to the army as a welcome surprise to the king.
The Governor of Paris and superintendent of the
finances had resumed his old course of life.   The
poorer inhabitants, scarcely yet recovering from

* *Mémoires de Sully.*

the effects of pestilence, famine, and civil war, gazed with wonder on the grand equipage of the Seigneur François d'O de Maillebois. His habits were more dissolute than ever, and he gambled more recklessly. Few of the nobility could com-pete with him in the splendour of his hôtel, and the display of silver and gold plate for the service of his table. His cooks were the *cordons bleus* of their calling, and prodigality reigned throughout his establishment. At a supper at which Rosny was present, amongst other rare dainties and artistic culinary productions, *pâtés*, or tartlets, composed of musk and amber, were served on small gold plates. These delicacies were said to cost twenty-five crowns each, which probably was their principal recommendation, for whether they were pleasant or otherwise to the palate is not stated ; but hippocras, it appears, was the proper wine or liqueur to be taken with them.*

Rosny was unable to secure for the king the privilege of sharing with the magnificent Seigneur d'O the sum the treasury then contained of the revenues of the state. Equally unsuccessful was his application, at the request of Colonel Liera-mont, Governor of Catelet, for a sum of money to discharge the long arrears due to the troops of his garrison, who were disposed to be mutinous if not promptly paid. The superintendent had nought to offer but regrets. The treasury was

* Pierre de l'Estoile.

empty.   By and by when the machine of the state
was again in thorough working order, and taxes
levied and collected with greater regularity, the
king's coffers would be better filled, if not over-
flowing.

Some heavy expense had lately fallen on the
treasury for the almost royal christening of
Gabrielle's recently born son, César, Monsieur,
so named with the king's approval.   Greater
pomp and ceremony there could scarcely have
been had the youthful César been heir to the
throne.   But the superintendent was liberal where
ladies were concerned.   He may have shrugged
his shoulders and uttered an expletive or two
when he saw the amount to be paid for the
Marquise de Monceaux's jewelry and *toilette*,
and the satin and velvet, instead of his favourite
gray suit, which the king had worn for the
occasion.   For the Seigneur d'O had brought
himself to regard the revenues of the state as his
own private purse, from which he magnanimously
defrayed the cost of such superfluities as the
above.

Another extra expense had also vexed him since
resuming the full exercise of his office ; for while
the League held Paris and other large cities of
France, D'O's receivers and treasurers could, of
course, only levy and collect taxes in the cities
under Royalist sway.   Having declared for Henri
IV. as a "politique" when Henri III. was assassi-

nated, his resources were to a great extent crippled by this division of the revenue of the kingdom. This made him a very wavering partisan, but the Leaguers knew him too well to desire his alliance.

The extra expense referred to above was for Madame Catherine's entry into Paris. She was absent from her brother's renunciation of Protestantism, but present at his coronation, when she occupied the place that would have been assigned to the queen. She had since, at Henri's desire, made her entry into Paris, where she was very frigidly received, — many of the people believing that the presence of this heretic princess in the capital betokened some dire calamity about to fall on it. D'O took little interest in the event, and probably shared in the superstition. Catherine was escorted by two or three hundred noble cavaliers, Protestant and Catholic, but, at her own request, with as little noise and ceremony as possible. Soon after, she retired to Fontaine-bleau. The apartments at the Louvre, usually occupied by the Queen of France, were being prepared for the marquise, with whom Henri now lived openly, and who was treated by him and his court with scarcely less homage than a queen.

The Baron de Rosny took leave of the Seigneur d'O, not too well satisfied with him, and, after sending to his château for a supply of cash, was soon on his way back to Laon. A few days only

after his departure, D'O was taken ill and died.
Notwithstanding his extensive peculations, he was
greatly in debt. His house was stripped by both
relatives and creditors of all his fine furniture,
plate, and valuables, before even his physician declared his illness dangerous — leaving him nothing
more than the bare walls. The only persons who
regretted him were the treasurers who shared in
his pecuniary depredations. Three of them are
said to have subscribed fifty crowns each as an
extra fee for the doctor whom, with the hope of
yet saving his life, they urged to try further reme-
dies. They proved unavailing, or possibly only
hastened his death. He desired to be recommended to the king. " He will learn," he said,
" much better when I am dead how I have served
him, than he would have done while I lived," which
very likely was the truth. His death was a happy
event both for the king and the kingdom. It
relieved Henri from much embarrassment in the
changes he was desirous of making in the regula-
tion of the finances. For successful changes in
that department there was yet some time to wait ;
but " at all events," he said, " henceforth the only
Governor of Paris shall be myself."

CHAPTER XVIII.

ON arriving at Laon, Rosny found the
king reposing on a mattress laid on the
ground. He had bandages on his feet,
which were cut and torn, and bleeding from his
exertions in the trenches. "The besieged," he
said, "had shown more vigour in repulsing than
the besiegers in attacking." Biron commanded,
but before leading his men to the assault, he asked
the king to promise him the governorship of Laon.
Being informed that should the city be taken that
post was destined for another, he expressed himself greatly dissatisfied, even muttering threats of
passing over to the Spaniards. Following the
tactics of his father, Biron determined, as victory
was not to benefit him, that there should be no

victory at all, and that Henri should be compelled to raise the siege and retreat.

Subduing his deep displeasure, the king affected indifference, which the ill-humour, bad feeling, and dissension amongst his officers too frequently, for the sake of maintaining peace in his camp, obliged him to do. He was, however, soon on his feet again and in the saddle — a host in himself — and being now surrounded by many brave men besides Maréchal de Biron, he resolved, thus reinforced, vigorously to press the siege. Twice the attempt to revictual the city was frustrated by his vigilance and activity, — the convoy of four hundred provision-wagons falling into the hands of his troops. The project of surprising his camp and forcing his lines was defeated, and Laon, having held out bravely during a two months' siege, was then compelled to capitulate, being without provisions, and the garrison and inhabitants in open revolt clamouring for surrender to the king. The honours of war were granted to the Comte de Sommerive and his cavaliers, whose bravery Henri greatly praised, at the same time charging the count with a message of peace to his father.

But Mayenne had hastened to Amiens, with the view of aiding D'Aumale to restrain the agitation of the *bourgeoisie*, who, when they knew that Laon had surrendered, sent word to Henri that as soon as the royal ensigns appeared before Amiens there would be a rising of the inhabitants. Général d'Humières, with a detachment of troops, was at once despatched to that city, where he was enthusiastically welcomed. Mayenne, taking advantage of the general excitement, made his escape, thinking his life in danger; while D'Aumale, who would have remained to resist, if possible, this outburst of patriotism, was compelled to follow. The cry was, "Spaniards or Frenchmen?" As the League was now but an empty name, "Frenchmen!" was the response; and there being no garrison to control them, the people of Amiens were their own masters when they chose to be.

The conquest of Laon, while adding greatly to Henri's military reputation, cost many of his bravest officers their lives. Amongst those the most deeply regretted was the gallant Anne d'Anglure, Baron de Givry, to whom Henri was much attached, and whom, in mind and character, he much resembled. Very devotedly Givry had served him from the time of the late king's assassination, when, with many young noblemen, he unhesitatingly joined the standard of Henri IV., saluting him as the "king of brave men, whom none but cowards would abandon." This young officer, who fought so valorously at Laon, is said to have recklessly exposed himself to danger, and sought death in the trenches, being passionately but hopelessly in love with one of the Duc de Mayenne's daughters.

From Laon Henri proceeded to Cambray, to receive in person the oath of the new sovereign prince of that important frontier town.* There a deputation from the inhabitants of Amiens waited on him, to beg that he would make his entry into his "good and loyal city." No conditions were imposed on him either at Amiens or Beauvais, which surrendered to him at the same time, — the governor of the latter town, General Sesseval, declaring that "he would not incur the reproach of placing his name on the list of those who had sold their king his rightful heritage."

Henri was magnificently received at Amiens. He rewarded the courtesy and the confidence of the people in him by exempting the city from the gabelle (salt-tax), as he had done at Abbeville, and by confirming all its ancient franchises and privileges. One of these was exemption from receiving a garrison, — an inconvenient arrangement for a frontier town. It was a similar exemption that deprived France of Tournay, and Amiens soon after found that, although it might be sometimes an advantage — as it had recently proved — yet it was a privilege more frequently open to evil results. In the *fêtes*, solemn processions, rejoicings, and thanksgivings that took place in honour

* The reign of this potentate was but of short duration. His petty tyranny exasperated the inhabitants, who aided the Spaniards to obtain possession of the city and expel him. It appears they did not gain much by the change of masters, as great trouble and distress alone resulted from their rebellious act.

of Henri IV. at Amiens, Gabrielle participated. The people were almost as anxious to see the king's beautiful mistress as to see the king himself. On other occasions, or when in consultation with his officers or ministers, if she was not visible, she was usually placed within hearing of what was going forward. If her views and opinions were rarely adopted by the king, he yet liked to hear them ; and although her influence over him was very great, the reproach of having abused it cannot justly be brought against her. She was generally considered gentle and amiable, cheerful, intelligent, and good-tempered — qualities for which Henri frequently said he loved her far more than for her great beauty. The festivities at Amiens being ended, Gabrielle returned to the Hôtel d'Estrées in Paris.*

Henri was still fully occupied with giving audience to the deputies from various towns in Picardy, all anxious either voluntarily to surrender,

---

* On the site of that hôtel, in the Rue de Rivoli, now stands the French Protestant church, the Oratoire, so named from having belonged to the famous Cardinal de Berulle, founder of the congregation of the fathers of the Oratory, for whom he bought the hôtel, and for whose use he built a chapel on the spot where Jean Chastel attempted to assassinate Henri IV. The chapel was afterwards transformed into a church for the same religious congregation. It came into the possession of the Calvinists in 1806. Rosny, who was present when the attempt on the king's life was made, says it occurred in his apartment at the Louvre, where a crowd of courtiers had assembled to congratulate him on his successful campaign.

or to treat with the king for that object on the most advantageous terms they could obtain. Château-Thierry, Péronne, Doullens, Montdidier, and Roie, all were willing to hoist the white banner, to begird themselves with the white scarf of the Bourbon, and to acknowledge Henri IV. as their legitimate sovereign.

Soissons, Ham, and La Fère (the king having ended the campaign by taking Noyon) were the only towns in the province where the Leaguers still held out, "waiting for the papal absolution." Mayenne had placed a strong garrison in each of them before taking flight for Burgundy, to the independent sovereignty of which — following his friend Jeannin's advice — he proposed henceforth, with great moderation, as he conceived, to content himself. To such an arrangement he could foresee no difficulty.

The subjection of Picardy was followed by the entire submission of the province of Champagne. The reigning Duc de Lorraine delayed not to make his peace with Henri IV. He also sold him his army for 900,000 crowns, the troops passing in a body from the service of the duke into that of France. The Duchesse de Guise was exceedingly anxious that her son should follow the example of the elder branch of the family. The Duchesses de Nemours and Montpensier added their entreaty to hers, these heroines of the League having been converted by

Henri's clemency, bravery, and gaiety of temper from inveterate opponents to ardent partisans.

The young duke was governor of Champagne, and was probably influenced rather by the state of feeling in the province than by the entreaties of the ladies of his family to bow the knee in submission to the king. He had delegated his authority in the northern part of his province to an adventurer named Saint-Paul, the son of a gamekeeper. In Guise's absence he acted as lieutenant-general, and like Balagny at Cambray, Saint-Paul assumed a title, Duc de Rethelois, the name of a small town he had assisted in taking. To keep the inhabitants who objected to his rule in check, he raised a sort of fortress and put a garrison in it, his intention being to set at naught Guise's authority, and, under Spanish protection, to establish himself independently in the north of the province. The *bourgeoisie* of Rheims complained loudly of the tyrant Guise had placed over them, and demanded that their city — the rest of the province speedily joining — should surrender to the king. As a first step towards that end, they sought their governor. Guise quickly appeared on the scene, and commanded the self-created duke immediately to remove his garrison. He haughtily replied that "he certainly would not," at the same time placing his hand on the guard of his sword. Enraged at his insolence, the fiery young duke drew his sword and plunged it into his arrogant lieutenant's heart.

Vitry, Mézières, and Rethelois, small towns in which Saint-Paul had placed his own lieutenants, were given up to the king; and as the municipality of Rheims had secretly determined to arrest their governor in the king's name if he did not at once surrender the city, Guise, who was aware of this, thought it well to choose the lesser evil; so making a merit of necessity, he yielded to the wish of the heroines. For this "voluntary submission" he expected enormous compensation. Rosny was the negotiator at the request of the Duchesse de Guise, and was astonished at his pretensions. Henri, however, consented to give him 400,000 crowns for the payment of his own and his late father's debts; also the government of Provence, in exchange for that of Champagne, with pensions and other advantages for himself or brothers.

This arrangement being agreed to and signed and sealed by the duke and the duchess, his mother, Rosny submitted it to the king for his signature. But a few minutes before, a deputation had arrived from Rheims informing Henri that the whole province of Champagne had declared against its governor and for submission to the king, whom they prayed not to bestow rewards on him, as the restoration of the province to the king was the act of the loyal inhabitants, not of the duke. For a moment Henri hesitated; much less was, indeed, conceded than had been claimed, or probably was expected, but Guise was at his mercy, and Rosny, devoted to the Guise family, anxiously awaited his decision. "No," he said at last, "I will change nothing;" then, hastily taking up the pen, signed the document and returned it to the baron. The deputation from Rheims sought no favours for themselves, but Henri insisted on making them a considerable present.

The Duchesse de Guise was so anxious for a perfect reconciliation that she desired that her son should make his submission in person. Henri consented, and the young duke, with the usual retinue of upwards of a hundred and fifty nobles and retainers, soon after came to do homage by bending the knee before his sovereign and embracing his thigh, according to the very ungraceful custom of the time. Henri received him with his habitual cordiality and "the usual three embraces"; addressed him as "nephew"; spoke in terms of high praise of his father — "one of the friends of his youth," he said, "though they were sometime rivals for the smiles and good graces of the ladies." Guise was unexpectedly much pleased with the gaiety and *bonhomie* of the Béarnais, and took willingly the oath of allegiance to him.

Some few days after, Madame de Guise entered the king's apartment at the moment the duke was presenting the *serviette* to his majesty (" who was about to take his usual slight repast after his dinner"). Availing herself of this opportunity, the duchess declared that "should the duke ever fail in his duty towards his sovereign, she would both disown him as her son and disinherit him." The king immediately rose and embraced the duchess, assuring her that "towards the Duc de Guise and his family he should henceforth cherish the tenderest paternal sentiments."

Great jealousy resulted from the favour the king had displayed towards the Guise family. Huguenots and Catholics, though from different motives, were alike dissatisfied. The pleadings of the duchess were said to have been addressed to his feelings of gallantry rather than to his sense of justice.* Rosny himself was accused of being too anxious to serve the Duchesse de Guise, owing to a marriage connection with her family. The duchess, though no longer young, was still a fascinating woman. Rosny says of her that "from the qualities of her mind and character she would have been the ornament of her sex in any other age than that which had lost all true ideas of vice and virtue." †

Rosny approved and probably advised the course the king adopted. By throwing a veil over the past he believed that there would be no recurrence in the future of that strife and bloodshed with

---

* The Duchesse de Guise was the Princess Catherine of Cleves, and first cousin of Henri IV. Her husband, Henri of Guise, took a prominent part in the Saint-Bartholomew massacre, and the Huguenots had not forgotten that, though the king appeared to have done so.

† *Mémoires de Sully*.

which the ambitious views of the powerful family
of Lorraine had for so long afflicted the kingdom.
Certainly there yet remained Mayenne to reckon
with. His prospects in Burgundy, even with
Spanish aid, were not promising, as the Burgun-
dians declined to accept a subject of the realm for
their sovereign. Matters were made still worse
by the summary decapitation of four members of
the municipality of Dijon for inciting the people
to take up arms and plotting to deliver the capital
of Burgundy to Royalist troops. Pride forbade
Mayenne to send in his submission to the king
until the long-deferred absolution should furnish
him with a pretext.

Other troubles occurred at this time, occasioned
by a rising of the peasantry, who in thousands had
taken up arms in various parts of France, in order
" to free themselves from the oppression and persecution of the numerous petty tyrants who imposed
and collected taxes and fines, and inflicted every
kind of torture upon them, crushing them to the
depths of poverty and to the condition of slaves."
Endurance was exhausted, and they now arose in
rebellion, "against those ' *croquants* ' "— as they
termed their oppressors — " to claim their right
to exist and be men."* They demanded an abate-

* This epithet, employed by them in the sense of oppressors
of the poor, was afterwards applied to the peasantry themselves
as " rebels in arms to oppose the rights and dues of their lawful
seigneurs, and to free themselves from the state of subjection to
which God had ordained them."— PALMA-CAYET.

ment of their burden of taxes and a lessening of
the number of the ruthless collectors.

The king at once remitted the whole of their
arrears of " taxes, fines, and subsidies," and
promised full inquiry into their complaints, and
a due consideration of their demands.   In some
parts this sufficed to put an end to the revolt,
in others a sort of guerrilla warfare was kept up
for a year or two.

Henri remained some time in Paris, for the
purpose of reorganising the financial department
of the government.   He suppressed the offices of
superintendent and treasurers, replacing them by
a council of eight members, and an honorary chief,
simply for the form ; to which post he appointed
the Duc de Nevers.   This reformed system seemed
at first to promise good results, and the king, well
pleased, then left the capital to revisit Picardy,
and — in pursuance of his grand designs for his
next campaign — to examine the strong places of
that province.

On returning from this expedition at the end of
December, the king, booted and spurred, hastily
entered the Hôtel d'Estrées, where Gabrielle then
resided.   A train of courtiers followed and numerous attendants, amongst whom there glided in
unperceived a youth of eighteen or nineteen, who,
on two gentlemen being presented to the king,
struck him in the face with a poniard.   The blow
was aimed at his heart ; but fortunately Henri at

that moment stooped to raise the gentlemen who bent the knee before him, and thus was wounded in the mouth, his upper lip being cut and front tooth broken. On receiving the blow he said, "Ah! cousin, you have wounded me!" addressing one of the gentlemen — the Comte de Montigny.

"Heaven forbid, Sire," he replied, "that I should wound or harm you. I have no weapon about me but the sword by my side."

In the scene of confusion and alarm that ensued the assassin thought to escape. But the Comte de Soissons, having seen him drop the poniard, laid his hand upon him, and he was immediately seized and questioned. At first he denied his guilt; then confessed it, said his name was Jean Chastel, that he was a student at the Jesuits' college, and was the son of a draper in Paris. Having already, although so young a man, led a life of fearful depravity, he was troubled concerning his salvation, but hoped to obtain at least some diminution of his punishment in the next world by doing the Church the service of killing the king, — a "permissible act," he said, the king not being "approved by the Pope." He acknowledged having heard his Jesuit preceptors maintain theoretically the lawfulness of taking the king's life. He determined, therefore, to put the theory into practice.

The king's wound was pronounced not dangerous, which was a great relief to many persons, but a disappointment probably to others. Rosny describes the terror he felt on seeing the blood flowing from the king's mouth. The king himself treated the matter, so far as his wound was concerned, very lightly, saying jestingly that he "had often heard from the mouths of trustworthy persons that the Jesuits did not like him, of the truth of which he was then convinced by his own mouth."

The wretched assassin was sentenced on the 19th of December, and condemned to make, on the following day, the usual *amende honorable* of traitors and regicides, before the grand entrance of Notre-Dame. His right hand, holding his poniard, was then chopped off, and he was put to the torture, but made no further confession. The execution took place by torchlight, and all the sickening horrors and demoniacal barbarities which at that period attended the punishment of such crimes then followed, ending with the poor creature's mutilated limbs being thrown into the flames, and, when consumed, their ashes cast into the river.

By the same decree, the "priests and students of the College of Clermont, and all others calling themselves of 'the Society of the name of Jesus,' were ordered, as corrupters of youth, perturbers of the public peace, and enemies of the king and the state," to quit Paris and other cities where they had colleges, within three days, and the kingdom within fifteen days, from the date of the decree. Chastel's father was banished ; the house in which his son was born was razed to the ground, and on its site a pyramid erected, on which was inscribed the sentence both of the assassin and the Jesuits. Seditious writings found in the college of Clermont were the cause of two Jesuits being hanged on the Place de Grève.   Several others, who had taken their departure, were executed in effigy.*

* Mathieu; L'Estoile; De Thou.

END OF VOL. I.

www.ingramcontent.com/pod-product-compliance
Lightning Source LLC
Chambersburg PA
CBHW021213090426
42740CB00006B/200